THIS WHISPERING
IN OUR HEARTS

CW00551577

Zelda

HENRY REYNOLDS

THIS WHISPERING IN OUR HEARTS

ALLEN & UNWIN

First published in 1998
Allen & Unwin
9 Atchison Street, St Leonards 2065 Australia
Phone: (61 2) 9901 4408
Fax: (61 2) 9906 2218
E-mail: frontdesk@allen-unwin.com.au
Web: http://www.allen-unwin.com.au

National Library of Australia
Cataloguing-in-Publication entry:

Reynolds, Henry 1938– .
    This whispering in our hearts.

    Bibliography.
    Includes index.
    ISBN 1 86448 581 7.

    1. Race discrimination—Australia. 2. Aborigines,
    Australian—First contact with Europeans. 3. Aborigines,
    Australian—Treatment—History. 4. Humanitarianism. I. Title.

323.119915

Set in 11/13 pt Bembo by DOCUPRO, Sydney

Printed and bound by McPherson's Printing Group, Maryborough, Victoria

10 9 8 7 6 5 4 3 2 1

CONTENTS

In memory of many humanitarians—men and women not individually noticed in this book—who struggled, often at considerable personal cost, to bring about a juster and fairer Australia.

ACKNOWLEDGEMENTS

The research on which this book is based was made possible by grants provided both by James Cook University and the Australian Research Council. Staff in libraries in both Australia and Britain have provided invaluable assistance. My colleagues at James Cook University have been both supportive and understanding when dealing with a colleague more often away than in Townsville. May Carlson, Kett Kennedy and Dianne Menghetti all assisted with the complications of a peripatetic lifestyle. Jean Willoughby efficiently turned longhand scrawl into impeccable text.

I benefitted from having access to three excellent unpublished Ph.D. theses by Christine Halse, Fiona Paisley and Geoff Grey. I have valued the friendly exchanges with James Cook colleagues working in similar areas, and particularly Noel Loos, Russel McGregor and Paul Turnbull. Marilyn Lake generously shared references and research materials and I owe her a special debt for her very large contribution to my understanding of the politics of 20th century feminism and the work of feminist leaders in the inter-war period.

John Iremonger and Rebecca Kaiser were invariably helpful, efficient and encouraging as the book took shape.

Margaret Reynolds taught me much about the humanitarian spirit while I played the role of understudy activist as we both came to terms with life in North Queensland and the fraught politics of race.

INTRODUCTION

MAJOR MORAL QUESTIONS underlie the history of Australian colonisation—

Were the Aborigines the true owners of Australia?

If so were the British justified in taking possession of the continent?

Was it legitimate for them to use force when they met resistance?

Should they have provided compensation for those they dispossessed?

They are questions which still concern us. They were there in the beginning.

They concerned James Douglas, 14th Earl of Morton and President of the Royal Society between 1764 and his death in 1768. He played a major role in promoting Cook's voyage into the southern oceans. On 10 August 1768 he wrote a long list of 'Hints offered to the consideration of Captain Cooke, Mr Bankes, Doctor Solander, and the other Gentlemen who go upon the Expedition on Board the *Endeavour*'. He paid particular

THIS WHISPERING IN OUR HEARTS

attention to the 'natives of the several Lands where the Ship may touch' and offered advice to the mariners, exhorting them:

> To exercise the utmost patience and forbearance with respect to the Natives of the several Lands where the Ships may touch.
>
> To check the petulance of the Sailors, and restrain the wanton use of Fire Arms.
>
> To have it still in view that shedding the blood of those people is a crime of the highest nature:— They are human creatures, the work of the same omnipotent Author, equally under his care with the most polished European; perhaps being less offensive, more entitled to his favor.
>
> They are the natural, and in the strictest sense of the word, the legal possessors of the several Regions they inhabit. No European nation has a right to occupy any part of their country, or settle among them without their voluntary consent.
>
> Conquest over such people can never give just title; because they could never be the Aggressors.
>
> They may naturally and justly attempt to repel intruders whom they may apprehend are come to disturb them in the quiet possession of their country.

Even if conflict broke out the native people should be treated with 'distinguished humanity' and considered as 'Lords of the Country'.[1]

Such moral concerns survived the long voyage to Australia. In 1807 Governor P. G. King prepared a memo for his successor William Bligh offering advice and summing up his knowledge of New South Wales. In a section headed 'Respecting Natives' he observed that he had been unwilling to force the Aborigines to work because he had 'ever considered them the real Proprietors of the Soil'.[2] It was a highly significant comment made on the basis of experience in Australia which stretched back twenty years to the arrival of the First Fleet in 1788. It was both an official note to a colleague and a confession of inner conviction. But had King thought like that all along? Had he expressed this view to colleagues? Did any of them also think the Aborigines were the real proprietors of New South Wales? Did King worry about the contradiction between his personal belief and the policies of his government which were premised on the doctrine of *terra nullius*? If he felt it improper to force the Aborigines to work, what did he think about occupying without negotiation or purchase the lands of the real proprietors?

King was not alone. Other settlers shared his scruples and worried about the morality of colonisation. The editor of the *Launceston Examiner* observed in 1847 that his contemporaries could not 'disburden their minds of the feelings of remorse in enjoying the soil' once the home of the exiled Tasmanian Aborigines.[3] An English visitor of the 1840s reached much the same conclusion, observing that the 'right to Australia' was a 'sore subject with many of the British settlers and they strive to satisfy their consciences in various ways'.[4]

This book is an account of the men and women who were unable to satisfy their consciences and who worried about the relationship between the Aborigines and the Europeans, who said so publicly and who took political action of one sort or another in the hope that they could change the way things were.

Unease about the morality of settlement has been apparent throughout the two centuries of European occupation of the Australian continent. In each generation people have expressed their concern about the ethics of colonisation, the incidence of racial violence, the taking of the land and the suffering, deprivation and poverty of Aboriginal society in the wake of settlement.

Some were so troubled by what they saw around them that they devoted themselves to the amelioration of Aboriginal suffering or to the denunciation of violence and brutality. In doing so they courted the anger, hostility and even the hatred of their contemporaries. They voiced the unspeakable, exposed carefully cloaked self-deception, dragged out hidden hypocrisies. For their pains they were seen as self-righteous, disturbing, dangerous, obsessive or mad.

There was sometimes an element of truth in these accusations. The Aboriginal cause often did attract outsiders, eccentrics, obsessive personalities. In some circumstances the cause itself overwhelmed its adherents as they steeled themselves in the face of disbelief, suspicion and hostility. Few other things so ensured alienation from mainstream society than a too great concern for the blacks. Those zealous in the crusade came to view with horror the progress that others glorified. They came to hate their own society for its unfeeling brutality. Resulting isolation fed further embitterment.

To those hardened against, or indifferent to, the fate of the Aborigines, such commitment was tantamount to betrayal of race, community, colony or nation. And it was more even than that. The humanitarians called so much into question. They cast doubt on the morality of the whole colonial venture. They burrowed beneath that sense of certainty necessary to push one's fortune in the new world.

The 'friends of the blacks' were seen to gratuitously assume an air of moral superiority, to consider themselves as more virtuous than the rest. Their contemporaries called them Exeter Hall enthusiasts, maudlin philanthropists, meddling pseudo-philanthropists, do-gooders, bleeding hearts, nigger-lovers and many other more abusive epithets.

The problem was that even mild remonstrance about the position of the Aborigines challenged the ethics of colonial progress which was premised on the exploitation of land taken from the real proprietors and even on the eventual extinction of the race. The editor of the *Rockhampton Bulletin* observed in 1867 that 'the disappearance of the black race before the face of the white man', was an inevitable fate to which 'we must of necessity submit as one of the conditions of successful colonization'.[5]

If Australia was morally flawed, the opponents of the humanitarians argued, the only solution was to climb back on board the tall ships and set sail for Europe. 'Let us therefore hear no more about the *right* or *justice* of our proceedings', a South Australian colonist wrote in 1839, 'or let every sincere objector on this ground, prove his sincerity, by at once leaving the country which he thinks he has so unjustly taken from another'.[6]

Colonisation, it was said, was not for those of tender or restless conscience. The brutal business had to be done. In a letter to the *Port Phillip Patriot* in 1842 'A Colonist' observed that the

> irretrievable step of taking possession of a country infers many minor wrongs to its inhabitants, besides

the first great act of spoliation; but he who would govern in a country so situated must steel his breast to their wrongs which are unanswerable.[7]

Moral choice was harder and harsher on the frontier. Refusal to participate in the brutal trade of dispossession was, by definition, a rebuke to those who did and one that was hard to forgive. Tacit disapproval was bad enough. Outright criticism was deeply provocative, profoundly contentious. Settler solidarity was not just comforting. It seemed necessary for survival. The shared guilt of the punitive expedition, the complicity in killing, bound participants together in close confederation. Dissenters who challenged the ways of the frontier were boycotted, bullied or banished. The pioneer Queensland grazier Ernest Thorn refused to allow a party of neighbouring settlers to use his boat to facilitate a nocturnal attack on a neighbouring Aboriginal camp. As a result he acquired a bad name which, he explained, 'followed me for many years, and rose up in judgement against me, in unexpected places, as a dangerous man'. His name was 'covered with opprobrium' and he was branded as a man 'who was false to his race, and unworthy of the confidence of decent white men'.[8]

But all over Australia there were men and women who stood up and demanded justice for the Aborigines, even on the most troubled frontiers and when conflict was at its height.

In the chapters to follow, attention will focus on humanitarian endeavour in three periods—the 1830s and 1840s, the 1880s and the years between 1926 and 1934. A few individuals will be chosen for detailed consideration—George Augustus Robinson, Lancelot Threlkeld,

Louis Giustiniani and Robert Lyon in the first period; John Gribble and David Carley in the second, Ernest Gribble and Mary Bennett in the third. Each was prominent in the humanitarian cause but the choice was arbitrary to some extent. Many other individuals could have been selected for special mention.

The book is about white humanitarians. It deals only in passing with Aboriginal resistance, protest and politics. While many of the Europeans who appear in the story were missionaries little attention is paid to their relations with the Aborigines, their attitudes, policies or evangelical endeavours. The focus throughout is on the political activism of humanitarians, their attempts to change the behaviour of their fellow Europeans and to encourage them to treat the Aborigines with 'distinguished humanity' and above all to eschew the indiscriminate and disproportionate violence of the punitive expedition.

Four humanitarians. Top left: Lancelot Threlkeld from an undated ambrotype portrait probably taken in the 1850s (Mitchell Library); top right: G. A. Robinson esq. from a lithograph by M. Gauol (National Library of Australia); bottom left: Rev. J. B. Gribble from The Problem of the Australian Aboriginal *by E. Gribble (Mitchell Library); bottom right: Rev. E. R. B. Gribble from* A Despised Race *by E. Gribble (Mitchell Library).*

I

THE CONCERNS OF
GENTLEMEN

Australia's first punitive expedition provoked the first clash of conscience. Following the spearing of one of his servants in December 1790, Governor Phillip decided to dispatch a military detachment to punish the tribe considered responsible. He instructed Captain Watkin Tench to take 50 men and capture two of the offending tribe and to kill and decapitate ten others. Tench suggested less stringent measures—six Aborigines captured of which two would be hung and four transported to Norfolk Island. If they could not be taken alive they were to be shot and beheaded. Tench explained that the Governor had determined to 'strike a decisive blow, in order, at once to convince them of our superiority, and to infuse an universal terror' in Aboriginal society.

While Tench sought successfully to moderate the Governor's instructions his younger colleague, the 29-year-old Lieutenant William Dawes, objected to the expedition itself. Although on duty at the time Dawes wrote to his commanding officer Captain Campbell refusing to take part in the venture. Both Campbell and

Phillip pressed him to obey orders and threatened him with arrest. After consulting the settlement's Anglican clergyman, Rev. M. Johnson, Dawes agreed to march with the detachment but subsequently told the Governor he regretted his decision. While reporting the incident to the Secretary of State, Lord Grenville, Phillip remarked that Dawes had 'very clearly showed that he would not obey a similar order in future'. A year later he refused to apologise to Phillip although requested to do so.[1]

It was a portentous clash of will, aspiration and conscience. Phillip was the man of Empire with a vision of flourishing colonial enterprise. If the Aborigines stood in the way they would be coerced, if necessary by means of terror. Dawes was an evangelical Christian, an enthusiast and humanitarian, a personal friend of William Wilberforce and associated with the nascent campaign against slavery which was soon to widen out and embrace the Empire's indigenous people.

Premonitions of violence were borne out during the first generation of settlement. While it didn't necessarily shake the confidence of governors and lesser officials in the colonial venture itself, they expressed deep disquiet about their inability to control the brutality unleashed on the frontiers of settlement. In 1810, just six years after arriving in Hobart, Governor David Collins issued an official statement deploring the 'abominable cruelties' which had been 'practised' upon the Aborigines by the Europeans.[2] His successor Thomas Davey was similarly concerned when he learnt that Aboriginal resentment had been 'justly excited' by settler brutality. In a proclamation of June 1814 he declared:

Had not the Lieutenant Governor the most positive and distinct proofs of such barbarous crimes having been committed, he could not have believed that a British subject would so ignominiously have stained the honour of his country and of himself; but the facts are too clear, and it therefore becomes the indispensable bounden duty of the Lieutenant Governor thus publicly to express his utter indignation and abhorrence thereof.[3]

Tasmania's third governor, William Sorell, reacted in a similar manner in 1819 when informed about the ways of up-country settlers. In a proclamation of 13 March he declared:

It is undeniable that, in many former instances, cruelties have been perpetuated repugnant to Humanity and disgraceful to the British character . . . The impressions remaining from earlier injuries are kept up by the occasional outrages of miscreants whose scene of crime is so remote as to render detection difficult; and who sometimes wantonly fire at and kill the men and . . . pursue the women for the purpose of compelling them to abandon their children. This last outrage is perhaps the most certain of all to excite in the sufferers a strong thirst for revenge against all white men.[4]

With settlement expanding rapidly in both New South Wales and Tasmania during the 1820s frontier conflict spiralled. Many more frontiersmen were living in remote locations where detection of crime was beyond the powers of fledgling governments. But as the wave of colonisation fanned outward from the port cities, urban critics arose who questioned the behaviour and attitudes born of the lawless frontier. They were met by advocates of rapid development in a debate which has continued in one form or another ever since.

Conflict around Bathurst in 1824 inspired a vigorous exchange of letters in the *Sydney Gazette* which canvassed contending views about frontier settlement, attendant violence and the nature of both up-country settlers and the Aborigines. The exchange began in July with a letter from a correspondent who chose the name *Fidelis* and who lamented the fate of murdered stockmen; 'so many defenceless and unprotected fellow men' who were stationed 'beyond the reach of succour, inhumanely murdered, robbed, or pillaged'. *Fidelis* called for the most determined measures to effect the 'suppression of such wanton atrocity and horrid murder' and to avenge the loss 'of our murdered countrymen'. Did not such Aboriginal attacks,

> call aloud for the extirpation of such lawless marauders? and do not lacerated remains of the unburied corpses and mangled limbs of individuals, who have breathed their last in agony, in the lonely sequestered forests . . . kindle feelings indescribable in the breast of every generous member of our community and demand immediate punishment.

Fidelis believed that the attempt to reason with the Aboriginal offenders would be 'attended with as much success, as would the application of eloquence to subdue or command any kind of undomesticated cattle'. So mercy should be 'unquestionably laid aside' until by a 'true sense of our superiority they would discontinue their murder and rapacity'.[5]

The humanitarian riposte came quickly. In the next

issue of the weekly paper *Philanthropus* denounced the view of *Fidelis* and introduced many of the themes which were to run through public discourse for many years. He began by affirming the humanity of the Aborigines and the common origin of all peoples. 'I think they have with myself and all other men', he declared, 'one common ancestor'. He was, therefore, willing to call them brethren, and to 'acknowledge them entitled to my compassion and fraternal respect'. Then in a direct challenge to frontier settlers he declared:

> Hence, I have been led to estimate *even* the least one of these, my despised and injured brethren, at more value than all the sheep and cattle on Bathurst Plains; than all the flocks and herds in the territory of New South Wales; than all the animals in the whole world!

But the Aborigines had a further claim on the settlers. They were the original proprietors of the country to whom was owed 'an equivalent, in such kind and manner as may afford or secure to them the greatest benefit'. This put their attacks on the Bathurst Plains stockmen in a different perspective. 'If we do not approve of their conduct', *Philanthropus* observed, how can we approve of the settlers' own behaviour 'in having first invaded their land, and in a great measure, deprived them of their pleasure and subsistence'. He concluded with a flourish:

> Rather than trespass any further, should we not endeavour now to make reparation, and so prove to them, and to all mankind, that we are not in principle, or in practice, less honourable than heathens; but that, on the contrary, we are humane and generous Christians—and really concerned for the welfare of these Aborigines.[6]

Fidelis had another challenger three weeks later. *Amicitia* was outraged by the suggestion that there should be a total extermination of the Bathurst tribes. While it might prevent further resistance it would be 'a needless, unmerited, and consequently a murderous destruction of our fellow men'. The extinction of human life was an act 'so transcendentally awful in its consequences' that it could only be justified by extreme necessity. Unless that could be established, the massacre of Aborigines would be 'foul and unpardonable murder'. And what, asked *Amicitia* did *Fidelis* mean by vengeance? Directly addressing his adversary he declared:

> If you mean anything more than legal punishment you mean more than you ought, more than can be sanctioned in a civilized and Christian country.

Punishment to be legal could only be inflicted on the guilty and be in proportion to the crime. Punitive expeditions would inevitably involve innocent victims and especially women and children. All talk of 'universal terror' overlooked the fact that the Aborigines were fellow subjects:

> They are recognized as such by the British Government, which has taken them under its control, and extends to them its protection . . . they are governed and defended by the same laws as ourselves so far as those laws are applicable to their condition . . . The general rule of our conduct towards the blacks must therefore be, to treat them in precisely the same manner as we should treat any other British subjects in like circumstances.[7]

In Tasmania in 1824 a similar situation was unfolding. Settlers and their flocks rapidly occupied the open grasslands between Hobart and Launceston. Aboriginal resistance intensified, bringing forth calls for punitive and pre-emptive action. As in Sydney, the community divided. Humanitarians viewed with growing alarm the spiralling calls for vengeance. In a letter to the *Hobart Town Gazette*, *Zeno* related Aboriginal hostility to the loss of their land and game leading to threatened starvation. The conflict of interest should be as far as possible 'averted by us in a just spirit of brotherly conciliation'. Addressing his fellow colonists he wrote:

> We ought to feel that we have invaded a domain from which our invasion has expelled those who were born, bred, and providentially supplied in it; that we have driven by our usurpation, families from their birth-place, and then completed our cruelty by destroying in sport, and consuming for profit, the principal means of their subsistence.

Because the settlers had been responsible for 'unprovoked aggressions' it was essential that they 'devise some way of compensation'.[8]

The first phase of humanitarian concern climaxed in a long, anonymous report sent from New South Wales in October 1826 to the Methodist Missionary Society in London. 'A letter from a Gentleman in New South Wales to a friend at ——' is 28 pages long and provides a savage assessment of the impact of colonisation. It is an important document requiring close examination. 'Strange to say', the Gentleman began, civilisation has been the scourge of the natives. Disease, crime, misery and death have been the 'sure attendants of our intercourse with them'. Could we but trace each poor individual's history, he lamented, 'what a tale it would unfold'. The results were not incidental to colonial progress. Indeed it was 'a sad truth to assert' that settler prosperity had been 'their ruin, our increase their destruction'. The colonial venture was marred with a fatal flaw. It was tragic, not triumphant. The fate of the Aborigines shadowed the land. With what pleasure, he asked rhetorically:

> can we possibly survey the rapid encroachment of Whites on these unhappy people? With what feelings can we look forward, but with those of deep regret, when we are assured that every new step which advances our interests is fatal to their existence? That every acre of land reclaimed by our industry is so much wrested from that pittance which Providence has bestowed on them.

The future for the Aborigines was bleak, the prognosis desperate for if 'such be the truth the ruin of the Aborigines is inevitable'. Tribe after tribe, he concluded, must successively endure the same measure of sufferings until total annihilation 'ends up the sad catastrophe'. 'Should such a state of things be realized', he declared:

> what will future generations think of our boasted Christianity, of our lauded Philanthropy when our posterity read in the early page of Australian history the miseries and ruin which marked our adoption of this land—when they find recorded that our proprietorship to the soil has been purchased at such a costly sacrifice of human happiness and life.

But there was more than moral outrage in the Gentleman's lament. He viewed the Aborigines as the legitimate owners of the land and was profoundly troubled by the fact that they were dispossessed without treaty, purchase or negotiation. Justice, he insisted,

> demands what humanity dictates and Christianity requires, that we should not usurp the possession of another's rights, however advantageous such may be to ourselves or however easy of accomplishment. How we have usurped the rights of others in possessing ourselves of their land without even the offer of an equivalent. And we have thus done, also, at the heaviest possible cost to the rightful proprietors, *viz, their certain ruin*. We are then deeply indebted to this unhappy people; debtors beyond what money can repay or restitution compensate—for Property may be returned, but life cannot.
>
> Deeply then are we in arrears to these injured Beings at whose expense we live and prosper.

The logic was relentless, the moral judgement unforgiving. 'None can defend our conduct towards the New Hollanders', the Gentleman declared bluntly, 'let us not therefore persist in it, and let them receive from our hands some reparation for the wrongs we have done them'.[9]

Debate about the morality and practice of colonisation intensified in the 1830s and 1840s. During those years settlement was propelled outwards from the already established districts close to the port cities of Hobart, Sydney, Adelaide and Perth. Wool became the great export staple; the pastoral interest grew in wealth and political power. At the same time the humanitarian movement reached the height of its authority, influence and moral certainty. With the triumphant abolition of slavery in 1833 the humanitarians turned their attention to the indigenous people of the Empire, a development symbolised by the important House of Commons Select Committee on Native Peoples in 1836–37 and the great expansion of missionary endeavour.

The humanitarian impulse collided with the drive to force the pace of colonial development and take up Aboriginal territory on an unprecedented scale. Colonial society divided deeply over the assessment of Aboriginal society, over indigenous rights and the obligations of the colonists towards those whom they had dispossessed. The army surgeon Thomas Bartlett who visited Australia in the early 1840s found that there were two points of view 'diametrically opposed to each other, respecting the character of the Aboriginal population'. He realised that the ideas had important practical implications. 'These opinions', he explained 'demand attentive consideration, as on them depends the justice, or otherwise, of the manner in which the natives are treated'. One class of settlers, which Bartlett was sorry to confess to his English audience, was a numerous one, maintained that the Aborigines were not 'entitled to be looked upon as fellow creatures'. As a result they adopted the harshest and most severe measures towards them. 'There are persons in these colonies', he observed,

> in what are considered respectable stations in society, who have the hardihood to defend savage butcheries that have been committed by the whites on the natives, by asserting they resemble so many wild beasts, and that it is proper to destroy them accordingly.

He was even more concerned with colonists who went so far in their attempts at justification to impiously declare that it was God's will that the 'black should recede before the white man'.

The second point of view was held by philanthropic individuals who were more common in Britain itself than in the colonies. They viewed with horror the 'inroad made into the possessions of the native' and the forcing of the 'unfortunate Aborigine' to submit to British law and to be administered by a people 'through whom they have endured much injury'.[10]

Philanthropic individuals arriving from Britain were often confronted by the brutality of language and sentiment employed in relation to the Aborigines. The missionary Lancelot Threlkeld was astonished, soon after he landed in New South Wales, when he heard a man boasting about how many blacks he had killed on his land.[11] A Congregational minister wrote home to England in 1840 about a member of the church from Liverpool who since arriving in Australia had adopted the opinions of the 'other Overland Desperadoes who glory in shooting the blacks'. He had breakfast in an Adelaide boarding house with a settler recently arrived overland from New South Wales who said that he had thanked God that he had shot the 'first Blackfellow on their journey'.[12] The Protector of Aborigines at Port Phillip, George Augustus Robinson, noted in his journal, after travelling on the troubled fringes of settlement, that when the settlers went into the wilds of Australia they 'at length become cruel'.[13] The British naval captain J. L. Stokes, after a sojourn in Australia, wrote that a portion of the colonists could not conceive how anyone could 'sympathize with the black race as their fellow man'. In theory and practice they regarded them as 'wild beasts who it is lawful to extirpate'.[14] The celebrated Quaker missionary James Backhouse was similarly struck by the manner in which colonial life brutalised settlers. After an extensive tour of the colonies he observed:

> Persons who before they emigrated would have shuddered at the idea of murdering their fellow creatures, have, in many instances, wantonly taken the lives of the Aborigines. And many of those who have desired to cultivate a good feeling towards them, have found them such an annoyance, as to have their benevolent intentions superseded by a desire to have these hapless people removed out of the way.[15]

The humanitarians were aware of the importance of harsh racial attitudes in loosening the strictures of conscience allowing otherwise moral men to engage in deeds of blood. Sydney's Baptist clergyman, John Saunders, argued in 1838 that a major step in the course of oppression was to degrade the opponent and to convince a sufficient number of people that indigenous people were 'not entitled to the full rights and privileges of humanity'. The task would be even easier if it could be successfully asserted that 'proposed victims are not men'.[16] Captain Stokes was also concerned to expose the role of ideology in allowing settlers to 'cast off the burden of benevolence and charity'. That the Aborigines were not men, 'but brutes', he declared, 'was their avowed opinion, and what cruelties followed from such a doctrine'.[17] Missionary Threlkeld made a similar assessment of the situation. If hostile settlers were able to succeed in persuading the community that the Aborigines were 'merely brutes' then the weight of guilt could be lightened. To shoot them down 'would be no more a moral evil, than destroying rats by poison'.[18]

James Dredge, the Assistant Protector of Aborigines at Port Phillip, argued that if it could be satisfactorily shown that 'the native blacks are anything but men' then their killers 'would be exonerated from the hideous stain of blood'. Those tempted to use violent measures would find nothing in the Aboriginal character which would incite them to the 'exercise of tender and sparing mercy'.[19]

The humanitarians may not have changed many minds, significantly ameliorated colonial behaviour or moderated the violence out on the vast frontiers but they clearly troubled many consciences and raised questions which didn't easily go away. In books, speeches, letters, reports and conversations the settlers grappled with the moral problems arising from the great brutality of the frontier, the appropriation of land without negotiation or purchase and from the nature of colonisation itself. In 1844 a young emigrant wrote home to his mother from the frontier in southern Queensland describing a vigorous argument he had just been involved in with his three companions. The young men had been disputing the 'moral rights of a nation to take forcible possession of a Country inhabited by savages'. He gave his mother a summary of the arguments:

> John and David McConnell argued that it is morally right for a Christian Nation to extirpate savages from their native soil in order that it may be peopled with a more intelligent and civilized race of human beings, etc etc. F. McConnell and myself were of the opposite

opinion and argued that a nation had no moral right to take forcible possession of any place. What is your opinion on the subject? Don't you think it a most heinous act of any Nation however powerful, however civilized and however christianized that Nation may be—to take possession of a country peopled by weak and barbarous tribes?[20]

There were many ways in which settlers sought to establish their right to Australia. In his book *The Present State and Prospects of the Port Phillip District* Charles Griffith explained that he felt an obligation to answer those who had doubts about the ethics of colonisation. He observed that many people, when arguing about the Aborigines retorted: 'Well after all, I do not see what right we have to come and take away the country from them.' Griffith saw it as a significant challenge. He believed that it was 'of importance that the right of colonisation should be settled in the first instance' because even some of those who were proponents of colonisation showed they had private doubts. 'In any case', he explained,

> it lies not in the mouths of those who have sanctioned that occupation, at this period to question its propriety; few do so openly, but there is an uneasiness in dealing with the subject which shows in many a consciousness that in their opinion our title is bad.

But if the title was bad the implications were serious indeed, suggesting that the only ethical thing to do was to abandon the new world and return to the old. Griffith observed that:

> if we have no right to occupy the country, no course of subsequent dealing can, in the forum of conscience,

cure the original defect of title; and the sooner that
we re-trace our steps, and that every European departs
from the shores of Australia, the sooner shall we have
shown a sincere regret for the injury we have already
caused the natives.[21]

Griffith had deployed one of the most commonly
used responses to self-righteous humanitarians. It was
used again and again. 'If we want a league of peace on
equal grounds', Alexander Harris wrote, there is 'no road
to it but to give up their land and forsake their country,
for this and this only is the true source of aggravation
. . .'.[22] In a letter to the editor of the Adelaide paper
the *Southern Australian*, a correspondent, *W.B.*, confronted the moral issues which were currently being
debated throughout the colonies. 'It is useless now', he
wrote,

> to speak about our right to come to New Holland
> and appropriate a part of it for our subsistence. It is
> now in vain to talk about the injustice of dispossessing
> the natives of part of their territories . . . everyone
> of us, by coming here has, in reality, said that we
> either had such a right—or not having the right, that
> we, at least, had the might and resolved to exercise
> it. Let us therefore hear no more about the right or
> justice of our proceedings in this respect; or, let every
> sincere objector on this ground, prove his sincerity,
> by at once leaving the country, which he thinks he
> has so unjustly taken from another.[23]

Some colonists were even tougher-minded in their
approach and openly proclaimed that Australia had been
conquered by the use of superior force and that similar
events had taken place throughout human history. 'It

must not be forgotten', Thomas Bartlett remarked, that the country was occupied by force, that the Aborigines attempted 'but in vain, to beat off the English settlers'. However much this question was mystified, he argued, it was evident that Australia was 'only held by the right of might'.[24] In 1847 the Perth barrister E. W. Landor savagely attacked those who talked and wrote about the British having a moral right of occupancy. 'We have seized upon the country', he thundered,

> and shot down the inhabitants, until the survivors have found it expedient to submit to our rule. We have acted exactly as Julius Caesar did when he took possession of Britain . . . We have a right to our Australian possessions; but it is the right of Conquest, and we hold them with the grasp of Power. Unless we proceed on this foundation, our conduct towards the native population can be considered only as a monstrous absurdity.[25]

A few colonists were able to synthesise the hard-headed views of E. W. Landor with appreciation of the suffering of the Aborigines. In May 1842 a correspondent using the name *A Colonist* wrote to the *Port Phillip Gazette*. He believed that:

> the inevitable step of taking possession of a country, infers many minor wrongs to its inhabitants besides the first great act of spoliation; but he who would govern in a country so situated must steel his breast to their wrongs which are unanswerable.[26]

Colonial experience changed preconceived views and prior expectations. In South Australia the Quaker Robert Cock was deeply disturbed to find that the local author-

16

ities had no intention of honouring a commitment made while still in Britain to set aside one-fifth of all land to provide a fund for Aboriginal welfare. Having bought land in Adelaide he felt morally obliged to pay interest on one-fifth of the original purchase price. 'I feel it my duty', he informed the local Protector of Aborigines in 1838, 'to pay to the proper authorities for the use of the natives this yearly rent'. He denied that the money was donation, grant or gift but 'a just claim the natives of this district have on me as an occupier of those lands'.[27] A few weeks earlier a correspondent using the nom de plume *Philaleh* wrote to the *Perth Gazette* expressing misgivings of a different sort, referring to the violent clashes between settlers and local Aborigines. He called on his fellow colonists to think again about the establishment of the colony:

> Let us look now to that act in which we are all parties concerned; namely the Settlement of Swan River . . . does it not strike us all with surprise that . . . we should have plunged into such a situation without consideration, without forethought. How few of us deigned to bestow even a thought upon the existence of a people whom we were about to dispossess of their country. Which of us can say that he made a rational calculation of the rights of the owners of the soil, of the contemplated violation of those rights, of the probable consequences of that violation, or of our justification of such an act? If perchance at any moment the murmurings of our conscience made themselves heard, were not its faint whisperings stifled by the bustle of business, or drowned in the din of preparations? Did we not swim the stream in a state of high wrought excitement, from the novelty of our

sensations and the rapidity of our course, without reflecting that this rapidity might be the indication of the vicinity of an awful cataract towards which we were hurrying in a heedless and blind security? Did it never occur to us then, that in thus extending the dominion of Great Britain, in thus acquiring a territory for our country, whilst seeking a fortune for ourselves, we were about to perpetrate a monstrous piece of injustice, that we were about to dispossess unceremoniously the rightful owners of the soil?[28]

Philaleh related the conflict which had embroiled many settlers in that unmediated grab for Aboriginal land. Instead of negotiating with the Aborigines and trying to purchase land for farming, the settlers were only too keen to get what they could and did not question the right of the government to sell the land. The boon of cheap land was a gift the settlers were all too eager to accept. He reflected:

we looked not too scrupulously to the title of the donor—we mounted this gift horse and rode proudly away, though at the hazard of being challenged by the real owner for the theft.[29]

Many of the conflicting and contradictory attitudes and values discussed above can be seen in the career of the prominent Sydney barrister Richard Windeyer, who had arrived in the colony in 1838 at the age of 29 to join family members already settled at the antipodes. He quickly established himself as a leading member of the Sydney bar, became a significant landowner, was elected to the Legislative Council in 1843 and played a prominent role in the cultural life of the community.

He arrived in the colony at a time when Aboriginal

issues dominated public debate, 1838 closing with the trial and execution of the Myall Creek murderers. From the start he displayed a degree of ambivalence towards the question of Aboriginal rights. He joined with prominent humanitarians in October 1838 in establishing a branch of the Aborigines Protection Society. But the humanitarians found him an uncertain ally. George Augustus Robinson was visiting Sydney at the time prior to taking up his position of Chief Protector of Aborigines at Port Phillip. He clashed with Windeyer at a committee meeting planning the public launch of the society. He recorded the exchange in his journal:

> Mr Windeyer said there was no tribes and depreciated the story of their being deprived of their rights of the soil since they had no rights. They were always treated the same as the whites . . . Then I said let the blacks go to England and take the lands. How would Englishmen like that.[30]

At the public meeting ten days later Windeyer was again out of harmony with the humanitarians. In his speech he confessed that he could not look upon the natives 'as the exclusive proprietors of the soil'. In fact he thought they actually 'had no right to the land'. Ownership belonged to the person who first bestowed labour upon it. He was himself owner of a large amount of land 'and he certainly considered he had a good title to it'. Moving beyond the question of land ownership Windeyer declared that he totally rejected 'the ridiculous notion that we have no right to be here'. If that view was ever accepted the colonists would 'have nothing to do but to take ship and go home'.[31]

While giving extensive coverage to the speeches at

the meeting, the pro-humanitarian paper *The Colonist* remarked:

> It may be proper to observe, that Mr Windeyer's speech was listened to in respectful silence, but it must have been obvious even to himself, that he failed to carry the judgement and feelings of the assembly with him.[32]

Windeyer further alienated his humanitarian contemporaries when he defended the convict stockmen charged with murder in the Myall Creek trials. But he retained an interest in the question of Aboriginal rights and sometime in 1842 delivered a public lecture on the topic: 'On the Rights of the Aborigines of Australia', the handwritten manuscript of which is held in the Mitchell Library in Sydney. The lecture is perhaps the most sustained and intellectually powerful attack on Aboriginal rights ever mounted in early colonial Australia.

Windeyer began with a sharp denunciation of traditional Aboriginal society. There were no social bonds, no law, no government. But his real target was the belief that Aborigines had some claim on the land or as he called it 'the fallacy of the Philanthropists . . . that the land *belongs* to them'. He took particular exception to the proposition that the Europeans 'had no right to take the land'. That claim, he argued, begged the whole question 'which is whether the land be theirs'. Europeans who ventured into the interior of Australia had met Aboriginal people and had assumed the land was 'more or less appropriated'. But the tribes didn't actually inhabit the land. Rather they ranged over it. 'That they have never tilled the soil, or enclosed it, or cleared any portion of it, or planted a single tree, or grain or root, is acknowledged.' As a consequence there was no ownership. Aboriginal occupation of the land did not 'by the law of nature establish any title to the substance of the soil'. It was, indeed, 'the height of absurdity to talk of the title of these men of the woods to anything not under the control of their bludgeons'.

It was a sustained attack on both Aboriginal rights and on the humanitarians who upheld them. In a sweeping peroration Windeyer declared:

> The consideration of the rights of the Aborigines to the enjoyment of their laws and customs, to the soil of the country, to its wild animals is done. The argument is sound, the chain of reasoning is complete.

And yet that was not the final word. His powerful analysis had not satisfied his own conscience. 'How is it our minds are not satisfied?' he asked. 'What means this whispering in the bottom of our hearts?'[33]

II

MISSIONARIES AND PROTECTORS

What motivated the missionaries, clergymen and other assorted humanitarians to take up the Aboriginal cause in the 1830s and 1840s when so many fellow colonists looked on with indifference or were keen to see the indigenous people and their legal rights trodden underfoot in the onrush of colonial progress?

A foundation stone of the humanitarian cause was the belief in the common origin of all human beings, that all people were created in the image of God, had descended from Adam and Eve and all alike had immortal souls. In what was probably the first letter submitted to an Australian newspaper on the question of the amelioration of the Aboriginal condition, in July 1810 *Philanthropus* called for suggestions which would advance that cause. He took it for granted that the 'Natives of New South Wales' were capable of instruction and civilisation, 'the great Creator having made of *One Blood* all the Nations of the Earth'.[1]

This belief was affirmed again and again in speeches, sermons, letters and conversations. 'I looked upon them as brethren', George Augustus Robinson declared in his

Tasmanian journal, 'not, as they have been maligned, savages'. He further emphasised, '. . . they are my brethren by creation. God has made of one blood all the nations of people, and I am not ashamed to call them brothers.'[2] The West Australian pioneer R. M. Lyon made a similar, if somewhat more inflated declaration:

> If ye pretend to doubt the sunburnt skin of the Australians, apply the lance to their veins . . . Examine the crimson fluid, as it pours out—there can be no mistake here—and say, Is it not blood of your own? Yes. The bleeding victims of your avarice are your brethren![3]

Not all missionaries had as favourable a view of Aborigines as Robinson and Lyon. To some they were degraded savages. William Horton wrote to the Methodist Mission Society explaining that the Tasmanians were the most destitute and wretched portion of the human family and that shape of body was almost the only characteristic which indicated they were human. But the orthodox doctrine about common human origins pulled at Horton's assessment from the other side. He explained that if it were not for his theology he would,

> without any hesitation affirm that they are a race of being altogether distinct from ourselves and class them amongst the inferior species of irrational animals. But as it is a revealed truth, that God has made of one blood all the nations of men that dwell upon the earth, however they may differ from each other in complexion, in features, in language and in manners, even the poor Aborigines of this Island are partakers of the same nature with ourselves, offspring of the same God and objects of his redeeming love.[4]

The humanitarians pitted the authority of scripture against the upsurge of scientific racism which was quickly seized on in the Australian colonies to justify death and dispossession as it was in the United States to provide intellectual buttressing to the institution of slavery. In using theology in this way they had the backing of the leading British ethnographer of the time, J. C. Pritchard. His *The Natural History of Man*, published in 1843, strongly condemned contemporary writers who asserted the 'Negroes, Hottentots, Esquimaux and Australians' were not, in fact, men 'in the full sense of that term, or being endowed with like mental faculties as ourselves'. Pritchard countered with the 'The Sacred Scriptures' which, he insisted, were received by all men of unclouded minds with 'implicit and reverential assent'. And their message was clear. The Almighty Creator had made of one blood all nations of the earth and therefore all mankind were the offspring of common parents.[5]

The humanitarians wielded their theology in other battles as well. The doctrine of human equality came sheathed in the authority of the scriptures. It should override colonial custom, and when it erred, secular law. Even though their advocacy made them unpopular the 'philanthropic individuals' believed they voiced a higher command which had direct application to the world around them. God, they believed, was on the Aboriginal side. 'Savages are men', wrote R. M. Lyon, and they possessed all the natural rights of men. To disregard their rights was to 'insult the supremacy of the Creator' from whom they emanated and who 'never authorized any nation to invade those of another'.[6] One of the most eloquent presentations of humanitarian doctrine was

given by the Baptist minister John Saunders in a celebrated sermon delivered in Sydney in October 1838.
George Augustus Robinson, who was in the congregation, thought it a very good sermon. He believed that
it was 'the first preached on behalf of the Aborigines'.[7]
It was a passionate, eloquent defence of human equality.
The Aborigine was the 'august possessor of a moral and
intellectual nature', the owner of an immortal soul. He
was 'our brother upon earth' and had a title to the mercy
of God and the inheritance of Heaven. He was, therefore,

> invested with all the natural rights which belong to
> humanity, and is entitled to all the charities which
> man is bound to show to man.[8]

William Thomas, who was on his way to Melbourne to
take up the position of Assistant Protector of Aborigines,
was also in Saunders' congregation. He transcribed parts
of the sermon in his diary. 'Does it seem strange',
Saunders asked those seated before him,

> to speak of the majesty of the New Hollanders, wilt
> thou despise the Saviour of the world, then despise not
> him who sprang out of the same stock, despise not him
> for whom Christ died, the Saviour died as much for
> him as he did for you, and he now reigns in Glory as
> much for him as for you, now by every sentiment of
> humanity and love you are bound to love him, to
> admit him into your fraternity and to treat him as
> fellow man . . . The New Hollander is a man and a
> brother.[9]

The humanitarians' attitudes toward the Aborigines did
not derive solely from their study of scripture. They

were by and large not the armchair critics that opponents constantly suggested. Many of them had close personal contact with Aboriginal society, recorded local languages and pioneered the study of ethnography in the Australian colonies. Nor were they the starry-eyed idealists of many reports. They found much about the indigenous lifestyle shocking but that was what their education and training had led them to expect of people who had never heard the Christian message. Theirs was the fate of people without God and without hope of salvation. The missionaries tried with very little success to change traditional practices which they found objectionable. But they were able to use their first-hand experience of Aboriginal society in their disputations with those who denigrated native life. R. M. Lyon wrote:

> I have seen them in almost all the common walks of life—I have met them by accident in the lonely desert—I have met them by appointment—I have walked and conversed with them—I have eaten, I have drunk, I have slept with them—I have performed the meanest offices for them when sick—I have taken the spear from them when quivering with rage—they have bathed my neck with tears of gratitude—and, after all this, I am to be told that I have no premises on which to ground my conclusions and form an estimate of their character.[10]

Often, despite themselves, missionaries and protectors found aspects of Aboriginal society to admire. 'Their kindness to each other', observed William Thomas, 'surpasses all commendation'.[11] The German missionary H. Meyer was impressed by child-rearing practices of South Australian Aborigines. The young were 'brought up with greater care, more than generally falls to the lot of children of the poor class of Europeans'. He noted that when a child cried it was passed from one to another and 'caressed and soothed'. The father would 'frequently nurse it for several hours together'.[12] Many of the pioneer missionaries studied Aboriginal languages, as William Dawes had done in the early months of settlement. They found them to be richer, more complex and more sophisticated than they had initially expected. Francis Tuckfield, a Methodist missionary at Port Phillip, found the local dialects had extensive vocabularies and combined great power and simplicity. He had never found his informants at a loss to express 'their thoughts or emotions, or to describe any of the qualities of matter with which they are acquainted'. While the language had some peculiarities these merely added 'to its precision and perspicuity'.[13]

Lancelot Threlkeld greatly appreciated the assistance he received in learning the language spoken around the shores of Lake Macquarie. The local people showed considerable patience while instructing the missionary, 'pronouncing again and again not without laughing at our stupidity in not understanding quickly'. Perhaps, he mused, they thought the Europeans had an innate deficiency of intellect.[14] When he published his *An Australian Language* he paid tribute to Biraban, or McGill, who was his 'almost daily companion for many years'. It was, he explained, 'to his intelligence I am principally indebted for much of my knowledge respecting the structure of the language'.[15]

The humanitarians were keen to establish that practical experience, as well as traditional theology, confirmed the intellectual equality of the Aborigines. The missionary William Watson declared that he had never found any deficiency of intellect 'in reference to things with which they are acquainted'. He believed the Aborigines would eventually 'equal if not outshine some of the now civilized and polished nations of Europe'.[16] The South Australian clergyman R. W. Newland informed the Aborigines Protection Society in 1840 that he would 'boldly affirm anywhere any time that finer formed men and more brilliant intellects are not to be found than some among the Natives around us'.[17] George Augustus Robinson was a persistent promoter of Aboriginal ability throughout his career in both Tasmania and Victoria. He noted in his journal in January 1830:

> God has given them the same portion of under-standing as ourselves. Their origins of intellect are as capable of improvement, and I am moreover con-vinced that they would as readily acquire any of those attainments by which human nature is distinguished, provided they enjoyed the means that are necessary for that acquisition.[18]

Ten months later he returned to the same theme. He denounced those who declared the Aborigines to be 'only a link between the human and brute species'. Nothing more false, he asserted, could proceed from the lips of men—'they are equal if not superior to our-selves'.[19] In 1836 while in Victoria he wrote:

> I hope ere long I shall be able to prove to the world that these people are not the degraded race has [sic] they have been represented that they have as much interlect [sic] as their opponents—the whites.[20]

Many of the humanitarians had direct experience of the brutality suffered by the Aborigines. They were outraged by the circumstances, censorious of the settlers, compassionate towards the victims. Assistant Protector of Aborigines at Port Phillip, James Dredge, wrote home to England explaining that he did not know how 'to repress the struggling fire in my bones' as he witnessed the 'awful tragedy in course of performance around me'.[21] Missionary Tuckfield responded to the violent frontier in a similar manner. He described himself, in a letter written to the Methodist Mission Society in London, as 'one who feels keenly—and bewails bitterly' the abuses which the Aborigines suffered.[22] George Augustus Robinson recorded in his journal the scene when a party of Aborigines were told of the murder of some of their relatives. The information, he wrote, was the occasion of 'general lamentation'. All wept bitterly. Robinson himself cried. 'I sorrowed for them', he explained. 'Poor unbefriended and hapless people. I imagined myself an Aborigine.'[23] Ten years later, out in the Western District of Victoria he came across the body of an Aborigine who had been shot by the edge of a stream. He was thrust into deep and painful reflections about the widows and orphans, of their 'deep lamentations', of their bitter indignation against 'the white and unrelenting persecutors and oppressors'.[24] The missionary Joseph Orton found that his experience in the colonies deepened his commitment to the Aborigines. He wrote:

> The mingled feelings of pitiful commiseration and compassionate desire which were wrought in my breast are not to be described—my soul truly went out after their welfare, I felt as though I could have

sacrificed every temporal comfort for their spiritual
advantage.[25]

Such views did not endear outspoken humanitarians
to their contemporaries. They were disturbing and even
dangerous agitators. They were not unaware of the
opposition they provoked. When George Augustus
Robinson began his mission to the Tasmanians he felt
as though he was threatened by 'a great tide of opposition' which was rolling against him with 'irresistible fury
threatening to overwhelm [him] in its mighty torrent'.
This did not surprise him because he knew when he
began to work with the Aborigines he would have to
'withstand a host of opposition'.[26] Missionaries in New
South Wales experienced similar hostility. When he first
arrived in the colony in 1826 Lancelot Threlkeld was
warned by the Attorney-General that there were many
people who would banish him and prevent every attempt
'of a missionary nature among the Blacks'.[27] Matters did
not change much over the years. James Gunther wrote
home to the Church Missionary Society in 1838 referring to 'that spirit of enmity so prevalent in this Colony
to missions among the poor Aborigines'.[28] The Quaker
James Backhouse informed the leader of British humanitarians, T. F. Buxton, in that same year that in Western
Australia 'persons have been subjected to great contumely in consequence of pleading the cause of blacks
and exposing atrocities upon them'.[29]

The missionaries and protectors were not surprised
by the hostility provoked. They saw the world as an
arena where good and evil, God and the devil were
struggling for supremacy. As often as not they welcomed,
and even courted opposition. 'I glory in this work',

Lancelot Threlkeld wrote in 1825 'because it is so much despised'.[30] The opposition encountered encouraged the humanitarians to believe that they were effectively confronting wrong-doers and wicked behaviour. It gave them proof of their own virtue and righteousness—reassurance they incessantly sought in their struggle against feelings of worthlessness. They were also strengthened in any conflict with the conviction that they were doing the work of God and following His instructions to man to preach the gospel to those who lived in spiritual darkness. All of this made them tenacious, determined and often fearless opponents.

George Augustus Robinson probably had more first-hand experience of the impact of settler violence than any other European. He was directly involved in the politics of dispossession from 1829 to 1849 in Tasmania and Port Phillip. In Tasmania he spent many months out in the bush travelling with Aboriginal companions at a time when conflict with the settlers still raged. He was informed on many occasions of atrocities committed by frontier settlers and understood the profound anger and hatred which they had provoked. While on the north coast he heard many stories of violence and kidnapping of women by the renegade European sealers who lived on the islands in Bass Strait. He wrote reflectively in his journal:

> Thus it is that their wrongs are handed down from generation to generation. How can we wonder at their committing outrages upon the white inhabitants? Who is there to avenge their wrongs? The children have witnessed the massacre of their parents and their relations carried away into captivity by these merciless

invaders, their country has been taken from them and the Kangaroos, their chief subsistence, have been slaughtered wholesale for the sake of filthy lucre. Can we wonder then at the hatred they bear to the white inhabitants? This enmity is not the effect of a moment. Like fire burning underground, it has burst forth. This flame of aboriginal resentment can and ought only to be extinguished by British benevolence. We should fly to their relief. We should make some atonement for the misery we have entailed upon the original proprietors of this land.[31]

Given their contact with Aboriginal communities and at least rudimentary knowledge of local dialects the missionaries and protectors were able to gain some understanding of the Aboriginal reaction to the traumatic loss of their land. This often informed their own view of the nature of colonisation and they tried thereby to moderate the behaviour of the Europeans and stir their conscience about the deepening tragedy being played out on an ever expanding frontier. With an under-standing of Aboriginal society came an appreciation of the importance of land and the deep emotion and spiritual ties which bound people to soil. The humani-tarians were among the first to reject the views of colonists like Windeyer who argued that the Aborigines had no recognisable form of tenure. The pioneer mis-sionary William Walker realised as early as 1821 that the Aborigines 'possessed some tract of country which they call their own'. Although they moved about from place to place in search of food they had a profound attach-ment to particular spots to which they were so 'senselessly bigoted' that if any attempt was made to settle them somewhere else they would understand the proposition 'no more than if you discoursed with them in Latin or Greek'. They were, in fact, a 'most bigoted race of people to the ground on which they were born'.[32]

The political and legal importance of the Aboriginal sense of property was clearly apparent to the humanitarian movement. Joseph Orton argued in 1842 that it was 'an important truth' which had been 'designedly or ignorantly overlooked' that the Aborigines had 'decidedly a property in the land of their birth which right is recognized and held sacred by themselves in their respective relations of tribes, families and individuals'.[33] Missionaries in contact with Aborigines who were losing their land were able to understand something of the anguish they suffered. Francis Tuckfield noted in his journal:

> they seem to be acquainted . . . with the relative possessions of the Black and White populations—they are conscious of what is going on—they are driven from this favoured haunt and from their other favoured haunts and threatened if they do not leave immediately they will be lodged in the gaol or shot. It is to the Missionaries they come with their tales of woe and their language is—'Will you now select for us also a portion of land? My country all you gone. The white men have stolen it'.[34]

Humanitarians employed some of their most powerful rhetoric to denounce the theft of Aboriginal land. In so doing they were at their most politically controversial, assaulting a central feature of the colonisation of Australia. It was not that they were against the establishment of British colonies. They spoke themselves of spiritual empires. They were zealous to evangelise the pagan, to save the souls of Aborigines and other indigenous people. They firmly believed they should both civilise and Christianise or at least radically change local cultures. The missionary could be more overbearing, more interfering, more insensitive than frontier squatters and stockmen. And they were characteristically profoundly self-righteous, often with the fixed stare and intense focus of the convert. None the less they were fierce critics of the practice of Australian colonisation. They deplored the promiscuous sexual exchanges between stockmen and Aboriginal women. When force was involved, as it often was, their concern turned to despair and anger at the ineffectiveness or indifference of government. The missionary James Gunther sought to preserve Aboriginal women 'from that frequent and almost constant intercourse with voloptuous [sic] Europeans' in order to 'perhaps rescue them from bodily and moral ruin'.[35] But his colleague William Watson reported that there was scarcely a man within 40 miles of his mission 'Bond or Free who is not living in adultery with these unhappy females'.[36] The traffic in children caused even deeper anger. Lancelot Threlkeld reported his horror soon after arriving in Newcastle that he had heard the shrieks of girls about eight or nine being taken by force by 'the vile men' of the town.[37]

Immediate experience of the frontier provided missionaries and protectors with first-hand knowledge of white hostility to black. George Augustus Robinson met a party of stockmen who had arrived with sheep from New South Wales. He fell into conversation with them but didn't let them know that he was the Chief Protector of Aborigines. They talked openly to him as they would with any other traveller. Robinson concluded that the general feeling towards the Aborigines was fierce and hostile. The men openly asserted that they would not hesitate to 'get rid' of the blacks provided they could do so without detection. It was, Robinson wrote later in his journal, 'the most cruel that could be'. The overlanders wished them 'to be burnt—hung—drowned—by any means they wished them got rid of'.[38] In a subsequent letter to the Superintendent of Port Phillip, C. J. La Trobe, Robinson reported that the 'ruthless stockman vaunts that he has killed and will kill blacks'. And even the gentlemen squatters were implicated. Those 'from whom better things ought to be looked . . . openly avow that if the blacks steal from them they will destroy them . . .'.[39] He had heard intelligent and respectable persons state:

> Well, Mr. Robinson I admit their situation is a hard one and I should be sorry to see them injured but then Sir really I do think under all circumstances the sooner they are got rid of the better.[40]

The violence and sexual exploitation was disturbing in itself and a symptom of a seriously flawed method of colonisation. 'It might have been supposed', John Saunders declared, that a Christian nation colonising the Australian wilderness, 'would have sought to bless the original possessors of the wild'. But so far from this the colonists had 'inflicted a series of wrongs' which had devastated those whom they should have helped.[41] R. M. Lyon believed that in colonisation the happiness, 'temporal and eternal' of conquered or adopted nations could not be the primary objective but it 'ought to be the ruling motive in all our colonizing proceedings'.[42] A central problem was the lack of any treaty or other form of negotiated agreement. The humanitarians were aware of the role of treaty-making in the colonisation of North America and venerated the memory of William Penn who had purchased land for settlement from the Indians in seventeenth-century Pennsylvania. After 1840 they compared Australian experience with the signing of the Treaty of Waitangi in New Zealand. 'There is no compact', declared R. M. Lyon, 'no covenant of any kind, between the British Government and the Aboriginal inhabitants of Australia' who, he believed, were ever ready to negotiate for the sale of some of their land.[43]

The lack of a treaty presented legal difficulties and aroused moral doubts. 'We have taken possession of the country', Lyon declared, 'on the simple ground that *might* is *right*'.[44] The editor of *The Colonist* believed that Britain's title to Australia rested on 'no better foundation than that of *might*'. The country had been seized by main force 'utterly regardless of the questions of *right*'.[45] John Saunders took the view that the settlers had robbed the Aborigines 'without any sanctions' that he could find 'either in natural or revealed law'.[46] In a letter to a friend in 1832 George Augustus Robinson explained that he had difficulty in finding any justification for the expropriation of Aboriginal land. He was 'at a loss to conceive by what tenure we hold the country for it does not appear to be that we either hold it by right of conquest or right of purchase'.[47] To strengthen his case he quoted a passage that he had found in John Locke's *Civil Government* to the effect that no body has a right to take away a country which is the property of the original inhabitants without their own consent, that if they do such inhabitants are not freemen but slaves under the force of war.[48]

Few humanitarians had any doubt that Australia was invaded although they were aware the process was quite different from the large-scale military assaults common in European history. 'We have invaded the territory of the New Hollanders', declared the editor of *The Colonist*, 'and have taken forcible possession of their rightful property'. John Saunders observed in similar vein that 'we descended as invaders upon his territory and took possession of the soil'.[49] In a letter to Governor Bourke in 1837 James Backhouse observed that it was

scarcely to be supposed that in the present day any person of reflection will be found who will attempt to justify the measures adopted by the British, in taking possession of the territory of this people, who had committed no offence against our nation; but who, being without strength to repel invaders had their lands usurped, without any other offer of reasonable compensation.[50]

Given their view of British settlement the humanitarians sympathised with Aboriginal violence characterising it as understandable resistance or even heroic defence of their homelands. This was another point of fierce disagreement with many others in colonial society. It was hard to find any middle ground on the question at all. To European frontiersmen and their supporters any justification of Aboriginal guerilla warfare was tantamount to treason. Immediately after the execution of the Myall Creek murderers in December 1838

the editor of *The Colonist* argued that given the illegit-
imate seizure of Australia there was little wonder that
Britain's 'piratical invasion should have been resented by
the lords of the soil'. Was it not perfectly natural, he
asked, 'that the native should feel himself an injured man
and strike back at the white settler'? The only wonder
was that

> under the provocation of these accumulated injuries
> and insults, the Aborigines have not slaughtered every
> European they have encountered in the solitude of
> their forests.[51]

R. M. Lyon became involved in a public debate
with a fellow colonist who denounced the Aborigines
of the Swan Valley because of their attacks on the
settlers. 'He forgets', Lyon observed, 'that we have
provoked these people to hostilities'. Taking possession
of the country and destroying the game gave them no
alternative but to resist or to perish. He similarly dismissed his opponent's complaints about the manner in
which the Aborigines conducted their attacks. 'Is it not
amusing to hear', he wrote,

> the invaders of a country complaining of the manner
> in which the inhabitants attack their enemies and
> defend themselves? The guerilla war in which Spain
> repelled the invader of her throne, was lauded from
> one extremity of Europe to the other.[52]

Another theme running through humanitarian discourse was the absolute obligation to provide for
compensation—or an 'equivalence' as it was often called
at the time—for the land that had been expropriated and
the violence and disruption which had accompanied it.

'Of how large a debt do Britons owe these Aboriginal natives', exclaimed missionary Watson, 'for the physical and moral injuries inflicted by their fellow countrymen'.[53] The barrister Sydney Stephen took up the question while addressing the public meeting which launched the Aborigines Protection Society in Sydney in October 1838:

> The great question was, whether we were to give them no equivalent for that which we had taken from them? Had we deprived them of nothing? Was it nothing that they were driven from the lands where their fathers lived, where they were born, and which were endeared to them by associations equally strong with the associations of more civilized people?[54]

The humanitarians took heart from the policies advocated by the 1837 House of Commons Select Committee on Native People assuming that it had become settled doctrine that the 'right of civilized states to take possession of barbarous countries' rested entirely upon the principle of 'a *full equivalent being given by the invaders*' [emphasis in original]. But in discussing this question the editor of *The Colonist* adopted the view of many humanitarians that apart from the provision of food and services the greatest and most valuable form of compensation was to communicate to the indigenous people 'the imperishable blessings of Christianity'.[55] This was a very common view among missionaries, protectors and other 'philanthropic individuals'.

R. M. Lyon was willing to contrast the wealth extracted from Australia by the Europeans and the poverty of the Aborigines living in or near the settled districts. 'The very dogs eat the crumbs which fall from their master's table', he observed, 'but not a crumb is allowed to the Australians'. In calling for an annual appropriation to be reserved for 'the rightful owners of the soil' he drew his readers' attention to the fact that:

> Of the thousands and tens of thousands, the annual proceeds of the sale of his [i.e. the Aboriginal] lands, and the hundreds of thousands that are annually accumulating in private fortunes from the agriculture and commerce of his country, not a single pound is appropriated to the improvement of his state in this world or his prospects in another. Robbed and wounded by the thieves among whom he has fallen, he is left bleeding in the bush and abandoned to his fate.[56]

While the humanitarians launched a political attack on contemporary society for the dispossession, violence and neglect of Aborigines, their most emotional response related to what they believed was the sinfulness of what was happening. They often turned their eyes upward to God and forward to the prospect of final judgement. They were convinced that God would deliver the justice denied on earth and that those whose hands were stained with blood would suffer from His wrath. Missionary journals are full of such premonitions and warnings. In a letter to the London Missionary Society, James Dredge referred to 160 murders of Aborigines that he could account for. The government appeared to be unable or unwilling to do anything to stay the 'widespread devastation, heartless cruelties, wholesale robberies and endless murder'. 'And shall not God avenge the blood of these people?', he rhetorically asked.[57] His colleague Francis Tuckfield had no doubt whatever that God 'most

assuredly heareth the voice of our Brothers' Blood'.[58]
R. M. Lyon warned the colonists:

> Our brothers' blood is upon our heads; and expiation
> ought to begin where the British flag was first stained
> with the guilt of a crime all but unpardonable, and
> committed against a people whose unprotected and
> sad conditions, ought instead of exciting our cupidity,
> to have commanded our commiseration.[59]

It was not just individuals who offended the Almighty.
Nations too could suffer divine retribution. For a time
they might recklessly pursue schemes of 'spoliation,
flattering themselves they will escape consequences'. But,
Lyon believed, they were indulging a vain hope. 'The
eye of the eternal is upon them',[60] he warned darkly.

By far the most eloquent and powerful account of
the dangers of divine retribution was given by John
Saunders in his celebrated sermon in October 1838. It
was a moment when the humanitarian movement was
at the height of its power. Governor George Gipps had
recently arrived in New South Wales bringing new
policies and attitudes to the Aboriginal question. The
Myall Creek murderers were soon to be brought to
justice. George Augustus Robinson and William
Thomas, who were in the congregation, were about to
leave to set up the Port Phillip Protectorate. The Aborigines Protection Society was established a few days later
with strong support from among the religious and pro-
fessional leaders of Sydney society. The sermon was
worthy of the occasion. It was reported verbatim over
three days in the humanitarian paper *The Colonist*.[61]

Saunders opened his assault on the conscience
of New South Wales with a text from the Prophecy

of Isaiah: 'Behold the Lord cometh out of his place to punish the inhabitants of the earth for their iniquity; the earth also shall disclose her blood, and shall no more cover her slain'. He declared that the conduct of the colonists towards the original proprietors of the soil was a theme of the highest interest. Having declared that the Aborigine was a man and brother invested with all the natural rights which belong to humans he unleashed a savage denunciation of colonial policy and behaviour. It was, he said, a solemn inquiry as to whether the Europeans had fully discharged their duty towards their brother or whether they had wronged him. 'Our influence', he declared, 'has been deeply fatal to the black'. He then set out to enumerate the series of wrongs. The colonists came as invaders, they stole the land, without 'compunction or the offer of an equivalent'. Secondly, the settlers had brutalised the survivors, teaching them new lessons in 'fraud, dishonesty and theft'. 'We came', Saunders observed, 'to eclipse what little they had of happiness'. Thirdly, he continued relentlessly, 'we have shed their blood':

> I speak not of the broils and murders which might find a parallel in the conduct of the white towards the white, but of those extra murders in which so many have fallen. We have not been fighting with a natural enemy, but have been eradicating the possessors of the soil, and why, forsooth? because they were troublesome, because some few had resented the injuries they had received, and then how were they destroyed? by wholesale, in cold blood.

His denunciation deepened. While disease and famine had done their part to exterminate the blacks, the musket, the bayonet, the sword and poisoned damper had also had their influence. Britain had avenged the death of her sons, not by law, but by retaliation at the 'atrocious disproportion of a hundred to one'. As the sermon mounted to a climax Saunders declared:

> The spot of blood is upon us, the blood of the poor and the defenceless, the blood of the men we wronged before we slew; and too, too often, a hundred times too often, *innocent* blood.

These were not just crimes against man but crimes against God. And if there was anything which called for a swifter and more severe punishment than another it was the shedding of human blood. 'It is a fearful thing to shed human blood', he said, 'it is an act which has the deepest malediction of heaven upon it—a curse from the dread power above'. But it was not just the individual murderer who had to be concerned. The nation itself was implicated. Unlike the sins of blasphemy, perjury, licentiousness, gluttony and drunkenness, the treatment of the Aborigines was the sin 'in which the whole colony' had been engaged and was therefore answerable. 'I do not select individual delinquents', he explained,

> but impeach the nation; for whether in ignorance, or with a guilty knowledge, we certainly have been culpable in our neglect and oppression of this despised and degraded tribe of our fellow-men.

And nations were not beyond God's reach. Unlike individuals they had no after-life; there could be no day of judgement. Nations were judged on earth, punished and rewarded there. The globe on which they dwelt was 'their hall of judgement and their field of doom'.

The Australian colonies had earned God's wrath. For shedding blood they would receive a prompt and con-dign visitation. 'Oppression, cruelty and blood', Saunders warned, 'gather clouds of vengeance, and provoke the threatening thunder of the Omnipotent, and attract the bolt of wrath'. The situation was, indeed, serious:

> When he maketh 'inquisition for blood' will he not find it here? And finding it, surely we have reason to dread his visitation. In what way he may chasten us it is not for me to suggest; he is a sovereign, and acteth according to the counsels of his own will; but it is only to glance at his resources, and we can at once discern abundant reason to fear; he could parch us with drought, scatter our commerce, pinch us with penury, and lower us with disease; the plague, the tornado, and famine are at his back; Above all, he could weary us with civil dissension, with the miseries of an overflowing wickedness, or with the power of a hostile sword. These things God in his infinite mercy, has restrained, but how soon could he let loose their malignant influence upon us! We have, there-fore, reason to dread the approach of the Lord when he cometh out of his place to punish the inhabitants of the earth for their iniquity.

But all was not lost. The colonists could appease divine wrath and escape retribution. A nation, like an individual, could repent. God would listen to the 'united aspiration of a contrite people and withhold his vengeful hand'. But the colonists would have to do more than feel remorseful. Heartfelt penitence would lead to change of policy. Above all the killing had to stop. Saunders conceded that it might be difficult to restrain the 'lawless aggressors' on the borders of the colony. The spirit formed under feeling of penitence would prevent whole-sale massacres and lead to 'wholesome regulations' having for their object the prevention of outrages. If public opinion was strong enough even the distant stockman could be held in check.

But a reformed public opinion was not enough. The next step was restitution. 'And do we start at this word', he asked:

> It is one an honest man never need shrink from; it is one a noble mind will never discard; it is one a religious man will cheerfully adopt. It is our duty to recompense the Aborigines to the extent we have injured them. It is true we cannot make atonement for the lives which have been taken, neither can we make reparation for the multitudes which have has-tened to the tomb by the profligacy we have taught them.

But Saunders apparently had few practical sugges-tions. He had little to say about land rights, reserves, financial compensation, education or health. His res-titution was to be a spiritual one which would overturn traditional customs and beliefs. The colonists had a boon in their hands 'above all price'—Christianity, and the numerous comforts which flowed from it and which were 'comprehended in the expressive word civilization'.

But while Saunders could come up with few concrete reforms there were other contemporary humanitarians who became deeply involved in colonial politics in an endeavour to improve the Aboriginal situation. Among the most prominent were George Augustus Robinson, Lancelot Threlkeld, Robert Lyon and Louis Giustiniani whose careers, aspirations, actions and tribulations will now be considered.

III

A REASONABLE SHARE IN THE SOIL: ROBINSON AND THRELKELD IN NEW SOUTH WALES, 1824–48

George Augustus Robinson was the best-known humanitarian in the Australian colonies. His reputation was built on his 'Friendly Mission' to the Tasmanian Aborigines which resulted in the end of hostilities and the removal of all the survivors to Flinders Island where Robinson was commandant for several years (1835–39) before accepting the position of Chief Protector of Aborigines at Port Phillip which he held from 1839 to 1849.

Robinson's relationship with the Tasmanians was characterised by a cluster of contradictions. It has been examined by numerous scholars.[1] For the present the focus will be on his attitude to indigenous land rights. Like many of his humanitarian contemporaries Robinson believed that Aborigines were the legitimate owners of the soil. Intimacy with numerous Tasmanians over an extended period of time gave him an appreciation of the importance they attached to their homelands. He regarded the tribes as nations, knew the boundaries of their various territories and thought of the tribesmen and women as true patriots. Despite his knowledge and understanding of the Aboriginal relationship with the land he almost certainly betrayed the Tasmanians by failing to deliver on his promise that they would be able to return to their homelands after a short stay on Flinders Island. There is much evidence to suggest that Robinson was deeply conscious of his part in the betrayal.[2] The Tasmanian colonial historian J. E. Calder recorded that Robinson was often heard to express regret that the promises made to the Aborigines 'on which they surrendered their liberties, were so faithlessly kept'.[3] An uneasy conscience provoked Robinson into angry defence of the expediture committed to the settlement on Flinders Island. 'Why cannot they be satisfied', he wrote in 1837 of settlers critical of the cost of his administration. 'Have they not got the birthright of these poor people?' he asked angrily.[4] When inadequate room was provided on a ship taking an Aboriginal party to Flinders Island he noted in his journal that less space had been provided than there would have been available on a slave ship. But the Tasmanians 'were not slaves they were free persons, the lawful proprietors of the land'.[5] He reacted in a similar manner when he first arrived on Flinders Island and saw the poor quality of the temporary housing which indicated that the Aborigines,

> were considered as bondsmen for the conduct pursued towards them was such as would be pursued towards bondsmen and this is the light in which they have been considered—Whereas they are or ought to be free men of the highest order—patricians not plebeians—for they not us are—legitimate proprietors of the soil—we hold by might not by right—oh, it is cruel not to provide abundantly for this remnant of the aboriginal race—parsimony in such a case is not

niggardliness but injustice—gross injustice—we have
desolated them—despoiled them of their country—
the land of their forefathers—and having placed them
on an isolated spot. The least we ought to do is to
abundantly supply their wants.[6]

Robinson took both his passion and his guilt when
he crossed Bass Strait to take up his new position in
Melbourne. He was widely considered to be ineffectual
as Chief Protector and few later commentators have
questioned that assessment. But one theme that can be
traced throughout Robinson's Port Phillip decade was
his concern for land rights, his belief that the Aborigines
should be provided with a 'reasonable share in the soil
of their Fatherland'.[7] On this question he was both
persistent and consistent.

He arrived in the middle of the squatting rush when
pastoralists from both New South Wales and Tasmania
were occupying vast areas of open grassland and stocking
them with sheep and cattle. In many cases the resident
Aboriginal clans were being driven off the land. Robinson soon became aware of what he called 'a Complete
System of Expulsion and Extermination'. The first squatters arriving in a district drove the Aborigines away as
did those who followed the pioneers and 'then on ad
infinitum' until they were 'driven onto hostile tribes who
destroy them'.[8] After travelling into the bush and seeing
the frontier situation at first-hand he jotted down in his
journal:

Mr— has about 100 Square miles—Mr— 90 miles,
Mr— 100. Thus 3 individuals own 200 miles of
country between them—and they think it is a hard-

ship if a native appears on their run imagining that a licence gives them a legal right to Expel the black.[9]

While staying overnight with squatters he learnt of the prevailing attitudes. He recorded a breakfast-time conversation with a Mr H—. Robinson broached the subject of the rights of the natives to the soil. His host would hear none of it, saying he would 'not give in to that' because it was never intended that 'a few miserable savages were to have this fine country'. Robinson observed that H. ran 7000 sheep and paid £70 per annum to the government and for that trifle he held 'half an English county'.[10]

As he travelled through the countryside Robinson made contact with parties of Aborigines, heard their grievances and sympathised with their desperate situation. One morning in June 1841 in the Western District a local clan group came up to his camp at dawn. Robinson asked them where their land was. They beat the ground and then 'in a dejected tone bewailed the loss of their country'.[11] Five years later when travelling along the Murray into South Australia he met an Aboriginal man who stamped on the ground making it clear that the land was his. He vehemently exclaimed 'belonging to me, belonging to me, my country'.[12] When reflecting on the results of one of his expeditions Robinson summarised the view of the Aborigines he had encountered:

> Some white men they said very good but plenty very bad, that these shoot too much blackfellow and take away their lubra and picaninnie and that by and by blackfellow all gone. They were poor now White man had taken their good country, no ask for it but

took it. Black men show white men plenty grass, and water and then White men say be off come be off and drive them away and no let him stop.[13]

As Robinson learnt more about the squatting system at Port Phillip he understood the important role Aborigines had played in the earliest phases of pioneering. They were not always hostile at the time of initial incursions and often guided overlanding parties across their country and showed them where to find grass and water. 'The natives', he observed, were the parties who first guided the white men 'through the intricacies of the forest' and led them to their runs, their springs and rich pastures. The white men who made their living by what was termed 'finding country' sold the information thus gained to speculators in runs who hurriedly occupied the land with stock.[14]

Soon after his arrival Robinson expressed his concern about the land question to senior government officials. In May 1839 he had a long conversation with the chief surveyor about providing space for the Aborigines. He observed that although the government was officially committed to their protection no provision had been made for Aboriginal ownership of country. He was shown a map of an area covering 30 miles square which was already marked off into allotments. He told the surveyor that if a similar map was 'Exhibited to the people of England' they would at once see the way the natives were treated. Their lands were sold 'from them' and no provision was made for their maintenance.[15]

Later in 1839 Robinson wrote to the Superintendent of Port Phillip C. J. La Trobe pursuing his growing alarm about the spiralling dispossession of the Aborigines he had been appointed to protect. He expressed his concern for the clans who were trying to find some refuge from the 'wide spreading encroachment and cupidity of the squatters'. He explained that he did not know of any land that had been set aside in a whole range of country which had been mapped and sectioned off for the Auctioneer's hammer. He argued that it would be an act of common justice for the tribes and remnant tribes to be allowed to select 'in their own districts small portions of land'. Many of the squatters with their twenty and forty square miles of country 'absurdly imagine' that a ten pound licence to squat confers on them the power to expel the 'primitive inhabitants from the land of their forefathers'. The Aborigines had been coerced and 'chased by horseman from their homes and native fires' by men who boasted that they never allowed an Aborigine to appear on their run.[16]

Robinson's confidence that the squatters had no right to expel Aborigines from their runs was undermined by a judgement made in the local courts in 1841 in the case of *R v. Bolden*. Bolden was indicted for shooting at, with intent to murder, an Aborigine named Tackiar. Justice Willis determined that a pastoralist holding a licence to occupy a run had a right to drive off trespassers by any lawful means. The Aborigines had 'no right to trespass unless there [was] a special clause in the licence'. If the Aborigines were stealing stock the use of firearms was justifiable.[17] The same rules would have applied to European thieves and trespassers.

Robinson was provoked into further action in the middle years of the 1840s when it became apparent that

the squatters would be given long leases over their runs.
Up till then he had refrained from officially raising the
question of land rights both because the pastoralists only
had annual licences and because he had been uncertain
about dealing with 'what might have been considered
at that time a vexatious question'. But in his annual
report of 1845 he proposed that the Aborigines be
granted a reasonable share in the country which had
recently been theirs.[18]

He returned to the question with much greater
confidence in his annual report for 1846. 'The claim of
the Aborigines', he wrote,

> to a reasonable share in the Soil of their fatherland,
> has not, I regret to say, been recognized, in any of
> the discussions, which, for so great a length of time
> have agitated the public mind on the question of the
> rights of the Squatters, to the occupancy of the Lands
> of the Crown . . . [therefore] the duty devolves on
> me to bring their Claim under the notice of Her
> Majesty's Government for a reasonable share in the
> Soil of their fatherland . . . especially as the Lands of
> the Crown are about to be alienated, and leased to
> the European Settlers for a period of years.[19]

He was deeply concerned that the legal authority
accorded to these lease holders would allow them to
drive the Aborigines from the land in question and that
they would be hunted from station to station without
any place to call their own. He referred to the similar
views of his colleague, the Assistant Protector E. S.
Parker, who warned that unless suitable reserves were
immediately formed 'every acre of their native soil will

shortly be so leased out and occupied as to leave them, in a legal view, with no place for the sole of their feet'.[20]

By the time Robinson wrote his next annual report he knew that the squatters had won the right to have leases for periods of between eight and fourteen years. 'What kind of treatment', he asked, would the native receive 'when all the Lands are leased for a period of years'.[21] Things were bad enough as it was. In some districts and in some seasons the 'greatest exertion' was required even by the healthy to procure a subsistence. The sick, the lame and the aged suffered want and frequently died from malnutrition. Elsewhere the traditional foods were totally destroyed and 'from their favorite haunts they are all but prohibited', every spot where water and grass could be found was overrun by stock. The squatters' runs often overlapped leaving the Aborigines only the rocky ravines and arid waste.[22]

Robinson re-iterated his belief that it was just and reasonable that the natives should have 'spots to call their own, and land whereon to settle'. He knew that such proposals were poorly received in the colonies. 'Improvable lands', he explained,

> are it is said too valuable, as they do not cultivate,
> and such lands are of great value to the White Settler,
> but if considerations of this sort were held to justify
> a compulsory transfer of property then there would
> be an end to the rights of all property whatever.[23]

Like other humanitarians Robinson was outraged by the contrast between the poverty of Aborigines living in the settled districts and the wealth that was being extracted from what until recently had been their land. Having referred to contemporary accounts of the value of pastoral industry he argued that a people from whose lands such wealth was derived was 'entitled to some consideration, in return for those great pecuniary advantages'. He continued:

> One would have thought that the immense *wealth* derived from their Lands, and possessed by the White Inhabitants would have obtained for them some consideration, and placed them in a different position.[24]

Robinson believed that by highlighting the Aboriginal plight and bringing 'under notice' the urgent need for reserves he had fulfilled his official duty to protect Port Phillip's traditional owners. He reminded his superiors of the wording of his original instructions from Lord Glenelg that he should watch over 'the rights and interests of the Natives' and protect them as far as possible from encroachments on their property and from acts of cruelty, oppression or injustice.[25] As was so often the case Robinson was seeking the approval of his 'betters' and hoping that he had not been too outspoken in his defence of the Aborigines.

It is likely that Robinson's long-winded annual reports received scant attention in Melbourne and Sydney. By the mid-1840s he was thought to be a tiresome and discredited officer; a pompous, prickly upstart. But his reports had a quite different reception when they eventually reached the Colonial Office in London. As he was compiling his 1848 report in December of that year his 1847 one was being given serious attention in Downing Street. His concern about Aboriginal access to land touched upon an issue which had aroused genuine, if intermittent, concern throughout the 1830s and 1840s. But Robinson's and Parker's pleas injected a sense of urgency into the discourse because the squatters now had security of tenure. Their call for a reasonable share of the soil was immediately picked up when it was read along with many other documents enclosed in a dispatch from Governor Fitzroy of New South Wales. Robinson was being taken seriously in a place, and in a manner, that even he may not have expected, his self-importance notwithstanding.

One of the officials who read Robinson's report emphasised the important issues with his pencil. He drew a line in the margin beside the twice repeated phrase regarding Aboriginal claims to a 'reasonable share in the soil of their fatherland' and further emphasised it by underlining the words when they first appeared and placing a large asterisk in the margin when they were repeated. The various officials wrote memos about the issue as the document crossed progressively larger desks in its ascent through the Colonial Office hierarchy. The first comment was from Thomas Murdoch in a memo to his superior Herman Merivale. He drew attention to, and directly quoted, the words of Assistant Protector Parker about there being no place, from a legal point of view, for the soles of Aboriginal feet. At the end of the quote Murdoch wrote: 'Fitzroy's attention should I presume be drawn. It would of course, be most unjust that the Natives should be extruded in the manner described ... from the soil of which till recently, they were the sole occupants.' In his turn Merivale observed that the request for reserves raised a number of serious questions. Australia was poorly supplied with water and with game. The Aborigines required room for wandering if they were to live after their own fashion. It would be difficult therefore to establish them on reserve land in the middle of territory occupied by scattered settlers. He suggested that Robinson be asked about the extent and location of the reserves he advocated and 'the manner in which he imagined they would subsist on such reserves'.

When the documents reached the Secretary of State Earl Grey the question of Aboriginal rights assumed even greater importance. The pleas of Robinson and Parker were being considered at the heart of the Empire. The irony is that in his long memo Grey also discussed the impending dismissal of Robinson and the winding up of the Protectorate. But on the question of Aboriginal rights Grey was adamant. Either with or without a machinery of protection, he wrote, 'the importance of doing whatever is possible for the preservation of the Aboriginal race must be strongly pressed upon the Governor'. [Words abbreviated by Grey have been rendered in full.] Grey apparently had second thoughts when he re-read his memo, crossed out 'importance' and substituted the far stronger word 'duty'. He then maintained that the expense of any measures for the amelioration of the Aboriginal condition 'ought to be the very first charge upon the [colonial] land revenue'.

Grey also addressed the matter of Aboriginal access to land. 'The question of reserves for natives is an important one', he observed. The Governor should be instructed 'to take care that they are not . . . driven off all the country which is divided into grazing stations and let under the recent regulations'. He foreshadowed measures to provide both land and maintenance for Aborigines to make up for the deficiency of game. Then

in one of the darkest comments ever made by a British
official or politician about Australian colonies he wrote:
'this is very important with a view to their preservation
from being *exterminated*' [Grey's emphasis].[26]

Two months after expressing his foreboding to his
departmental officers Grey signed a dispatch to Governor
Fitzroy which contained the Colonial Office's considered
response to the question of Aboriginal rights and pastoral
leases. It addressed the concerns expressed by Robinson
and Parker but it also encompassed the practical questions
injected into policy making by Herman Merivale about
the nature of Australian geography. Thus Grey referred
to the requests for the creation of reserves in every large
district and observed that while such a scheme was
appropriate elsewhere in the world Australia's soil and
fertility demanded a different answer. The dryness of the
continent and the need to use large areas of land for
grazing called for a peculiarly local solution. In fact:

> . . . the very difficulty of thus locating the Aboriginal
> Tribes absolutely apart from the Settlers renders it
> more incumbent on Government to prevent them
> from being altogether excluded from the land under
> pastoral occupation. I think it essential that it should
> be generally understood that leases granted for this
> purpose give the grantees only an exclusive right of
> pasturage for their cattle, and of cultivating such land
> as they may require within the large limits thus
> assigned to them, but that leases are not intended to
> deprive the natives of their former right to hunt over
> these Districts, or to wander over them in search of
> subsistence, in the manner to which they have been
> heretofore accustomed, from the spontaneous produce

of the soil except over land actually cultivated or fenced in for that purpose.[27]

Grey concluded that the rights of possession conferred on a lessee by a lease for pastoral purposes did not include a right to exclude Aboriginal people. The pastoralists' 'exclusive rights of pasturage' co-existed with Aboriginal rights to live on, travel over and obtain their subsistence from leased lands, although Grey accepted that in the case of land cultivated and enclosed 'for the purpose', a lessee would have unqualified rights of possession.

> The rights of the lessee and Aboriginal people were 'mutual rights'—a distinct understanding of the extent of their mutual rights is one step at least towards the maintenance of order and mutual forbearance between the parties. If therefore, the limitation, which I have mentioned above on the right of exclusive occupation granted by Crown Leases, is not in your opinion fully recognized in the Colony, I think it is advisable that you should enforce it by some public declaration, or, if necessary, by passing a declaratory Enactment.[28]

In the following year Grey returned to the question and in a dispatch to Governor Fitzroy he again explained the relationship which should exist between Aborigines and pastoral lease holders. There could be little doubt, he explained,

> that the intention of Government was, as I pointed out in my Dispatch of 11 February last, to give only exclusive right of pasturage in the runs, not the exclusive occupation of the land, as against the Natives using it for ordinary purposes.[29]

By the end of 1850 the Imperial government had determined that all pastoral leases issued in the Australian colonies should contain a clause, or reservation, 'conveying to the Natives the continuance of rights'.[30] In the Wik judgement of 1996 the High Court determined that those rights still survive and have not been extinguished by the issuing of a pastoral lease.

George Augustus Robinson betrayed the Tasmanians and received great benefits from doing so. But his determination to bring the plight of Victorian Aborigines 'under notice' of the authorities was to have major consequences over the vast pastoral lands of the continent. They are still being felt.

Lancelot Threlkeld and George Augustus Robinson had much in common. They were both born in 1788 and grew up in London in poor families with semi-skilled artisan fathers. Both were largely self-educated and like many young men of their class background became involved in the evangelical revival, Threlkeld as a Methodist and Robinson as an Anglican. Threlkeld experienced sudden conversion and became an itinerant field preacher. He was accepted for missionary work by the London Missionary Society in 1815 and set sail for Polynesia in January 1816. Robinson remained in England till 1823 but both men arrived to settle in Australia in 1824. Threlkeld established a mission to the Aborigines on the shores of Lake Macquarie near Newcastle in 1826 and remained in the district until 1841, first under the auspices of the London Missionary Society and then from 1829 with the support of the colonial government. Robinson began his work with the Aborigines as a government official on Bruny Island in 1829.

The arrival of the two immigrants coincided with the rapid expansion of settlement and the outbreak of serious frontier conflict in the Tasmanian Midlands, on the Bathurst Plains and along the Hunter Valley.

Threlkeld was confronted by racial violence as soon as he arrived in Newcastle prior to setting up his mission. There was constant friction between the male convicts and the Aboriginal fringe camps and Threlkeld attempted to prevent the forcible abduction of black women and girls. One evening in December 1825 he heard a shout which attracted his attention and saw a white man beating the Aborigines who called out to him for help. He ran up to the scene demanding to know what was going on. The European replied that the blacks had insulted him. But on enquiring further he found that the assailant had arrived in the camp demanding to take away a ten-year-old girl who had run off and was hiding in the water. The girl's father had refused to give his permission for the girl to go away, was being beaten for his trouble and had deep wounds on both his head and back. Threlkeld was infuriated and told his countryman that he would have him charged 'as no one should wantonly insult the Blacks, with my knowledge with impunity'.[31] The following day he laid a complaint against the man for assault. Two of the three magistrates on the local bench were hostile to Threlkeld but eventually they agreed to hear the charge. The man was reprimanded and discharged.[32]

Threlkeld had intimations of the violence out on the frontiers while he was still in Sydney, writing to the London Missionary Society in February 1825 that at a meeting he had attended a prominent landowner advocated the shooting of all the Aborigines.[33] Once he settled at Lake Macquarie the Aborigines frequently brought him news of atrocities committed by settlers in the district. In his second half-yearly report to the London Missionary Society in June 1826 he referred to the local outrages and then speculated about the aggregate throughout the colony and what 'must be the feelings of the Aborigines' mind against the whites?' As with many other humanitarians he was deeply troubled by the already entrenched tradition of the punitive expedition which by its very nature was likely to be both random and excessive. He had no doubt that murderers, whether black or white, should be executed. 'But let it be the *Murderer*', he cried in anguish, 'not his wife, his children, his friends, his relatives, his race'.[34]

A few months later he was writing home to England again with news of continuing violence. 'We are in a state of warfare up the country here', he observed, 'the blood of the blacks begins to flow'. Two stockmen had been speared in revenge for the earlier deaths of four Aborigines who were 'deliberately shot without any trial or form whatever'. For their part the settlers were demanding martial law and massive retaliation. He was in a very difficult situation. The mission was unpopular and hostility to it increased as tensions rose. 'No one can tell how I am perplexed respecting the Aborigines', he explained. If he spoke out he outraged his countrymen. If he didn't he had to confront his own demanding standards. He wrote: '. . . if I don't speak then my conscience says I become accessory to their death'.[35] He hoped that God would give him the wisdom and strength to act faithfully and provide refuge in times of trouble.

But Threlkeld's unpopularity with the settlers was not surprising. He took a very jaundiced view of the whole process of colonisation. 'No man', he wrote bitterly, 'who comes to this Colony and has ground and corn can dispassionately view the subject of the blacks, their interest says annihilate the race'. He was censorious of those who were accumulating wealth from their expropriation of Aboriginal land and who did not devote a portion of those riches to assist the dispossessed or take up the cause of philanthropy. Like his brother missionaries he wielded the threat of God's displeasure, asking rhetorically, 'will not the cry of a brother's blood, occasioned too often to be shed through the thirst for wealth . . . ascend into the ears of God?' And will not 'the wealthy possessors of the land', by apathy to the Aborigines, 'subject themselves to that imprecation of the Angel in the day of Retribution, "Curse ye bitterly the inhabitants thereof, because they came not to the help"'.[36]

Threlkeld was distressed by the brutal language used in relation to the Aborigines. In a letter to the London Missionary Society in 1826 he declared that he would forbear from repeating the 'many revolting things which had been said publicly in the Colony' and in the presence of leading citizens who should have been the 'real Champions for such injured persons'.[37] But the erroneous impressions did not arise solely from ignorance of Aborigines' habits and customs. Threlkeld argued that it was a time-honoured tactic of those who wished 'determinately to carry a point' first to brand with obloquy their intended victim 'and then destroy him'. So the murderers of the blacks 'boldly maintained that the blacks were only a specie of baboon, that might be shot down with impunity, like an Ourang Outang [*sic*]!'[38]

The violence which disturbed Threlkeld when he established his mission in 1826 was merely a prelude to what was to occur in the following decade as the settlers fanned out in ever increasing numbers along the broad river valleys of northern New South Wales. As pressures on them increased the Aborigines responded, spearing shepherds and stock, driving off whole flocks of sheep, firing huts and grass. Punitive expeditions, both official and private, struck back exacting revenge out of all proportion to the intensity of Aboriginal resistance. Threlkeld gathered information about the border war from many sources and began to compile a catalogue of the various atrocities which was then passed on to government officials, churchmen and members of the judiciary by means of conversations, letters, reports and speeches. He prepared a document for the Supreme Court judge Justice William Burton and in April and October 1838 had long interviews with Governor George Gipps.[39]

His speech to the public meeting in Sydney in October 1838 which launched the Aborigines Protection Society was characteristic of the man. He began by saying that he had seen circumstances for many years that had pained his mind in the conduct of Europeans towards Aborigines. 'If the natives did wrong', he argued, 'let them be punished on *Christian principles*'; let not the innocent be punished for the guilty. The whites, he believed were generally the aggressors, and he told his audience that he could, if necessary make out a list of 500 blacks who had been slaughtered by the whites, and that 'within a short time'. He then turned his attack on the editors of the pro-squatter Sydney newspapers who stood charged 'with criminality in the sight of God' for having inflamed the public mind against the Aborigines. While they could shelter from the public behind the editorial 'we', that would avail them nothing when they were called to answer for their deeds 'before the Judge of all'. Threlkeld concluded his speech with the assertion that:

> He should strongly maintain the principle that the Aborigines were entitled to protection and compensation from those who had forcibly deprived them of their patrimony.[40]

Threlkeld detailed the atrocities he had heard about in his official annual reports to the government, particularly in his seventh report, for 1837 and the eighth report, for 1838. In the seventh report he declared that if an inquiry was held into the conduct of some Europeans towards the blacks it would discover that a 'war of extirpation' was underway. Anyone who tried to speak about the situation faced intimidation from a 'lawless banditti' who by combination and cruelty defied British law 'to its very teeth'. Threlkeld spelt out a list of horrors that had been reported to him, including:

> the ripping open of the bellies of the Blacks alive;— the roasting of them in that state in triangularly made log fires, made for the very purpose;—the dashing of infants upon the stones; the confining of a party in a hut and letting them out singly through the doorway,

to be butchered as they endeavoured to escape, together with many other atrocious acts of cruelty, which are but the sports of monsters boasting of superior intellect to that possessed by the wretched blacks.[41]

Threlkeld returned to the theme in his report of the following year. He noted that a recent report of the New South Wales Legislative Council had provided a list of fifteen Europeans killed by Aborigines between 1832 and 1838. But at the same time 'a secret hostile process' had been carried on against the Aborigines by a party of lawless Europeans which had 'unblushingly and openly appeared', to the loss of upwards of 500 Aboriginal lives within the last two years. But this time Threlkeld indicted not just the 'lawless banditti' but Major James Nunn, the colony's senior military officer. The death toll of 500 included the 200 or 300 'said to be slaughtered in the engagement which it is reported took place betwixt the horse police, commanded by Major Nunn, and the Aborigines of the interior'.[42]

The missionary's anger at the campaign by Major Nunn along the Gwydir and its tributaries in January 1838 runs as a broad thread through his 1838 report. He referred with fury to the 'cold hearted, bloody massacres by men called Christians'. Then in a direct reference to what he knew of Nunn's behaviour after the campaign he scorned those who could 'boast of their exploits in "popping off a Black the moment he appeared", regardless to his innocence or guilt'. He continued the attack with cutting sarcasm, observing that 'the gallantry displayed' in attacking the Aborigines 'had better been displayed in the field of honour with more equal enemies, and in a much more noble and righteous cause'.[43]

His sympathy for the Aborigines is as clear as his anger at the Europeans. Retaliation had to be expected and therefore guarded against. Massacre and atrocity would naturally feed the fires of revenge. They could not be condemned for their resistance because they were in exactly the same situation as the ancient Britons when their country was invaded by the Roman legions and the Roman claim to Britain was about as just and right in principle as that of Great Britain to New South Wales. Threlkeld had compared the Aboriginal situation to that of the ancient Britons throughout his career as an advocate for reform. Ten years earlier he had written:

> We view the conduct of Charactacus, leading the Aboriginal Britons and opposing the invading Romans with applause, and Boadicea, queen of an Aboriginal tribe . . . with sympathy. But the Aborigines of Australia, who have no combined numbers, no political power, to render themselves respected, or rather feared, by the invaders of their country, are driven, indirectly, from their districts, as other wild beasts of the desert, without Sympathy, when the civilized hand cultivates their soil![44]

Before his report was completed Threlkeld returned once again to that recurrent theme of the humanitarians of the period—their moral doubts about the taking of Aboriginal land and an even more general concern about the manner of Australian colonisation which had seen indigenous land sold off section by section 'till there be no place for the Aborigines—that the European may be placed alone in the midst of the earth'.[45] As a nation, he declared,

> we have *placed ourselves* in a position that has *compelled* the Aborigines to become *our neighbours*, and we have worked ill towards our neighbours, because we, the many dispossess the few Blacks of their rights of birth, which convey to them a certain district, in which they seek and obtain their means of subsistence. Our might deprives them of this right, without remuneration: and Immigration, so beneficial to us as a Colony, in increasing our population, decreases in an incalculable ratio, our neighbours as a people, by taking away the common hereditary privileges which they have possessed since time immemorial.[46]

Few contemporaries read Threlkeld's 1838 report. His two previous ones had been published and were available to the public. The recently arrived Governor Gipps showed interest in the 1837 report and asked Threlkeld to call on him to discuss his account of frontier violence. But in 1838 Threlkeld had gone beyond general accusation and reference to anonymous assailants. He had named Major Nunn, the commandant of British forces in the colony as the mass murderer of several hundred Aborigines. Despite his humanitarian leanings this was too much for the Governor. The report was filed away and the official copy eventually disappeared.[47]

Threlkeld remained on his mission until 1841 when Gipps informed him that he was to lose his funding. He left the district at the end of the year and moved to Sydney. Gipps delivered the coup de grace with 'never a word of thanks for his 27 years hard labour'.[48] By then the Governor's determination to protect the Aborigines was faltering. The humanitarian movement was at its zenith in 1838 with the trial and execution of the Myall Creek murderers in December, a development which Threlkeld's exposure of frontier violence had helped bring about.

IV

GREAT DISPLEASURE: LYON AND GIUSTINIANI IN WESTERN AUSTRALIA, 1829–38

The Quaker missionary James Backhouse left Australia early in 1838. On the voyage from the Swan River to Mauritius he met fellow passenger Dr Louis Giustiniani. When he arrived in Port Louis he was introduced to Robert Menli Lyon who had left Western Australia a year or two earlier and was the professor of Greek and English at the Royal College. Backhouse took an interest in the two men because they had promoted the Aboriginal cause in the Swan River colony. Both had suffered as a consequence and were in a sense political exiles. In a letter to the great British humanitarian Thomas Buxton, Backhouse mentioned their experiences and explained how both men had been subject to 'great contumely' because of their views.[1] Robert Lyon had taken a 'very commendable interest in the welfare of the Aborigines'. As a result of his belief respecting their 'capacity for amelioration he had strong prejudices to contend with' and in defending their cause he subjected himself to the 'great displeasure of many of the settlers'.[2]

Lyon and Giustiniani were quite different from their eastern Australian contemporaries Threlkeld and

70

Robinson. They were both highly educated. Giustiniani had the 'education of a Scholar in the dead languages' and had been in the habit of 'preaching in four living ones'.[3] He had a medical degree as well. Lyon wrote with flair and alluded easily to classical and contemporary literature. Both men had confidence and sophistication beyond the reach of the self-educated Robinson and Threlkeld. However, they shared with them an evangelical fervour and a commitment to the protection of Aboriginal rights. Like Threlkeld, Giustiniani came to Australia as a missionary appointed by the Western Australian Missionary Society established in Dublin and London in 1835. Lyon arrived as a settler in 1829 and in a similar manner to Robinson was moved to take up the Aboriginal cause by the tragic events he saw unfolding around him.

Lyon travelled extensively in the new colony and had friendly contact with the local Aborigines. He believed them to be a 'harmless, liberal, kind-hearted race'. They had initially shown little hostility to the Europeans. In a letter to the Colonial Office in 1833 he explained that they not only abstained from 'all acts of hostility when we took possession but showed us every kindness in their power' even though

> we were invaders of their country, & they had therefore a right to treat us as enemies, whilst any of us lost ourselves in the bush and were thus completely in their power, these noble minded people shared with us their scanty & precarious meal; lodged us for the night and in the morning directed us on our way.[4]

Like other humanitarians Lyon studied the dialects and customs of the clans living close to the settlement and believed their culture and way of life was intimately related to the environment. Their circumstances were entirely due to the situation in which they were placed 'and not to any mental inferiority'. In no point were they inferior and in many ways they were superior 'to those of the same grade with themselves in civilized life'. The settlers who insisted they were savage were 'entirely ignorant of their manner and disposition'.[5] Their apparent 'want of ingenuity' had been caused by the nature of the country, the climate and their mode of living.[6]

But Lyon believed that the settlers felt compelled to vilify the Aborigines in order to justify the invasion of their territory. None of the normal justifications used in European inter-state diplomacy had any purchase at the antipodes. There had been no breach of treaty, no unprovoked aggression or insult offered to the national flag. The tribes around the Swan River were totally unaware of England 'till British arms gleamed on their shore'. Those who advocated the adoption of a hostile attitude towards them were 'driven to the alternative of inventing some view of the case that would justify such a line of conduct'. The plan hit upon, Lyon argued, was 'to render them odious to the public at home, by representing them in the worst light'.[7]

Lyon watched with mounting concern the escalation of violence around the fringes of the colony and the growing demand from the settlers that the government sanction punitive actions. Hearing that a public meeting was to be held at Guildford he decided to attend because he feared that 'sanguinary measures would be determined upon'. He gave a report of his speech to the Colonial Office:

Gentlemen: Have you not a fatherland?—So have the aboriginal inhabitants of this country. Have you wives and little ones? So have they. Have you scenes of childhood, endured to you by the recollection of many an endearing association? So have they . . . Have you the rights of men? What has expunged theirs from the book of Nature? Have you lands that have descended to you by inheritance? So have they. These lands have descended to them from their fore-fathers from time immemorial. And their title deeds require not the wrangling of lawyers to prove them to be correct. They have the seal of Heaven— the sanction of Him who 'divided to the nations their inheritance'. They are indisputable. Reflect. You have seized upon a land that is not yours. Beware, and do not . . . add to the guilt of dipping your hands in the blood of those whom you have spoiled of their country.[8]

Whether Lyon's oratory had any effect on the meeting is impossible to tell but the decision was made to restrict force to acts of justifiable self-defence. But violence persisted. The settlers came to fear the influence of Yagan and a reward of £20 was put on his head. Lyons' view was that he was a patriot who had 'distinguished himself in the defence of his country'.[9] He had displayed feelings which had 'immortalized Tell of Switzerland and Wallace of Scotland'.[10] But Lyon came to have much more than an abstract admiration for Yagan.

He was travelling to Perth on the day that Yagan and two companions were 'ensnared by stratagem', taken bound hand and foot and thrown on the ground in front of the guard house. As Lyon neared the town he saw men, women and children running towards the central meeting place. A woman carrying a baby cried out to him as she ran: 'Oh that terrible man is taken'. When he reached the Governor's residence he found the Governor, council members and a large crowd surrounding the three captives 'lying on the ground, in fearful expectation of the doom that awaited them'. Lyon approached the Colonial Secretary suggesting that he might visit the prisoners in prison in order to learn the local language but was rudely rebuffed. He then spoke to the Governor and remonstrated against the planned execution urging him that the men were guilty of no crime but that of fighting for their country. 'We might call their deeds murder', he argued, 'so might they ours'. But they had a right to make war 'after their own manner'. Consequently Yagan and his two compatriots were prisoners of war and it would be contrary to both the law of nations and the usages of war to put the captives to death.[11]

Governor Stirling agreed to allow Lyon to have access to the prisoners. With a small military guard the party was marooned on the barren, rocky island of Carnac lying about ten miles off the coast between Fremantle and Rottnest Island. Lyon and the prisoners remained there from 8 October to 15 November 1832 when Yagan and his companions stole a boat and escaped to the mainland. While on the island Lyon busied himself learning the local language as projected. A week after arrival he wrote to the Governor enclosing a vocabulary and explaining that 'the whole tribe are bards'. Their history and geography was handed down generation to generation in verse. He later wrote that he was constantly annoyed by the claims that the local language was 'an unintelligible jargon'. It was, he declared, an interesting language and one which would richly repay the 'labour of acquisition' both to the 'Christian and the man of letters'.[12] On the first Sunday he assembled the small party for divine service. Carnac, he remarked, heard the sound of prayer for the first time since creation.[13] The pleasure he derived from being the first to 'announce the name of Jesus' to those who were 'utter strangers to revelations' and had never heard of the advent of a Saviour made the rock on which he slept 'softer than a bed of down'.[14]

As Lyon worked, ate and slept with the three prisoners he acquired information about traditional society which he published under the title 'A Glance at the Manners and Language of Aboriginal Inhabitants of Western Australia' in the *Perth Gazette* in March 1833. He developed a close relationship with Yagan and came to admire him, writing an appreciative sketch of his appearance and character:

> He was tall, athletic and muscular, with a strong dash of the savage in his countenance. When placid, animated in conversation, or even a little excited, no peer in the realm could excel him in dignity or demeanour or urbanity of manners. The passions of the savage, however, occasionally flitting across his brow and playing behind his bronze coloured countenance, kept confidence in check; and yet, when conciliating, he exhibited a disposition so candid, cordial, and generous, that the most timid could not but feel at perfect ease in his company, be it where it may, whether in the midst of the city or the solitary desert. He was altogether a noble, a princely character—one of nature's best productions.[15]

While reporting to the Governor after his return to the mainland Lyon was sanguine about the possibility of reaching an accommodation with the local tribes. He believed that if he had been a few weeks longer on Carnac the three prisoners could have been used to negotiate a treaty between the traditional owners and the newcomers. Without that Swan River would experience the sort of intense conflict which was just coming to an end in Tasmania. He warned the Governor that the Aborigines were courageous, strong-willed and determined to maintain their independence. 'Such are the men', he observed, 'you have to deal with in the natives of Western Australia'. The best policy was clearly to make peace with them before they acquired a knowledge of European manners and tactics. Otherwise the peace of the settlement would be sacrificed for many years at a cost to both government and community of which there appeared to be 'no conception'.[16]

Lyon's call for a negotiated treaty and for greater understanding of the desperate situation of the local clans who were finding it increasingly difficult to acquire enough to eat did not earn him the affection of his fellows or the ear of government. In a letter to the *Perth Gazette* in April 1833 he rhetorically asked the colonists: 'How long will it be before you take pity upon this people? Are your hearts made of adamant?' 'Have they no compassion?' 'My enemies', he wrote, 'may sneer, lampoon and defame. I regard them not.' His endeavour to prevent 'a war of extermination' and to introduce the true God to the 'unfortunate savages', would eventually be judged by future historians.[17]

Lyon's greatest moment came in June 1833 when

settler demands for punitive action were burgeoning once again. He attended a meeting of the 'magistrates, gentlemen and yeomen' of the colony at Guildford and delivered a long and impassioned plea for conciliation. It was inflated, rhetorical and strangely archaic in manner. How it was received is unknown. But it is one of the most distinguished humanitarian speeches delivered in colonial Australia, ranking alongside John Saunders' sermon of 1838. It deserves lengthy quotation.

'Again the war shout echoes from hill to hill', he began, 'again our ears are assailed by the din of hostile movements throughout the settlement'. He asked his audience that before they were 'hurried away by the fury which seems to possess the minds of so many' they would allow him as 'the friend of this unfortunate race', to remonstrate with them. He then posed the 'awkward question' of whether the Aborigines were British subjects or not. If they were they should have all the attendant privileges and especially trial by jury. In reality they were left to the mercy of 'any ruffian who chooses to level a gun at them'. What was more they had no means of communicating with Europeans. It was the duty of the settlers to possess themselves of the native language for without that they might as well 'call the Kangaroos of the forest British subjects'.[18]

> But if ye have taken their country from them, and they refuse to acknowledge your title to it, ye are at war with them; and, having never allowed your right to call them British subjects, they are justified by the usages of war in taking your property wherever they find it, and in killing you whenever they have an opportunity. Ye are the aggressors. The law of nations

will bear them out in repelling force by force. They did not go to the British isles to make war upon you; but ye came from the British isles to make war upon them. Ye are the invaders of their country—ye are the plunderers of their wealth—ye destroy the natural productions of the soil on which they live—ye devour their fish and their game—and ye drive them from the abodes of their ancestors.[19]

He then turned his attention to the colonial assumption that Aborigines lacked attachment to the soil because of their nomadic lifestyle. After a long digression about the universal characteristic of humans to feel devotion to the land of their birth he declared:

Think not, then, that the Aboriginal inhabitants of Australia, offspring of the same great parent with yourselves, and partakers of all the kindred feelings of a common humanity, can resign the mountains and seas, the rivers and lakes, the plains and the wilds of their uncradled infancy, and the habitation of their fathers for generations immemorial, to a foreign foe, without the bitterness of grief. What, though the grass be their couch and the tree of the forest their only shelter, their blue mountains, and the country where they first beheld the sun, the moon, and the starry heavens, are as dear to them as your native land with all its natural and artificial beauties, its gilded towers and magnificent spires, is to you.[20]

Lyon then turned his attention to the persistent conflict, warning his listeners that even if the Aborigines were not subjects but national enemies it was still not legitimate to 'hunt them down and kill them, as if they were so many wild beasts'. He continued:

But what shall we say to the barbarous practice of firing upon them wherever they are seen—a practice, unconfined to the lower orders, and common to some from whom better things might be expected! Apart from the fiend-like wickedness of thus wantonly destroying human life, what will such a course of proceeding profit you in the end? They have tendered their services to you as hewers of wood and drawers of water; could the most despotic conqueror—the most iron-hearted tyrant—require more? The very powder and ball ye expend in shooting them would *purchase* their lands.[21]

In an increasingly emotional plea he asked his fellow settlers whether the defenceless Australians would find in them 'no compassion, no trait of a kindred humanity, nothing but tigers, bears, wolves, and beasts of prey?'[22] He was particularly censorious of the colonial habit of denouncing Aboriginal attacks on the Europeans as illustrative of savagery and treachery. How hard is the fate of this people, he observed:

They may stand to be slaughtered; but they must not throw a spear in their own defence, or attempt to bring their enemies to a sense of justice by the only means in their power,—that of returning like for like. If they do—if they dare to be guilty of an act which in other nations would be eulogized as the noblest of a patriot's deeds—they are outlawed; a reward is set upon their heads; and they are ordered to be shot, as if they were so many mad dogs! Thus, in the barbarous manner, ye practice what in them ye condemn, the law of retaliation.[23]

He then explained that the whole country was divided into districts and that no tribe could move onto the land of another. Their 'sad condition' was that they were caught between the 'British banner, frowning destruction' and behind them the spear of the neighbouring tribes. 'Remember, too', he declared,

> that ye have never attempted to make peace with them. Every cessation of arms has been only a tacit truce—a calm that preceded a storm. And while ye act upon a wavering uncertain policy, the war will assume a more sanguinary character on every recurrence of hostilities, till it become interminable, and, staining your title deeds with blood, involve the destruction of one of the most interesting races of Aboriginal inhabitants now to be found on the face of the globe.
>
> There are still two courses open for you to pursue—either a decidedly pacific one, or a decidedly hostile. To the adoption of the former, I know of no obstacle that may not yet be easily surmounted. They have all along shown themselves ready to be reconciled, desirous to live in peace and amity with you, and even willing to be taught your manners, laws, and polity. It remains for you to consider the consequences of adopting hostile measures. A bad name to the colony, a stop to emigration, and a depreciated property, are but minor evils. An exterminating war, the flames of which, spreading with increasing fury among the surrounding tribes as the settlement extends itself, must be the consequence. An exterminating war over a continent as large as Europe, and abounding with tribes unknown and innumerable! The very thought is appalling . . .
>
> Taking advantage of your distance from the mother-country, ye may flatter yourselves with the idea that it is possible either to commit the infamous

deed of extermination clandestinely, or that ye can persuade the world that ye were not the aggressors. Vain thought! . . . The fate of Cain will be yours, Ye may enjoy the blood-stained spoils of an innocent, unoffending people; but ye cannot bury the crime ye perpetrate in the graves of your victims, nor escape the eyes of Him who has drawn the lines of demarkation around the inheritance of every nation. Your fallen countenances will betray you. The voice of your brother's blood will cry from the ground where it is shed. The land of your fathers will abhor you; and the page of history will brand you to the latest posterity with the guilt of the unparalleled deed.

Choose for yourselves. If ye determine upon a war of extermination, civilized nations will be mute with astonishment at the madness of a policy so uncalled for, so demoniacal . . . When your doom is passed, your own children, for whose sakes ye have invaded the country, will join with the disinherited offspring of those ye have slain to pour a flood of curses on your memory.

If ye have any feelings of compunction, before the die be cast, let the Aboriginal inhabitants of Australia live. Ye have taken from them all they had on earth. Be content with this, and do not add to the crime of plundering them that of taking their lives. Let them live that they may be put in possession of a title to a better country—a country where the invading foe dare not enter.[24]

When Lyon sailed for Mauritius he must have been aware that the policies he advocated of negotiation and conciliation were not going to be adopted. The violence he foresaw and feared continued until the 1920s as European settlement edged across the landscape. When he returned to Australia and settled in New South Wales in 1839 he found a familiar scene. In returning to the ideas which had obsessed him in Perth he wrote an obscure and eccentric book the full title of which was *Australia: An Appeal to the World on Behalf of the Younger Branch of the Family of Shem*. For the already crowded title page Lyon composed a five-line poem in ancient Greek providing a translation which read:

> So greatly have Australia's sufferings
> Moved me, that, impell'd by sorrow, I came here
> To tell them, undismay'd, to earth and skies.
> I heard the voice. I heard the loud lament,
> I saw the tears upon her sable cheek.[25]

The book was in two parts. It incorporated most of Lyon's West Australian articles, letters and speeches. But it opened with a series of highly rhetorical letters to members of the Royal Family, the British Houses of Parliament, the Secretary of State for the Colonies, the Governor of New South Wales, the Bishop of Australia and the people of New South Wales. In a final letter to the reader he solicited funds to assist 'the writer' who was determined to live 'on bread and water till the Salvation of Australia is accomplished'.[26] But he urged his readers not to waste their time trying to 'gratify a vain curiosity by idle conjectures respecting his name'.[27] It should suffice to know that the book was the voice of one crying in the Australian wilderness.

The letters embodied many of Lyon's criticisms and concerns about the nature of Australian colonisation. In his appeal to the House of Lords he recalled that millions of pounds had been spent to rescue Africa from slavery. 'Will ye allow Australia to perish?', he asked. 'Will ye suffer the British flag to be indelibly stained by the extermination of one of the most interesting races of the human family?'[28] In the first four letters to the Secretary of State he observed that there had been no compact or covenant between the British government and the Aborigines. The settlers had taken possession of the country on the simple grounds that might was right. They had neither legal nor moral right to seize the uncultivated land. There was no more right for the Crown to so act than there was to take possession of the 'untilled land of the nobility and gentry of the United Kingdom'.[29] The United States government, Lyon observed, acknowledged the right of the Indians to the soil and, therefore, acquired additional lands by purchase. 'What a contrast to the policy of the British', he declared, 'who act the part of the assassin and possess themselves of the lands they require by powder and ball'.[30]

In his letter to the people of New South Wales Lyon looked forward with profound concern about the fate of the 'innumerable and yet unknown tribes of the interior'. Were they to be

neglected till, surprised by the striding march of colonization, they perish by the blast of European morals, or be exterminated by the powder and ball of unprincipled adventurers, aided perhaps by the police, the military, and those bearing Her Majesty's Commission. To suppose, whatever may be the disposition of the representatives of the Sovereign, that colonial governments, hampered as they are between orders from home on the one hand, and clamour in the colonies on the other, will ever grant funds adequate either to the urgency or the magnitude of the object, would betray great ignorance of human nature.[31]

But Lyon hoped that eventually sufficient funds would be provided for amelioration and reparation. Assistance in such a cause 'kindly, promptly and liberally' supplied would command the 'benedictions of generations yet unborn'.[32]

Lyon and Giustiniani were both outsiders in the small Swan River colony. Their passionate involvement in the Aboriginal cause was sufficient to set them apart. But there were personal reasons as well. Lyon was an eccentric; Giustiniani an exotic—a sophisticated Italian convert to Anglicanism who was denounced for daring to criticise British policies and manners. But unlike Lyon he became involved in the colony's petty politics, siding with the democratic faction associated with the *Swan River Guardian* in opposition to the oligarchs and their mouthpiece, the *Perth Gazette*. He became a marked man. In January 1837 he defended himself in a letter to the *Guardian* complaining of the 'constant laceration of my character'.[33] The editor of the paper observed that the government officials and their allies 'yelp after Dr Giustiniani like a pack of hounds'.[34]

When Giustiniani took up the Aboriginal cause the denunciation intensified. He began his crusade when early in 1837 the editor of the *Perth Gazette* declared that it was a prevalent opinion that 'forcible measures' would be required to subdue the clans resident in the York district, that 'a second Pinjarra' was called for, evoking memories of the bloody punitive expedition of October 1834. In a letter to the *Guardian* Giustiniani declared that what the opposing paper was advocating was 'an entire extirpation of that unfortunate race, who have no other crime (except they were born in the Country, which we have taken from them)'.[35] He challenged his opponents to read and accept the principles which the Secretary of State for the Colonies, Lord Glenelg, had laid down in a dispatch to Governor D'Urban of the Cape of Good Hope in January 1836 dealing with conflict between settlers and indigenous tribes. 'Whether we contend with a civilized or barbarous enemy', Glenelg declared, 'the gratuitous aggravation of the horrors of war, on the plea of vengeance or retribution, or on any similar ground, is alike indefensible'.[36] It was a particularly pointed text to deliver in Australia in the 1830s.

A week later the missionary set out a series of principles which should inform the relations between Aborigines and settlers. The first was amelioration of their 'destitute condition', all the more imperative because they had a right to claim a remuneration in return for the loss of their country which was exacerbated after each exploring expedition. His second principle was equality of justice and the third the renunciation of punitive expeditions which would mean:

> No human blood spilt any more;—no Settler shall have a right any more, to take the Law in his own hands, to punish, or to shoot a Native without the concurrence of the next Magistrate and proper trial before the bar of Justice.[37]

Giustiniani went further, threatening to expose the colonists before the 'enlightened British Public, and the whole civilized world'. It was going too far. A correspondent 'John Bull the Younger' hit back in a letter in the *Gazette* explaining that the missionary's affront to the settlers might have been acceptable if he were a Briton,

> but the idea of our government being ridiculed and sneered at by a designing foreigner and his having betrayed his intention of raising himself to notoriety by exciting dissensions and placing in a false light our conduct to the world, is more than I can pass in silence and I feel myself in duty bound, as a member of the family to which I belong, to undeceive the public and unmask the braggart.[38]

Giustiniani replied in the rival paper a few days later. His assailant was a 'defender of the blood cause', whose invective could not 'wipe away the stain of cruelties committed towards our unfortunate Aboriginal inhabitants'.[39]

In reply to the charge that his views were those of an outsider Giustiniani wrote several letters outlining the humanitarian principles which were currently informing the policies of the Colonial Office under Lord Glenelg and contrasted them with colonial practice which he characterised as being infused with 'a blood principle of the twelfth century'. He referred to a recent incident in which a party of soldiers had fired into an Aboriginal camp at night. 'Every transaction of this kind between two enemies who must live together', he warned,

> is but an Armistice; and not a real peace. The glaive [i.e. the sword] is only deposited for the next Combat, and that unhappily consists not (as in civilized life) in words, or in the Press, but in Guns and Spears. It is not a victory over principles, but a destruction of human life.[40]

He continued to plead against the use of indiscriminate violence which he insisted would eventually be self-defeating. Even if the settlers shot 100 Aborigines would the remainder be better informed, he asked? Would they have a clearer conception of British law or would they become pacific, useful members of society? The pause of action produced by terror was not a real peace or a voluntary submission to a conqueror. Victims of injustices would never forget them and if they were 'forced to bend to injustice' it would only be until they became strong enough to resist it.[41]

Sporadic violence continued to trouble the colony. Talk of punitive expeditions abounded. In August 1837 Giustiniani wrote to the Colonial Secretary with the information that a party of settlers 'who wish to be called Gentlemen have entered into a *conspiracy* to shoot the Aboriginal inhabitants across the Hills, indiscriminately': one of the party had declared that he would kill ten men, women and children before he returned from the 'bloody crusade'. Giustiniani begged the Governor to intervene in the name of the British Constitution, British law and humanity and Christianity. Failing that he declared he would appeal to the Colonial Office.[42]

Giustiniani wrote a series of letters addressed to Lord Glenelg which were published in the *Swan River Guardian* in November and December 1837. He expressed outrage at a punitive expedition which had taken revenge for the murder of five settlers. Aboriginal informants had told him that eighteen of their countrymen had been killed, or as Giustiniani phrased it, had been 'immolated to the vengeance in the most cruel manner'. But none of the victims had been tried, nor had any evidence been brought against them 'before the deadly weapon of the armed European prostrated them on the ground'.[43] Warming to his task, he thundered:

> Barbarities of the middle ages have been committed even by boys and Servants, who shot the unarmed women, the inoffensive child, and the men who kindly showed them the road in the bush; *the ears of the corpses have been cut off*, and hung upon the kitchen of a gentleman, as a signal of triumph![44]

In a later letter entitled 'The Logic of the Swan River' Giustiniani returned to the question of whether the Aborigines were British subjects contrasting their treatment with that accorded to the settlers. He wrote with deepening bitterness:

> If a white man kills another white person, he is hung, but no innocent white man is obliged to suffer death for the guilty. What was the conduct towards the Natives?—Have not Magistrates been leaders of a Bloody Crusade, running through the bush like infuriated beings, without even asking the names of the unfortunate beings? Have they not left them a prey to the birds of the air, and food for the insects of the earth? The least that an inhuman Magistrate can do is to bury the dead.[45]

Giustiniani decided to defend three Aboriginal men indicted to appear before the quarter sessions of October 1837. Neu-anung was charged with stealing two bushels of wheat. The only evidence against him was that two months after the theft he was wearing an empty wheatsack on his shoulders. He was convicted and sentenced to six months imprisonment. Durgap was arraigned for stealing some dough from a house and was sentenced to seven years transportation. Go-goot pleaded guilty to stealing ten pounds of butter and was also sentenced to seven years transportation. In his address to the jury Giustiniani referred to the privations which the Aborigines had been exposed to. They had been deprived of their food, had 'no Parish where to go', had not been taught any kind of work and were ignorant of British law. Given their anomalous position in the colony 'the legal proceedings were ridiculous'. His advocacy achieved little. The chairman of the quarter sessions 'uncourteously interrupted the Reverend Gentleman several times in the course of his address' and eventually told him to sit down.[46]

By the end of 1837 time was running out for Giustiniani. His attempt to buy land was rejected because he was a foreigner. His application for naturalisation was rejected. He had few friends left in the colony. Attacks on him in the *Perth Gazette* intensified. He hoped the 'enlightened British Public' would not be moved by the 'dark insinuations, and bitter acrimony of the Government scribblers'. But clearly the pressure was beginning to tell. He bravely announced that his principles could neither be bought with money 'nor annihilated by haughty frowns or malicious tongues'.[47] In one of his last letters to the local press he wrote:

It is the duty of every Minister of Christ, whenever he is personally attacked to overcome the evil by doing good, and according to that principle of our blessed Saviour I have never answered the personal attacks of the Government Journal but only continued the good work of Christ by defending the Natives, protecting the innocent, and exposing cruelties. Now the work of Satan is so far advanced that even my character is in the most violent, and the most cruel way attacked.[48]

It was a rearguard action. A few weeks later Giustiniani sailed with James Backhouse for Mauritius never to return. His crusade was taken up 50 years later by another Anglican missionary, John Gribble.

V

AGITATION AGAINST ASSASSINATION: QUEENSLAND, 1860–80

Aboriginal Australia had no cause to celebrate when power passed from the Colonial Office to the new parliaments in Sydney, Melbourne, Adelaide and Hobart in 1856. They had even less reason to applaud when Queensland was separated from New South Wales in 1859. The new northern parliament was dominated by pastoralists and their urban friends, partners and business associates. Rapid occupation of the land was the central purpose of the inexperienced and impoverished government. The humanitarian movement was weak and underdeveloped and exercised little restraint on the drive to dispossess the independent Aboriginal tribes beyond the rapidly moving fringe of settlement. The Native Mounted Police Force, inherited from New South Wales, became the main instrument of the policy to crush Aboriginal resistance in advance of the pioneer. It was cheap, effective and brutal. It was also a para-military force of dubious legality and evil repute. The force was constantly attacked during the twenty years 1860–80 by individuals from all parts of the colony, by townspeople and frontier settlers alike. Public disquiet culminated in

1880 with a long and sustained campaign by the Brisbane weekly newspaper, the *Queenslander*. Despite criticism from both inside and outside the colony the government characteristically ignored the protests and resisted all attempts to institute an inquiry into the force which continued to operate in the more remote parts of Queensland until the end of the nineteenth century. Some of the most effective attacks on Queensland frontier policy were launched by a minority of humanitarian-inclined squatters who were convinced that the Native Police exacerbated rather than suppressed resistance and in the process was guilty of widespread atrocities which compromised the reputation of the new colony.

In a letter to the editor of the *North Australian* in July 1860 a correspondent using the pseudonym 'A Squatter' denounced the marauding force and the 'dreadful deeds now done in the Queen's name'. He believed that the need to cover up the systematic brutality meant that whole neighbourhoods became accessories 'after horrible facts'. The most cold-blooded murders were consequently hidden until he believed that the whole community was 'becoming awfully debased'.[1] Another correspondent, 'Justice', wrote with similar concern about the spreading influence of community tolerance of punitive violence on the frontier. He sought to prevent 'that abominable feeling becoming a principle in the minds of the men of Queensland, that to kill a blackfellow in cold blood is not murder'.[2] The Mortimer brothers of Manumbar station used another form of protest, placing an advertisement in the Brisbane *Courier* in February 1861 which ran:

To the Office in command of the Party of Native Police, who shot and wounded some Blacks on the Station of Manumbar . . .

Sir—If in future you should take a fancy to bring your troopers upon the Station of Manumbar on a sporting excursion, we should feel obliged if you will either bag or bury the game you shoot, as it is far from pleasant for us to have the decomposing remains of four or five blackfellows lying unburied within a mile or two of our head-station. If you will do neither, please be kind enough to remove the corpses from the waterholes near the head-station, from which we sometimes use water for culinary purposes. As most of the blacks you left dead on our run were feeble old men, some of them apparently not less than eighty years of age, will you please to inform us whether these hoary sinners are the parties chiefly engaged in spearing bullocks, &c.; or whether you just shoot them because the younger ones are too nimble for you. Besides the four or five you left dead on our run, you have wounded two of our station blacks, who have been in our employment during lambing, washing and shearing, and all other busy times, for the last eight or nine years, and we have never known either of them to have been charged with a crime of any kind. One of them came to the station with a bullet-wound through one of his thighs, another through one of his hands; the other had a bullet-wound through one of his arms. These blacks, being in our employment, very naturally look to us for protection from such outrages; and we are of the opinion that when you shoot and wound blacks in such an indiscriminate manner, you exceed your commission, and we publish this that those who

employ and pay you may have some knowledge of
the way in which you perform your services.

We have, &c
T. & A. Mortimer
Manumbar, Feb.22, 1861.[3]

The well-educated and well-connected squatter
Charles Dutton conducted a longer and more systematic
campaign against the Native Police. He wrote to the
government in March 1861 in fury about the behaviour
on his station of a Native Police detachment under the
control of Lieutenant Patrick. Dutton was unusual at the
time in that he encouraged the local Aborigines to live
on the station. In what Dutton called an impertinent
and dictatorial tone the Lieutenant ordered the Aboriginal camp to disperse and destroyed their possessions,
telling Dutton that his orders were to disperse all 'armed
mobs'. But the young squatter refused to accept that
such behaviour had official sanction. Here, he wrote,
was a small group of eight men and seventeen women
and children who had camped near his head station
awaiting the arrival of the bullock wagons carrying
promised tomahawks and blankets and they were 'rushed
out of their camp' and threatened with shooting if they
dared to stand their ground, their implements of chase
carried off and destroyed. Could anything be more
repugnant, he asked, to 'every feeling of humanity . . .
every principle of justice and good faith'. He observed
that the Aborigines asked him why they were shot and
paraphrased their complaints:

they say bail mine kill white fellow, bail kill [animals],
bail take rations what for shoot him?

How are they to be answered, how appeased, he cried, and angrily replied: 'There is but one answer you are black and must be shot.'[4]

Dutton talked to Patrick about his recent attack on an Aboriginal party on the Comet River and referred to it as an unfortunate and untoward event. The policeman immediately justified himself; Dutton reporting him saying,

> other Police Officers before they had been in the Force a fortnight had sent in dispatches (I use his own words) of lots of blacks shot and here he had been in the force six months before he had shot a single black.

Dutton warned the government that Patrick's behaviour was a serious threat to the peace of the district. And his foreboding was prophetic. At the end of the year nineteen members of the Wills family and their workers were killed on Cullinlaringoe station. Insistent calls for indiscriminate and massive revenge rang through the colony. Dutton was brave enough to write to the press complaining that the rampaging punitive expeditions were creating a situation where there was 'a total subversion of the law'.[5] He related the attack on Cullinlaringoe to the understandable if not excusable desire for revenge for Patrick's earlier bloody foray. There are some, he wrote, who believe it is unnecessary to ask why a black has committed a murder. 'The cause', they argued, 'was sufficiently accounted for by his savage and bloodthirsty nature'.[6]

Two months later Dutton returned to the subject with a more general, and more telling attack, on the Native Police Force. He began by referring to a recent incident in his district when the police had deliberately ridden down and trampled a young Aboriginal woman who was shepherding sheep on a neighbouring station, 'bruising and lacerating her dreadfully'. The treatment of the young woman and of Aborigines in the district generally was

> a thorough exemplification of the serious abuses that must result from entrusting to any body of men ill-defined and unascertainable powers—powers which, in practice and according to their interpretation, usurp the functions of magistrate, jury and judge. The exercise of this power is too clearly and distinctly claimed for them by the Executive, and acted upon with that measure of justice which too surely follows the possession of irresponsible power of life or death . . .
>
> If no other argument could be adduced in condemnation of the Force as at present constituted, the mere fact of one white man arrogating to himself greater powers than any tribunal in the land, with the ultimate control of six or ten men, with all the elements of mischief at their command—men who, acting together, are in reality, religiously, socially, and legally irresponsible—should suffice to convince the public that some check is needed.[7]

The reading public may have noticed Dutton's angry letters but the government was unmoved. In the bush Dutton was thought to be a dangerous man, one who harboured blacks thereby endangering his fellow countrymen.[8]

His view of the Native Police was supported by the prominent colonist Gideon Scott Lang who delivered a lecture on 'The Aborigines of Australia' in Melbourne in 1865 and later published the text as a pamphlet. Lang had been a pioneer pastoralist in South Australia, New South Wales and southern Queensland. He explained that he had been in the colonies for 24 years, eleven of them in the bush during which time the Aborigines had been a 'constant subject of interest and inquiry'. For three years he had been in a state of 'active hostility or dangerous peace'.[9] He was, he declared, 'no blind partizan of the blacks',[10] but he believed they could be managed without fighting. Consequently his attack on the policies of the Queensland government carried more weight than similar criticisms from townspeople.

Lang believed that in Queensland there had been greater destruction of Aborigines in occupying new country than in any other colony. But in the years since the establishment of the self-governing colony the destruction had been 'wholesale and indiscriminate and carried on with a cold blooded cruelty on the part of the whites quite unparalleled in the history of these colonies'.[11] While many northern settlers were men of benevolence who wished to save and civilise the blacks there were others who were 'cowardly cold blooded murderers' and who were able to do as they pleased because it was the 'rule and custom to arrange the black question by killing them off'.[12] Lang attributed the obvious moral corruption of the settlers to the extensive use of the Native Police who made it unnecessary for the frontier squatters to attempt to come to terms with the resident Aborigines. Now they had the Native Police to 'crush them out like so many ants' any more 'tedious way of quieting them is a useless risk and waste of time'.[13]

Lang accused the Queensland government of adopting a policy of extermination. In the past blacks had been massacred cruelly and indiscriminately but now 'all, all, without exception are to be given up to destruction'.[14] Wholesale execution, without either warrant, apprehension, judge or jury, had been institutionalised. He wondered whether Queensland could any longer be trusted with the colonisation of the enormous country placed under its rule by the Imperial government. Like many other humanitarians Lang looked to the Colonial Office for deliverance. But if the British failed to intervene 'on their head be the blood'.[15]

But no assistance came from Britain. Lang himself concluded that his attack on the Queensland settlers had been counterproductive. He later wrote a note on his own copy of the pamphlet to the effect that

a simple expression of opinion from home, from *The Times* for example, would have done much good. The effect of this pamphlet, after they had abused me for months, was to cause the formation of a protection society by Squatters, and they ceased to boast of murder as a meritorious action, but that massacre still goes on, and that most wantonly.[16]

Humanitarian-inclined squatters were not alone in their disgust with the Native Police. Residents of pioneer townships were often sharply aware of the force's bloody work. They saw the troopers riding to and from their hinterland patrols and occasionally raids were made of camps near or even in the towns themselves. A Rockhampton resident wrote to the Brisbane *Courier* in 1861 highly critical of the 'mismanaged and most disgraceful force'. Only gross cowardice or culpable blindness to the facts could allow people to argue in its favour. 'This very town', he explained, had witnessed scenes in its neighbourhood 'which one hardly dare relate'. He instanced 'the bloodiest of murders' committed upon the innocent natives followed up by the greatest solicitude upon the part of those who saw the deeds that they should not be talked about. The town had witnessed

> a drunken officer too beastly almost to sit upon his horse, ride forth with the avowed and inflamed intention of 'shooting down the wretches' and in a very few hours afterwards its inhabitants have been busy again in shielding the miscreant from his proper doom.

The correspondent called on every father, mother, sister and brother in Queensland to join in a 'holy cry' to do away with the force which was 'fast demoralizing the whole community, and turning Christians into abject and wicked apologists of men'.[17]

It was a common concern of the humanitarians. Six years later another Rockhampton resident expressed grave concern that news of frontier atrocities was so easily accepted, when in any part of Britain they would elicit 'universal indignation'. He feared that the whole community was becoming brutalised:

> Already the evil leaven has begun to work. I have frequently felt grieved and indignant at the levity with which many of the colonial youth speak of these outrages upon the blacks.[18]

Events in Maryborough in 1860 bore out both the worst fears about the Native Police and of broad community support for its activities. On the morning of

3 February Lieutenant Bligh led his detachment into the town and dispersed the local Aboriginal camps and shot the residents as they ran. An 'excellent and industrious' young man known to the Europeans as 'Young Snatchem' was driven into the river near the town wharf. As men, women and children looked on, the police pursued him in a rowing boat. Bligh eventually shot him in the back. An old one-eyed man, 'a constant attendant in the town, against whom there had never been a charge', was captured, marched handcuffed into the bush and assassinated.[19] Early the following week a public meeting expressed strong support for Lieutenant Bligh and opened a subscription to buy and present him with a ceremonial sword to commemorate the event.[20]

It was too much for local humanitarians. Writing a year later a deeply troubled Maryborough resident referred to what he called 'the foulest day the town had ever known'. The most horrifying aspect of the affair was the community approval of the murder of local Aborigines who had lived peacefully and had worked in the town for years. 'It seems incredible', the troubled resident wrote, 'and a lapse of twelve months since the hideous circumstance only makes it more incomprehensible to understand—more humiliating to ponder over'. He could never walk through the town 'without blushing for that meeting'. But he was gratified to find that many who attended 'that awful meeting—who subscribed to that weapon of blood', were now thoroughly ashamed and repentant of the day and the act. He hoped his fellow townspeople would

repudiate their own act. A testimonial to the common hangman would be more appropriate—after each 'operation performed'—than this one to Bligh. What honor can there be?—What courage is required?—What noble qualities are displayed in occasionally slaughtering the naked, unarmed, flying savage? It was a mockery of all the attributes of greatness and goodness to pretend to discover in Mr. Bligh's conduct on 3rd February 1860, that which entitled him to public praise and to wear a sword!![21]

But while some Maryborough citizens were repentant Lieutenant Bligh was never questioned about his actions and things went on as before. In 1867 the small mining community of Morinish learnt the meaning of the term dispersal. Townspeople were woken a little before sunrise by hearing a volley of shots coming from the direction of the town camp a few hundred yards down the main road. Those who were already up rushed towards the camp where a scene presented itself 'alike brutal on the part of the perpetrators, and revolting to the feelings of those who saw it'. The camp was deserted but around the fires were remnants of blood-covered clothing and trails of blood leading in every direction. Eventually the bodies were discovered in the surrounding bush. The wounded staggered into town—a girl with a bullet through her thigh and a little boy with a similar leg wound. Horrified townspeople were told that the attack was a reprisal for the murder and mutilation of a shepherd on a nearby station. But it was eventually learnt that the outrage had amounted to no more than the theft from a shepherd's hut of sugar and tea. That was the only justification for the 'horrible tragedy and disgraceful butchery'.[22]

The 'Miner on Morinish' who wrote in outrage to

the *Rockhampton Bulletin* may never have learnt that a copy of his letter was sent to the Aborigines Protection Society in London and republished in the *Colonial Intelligencer* in 1868.[23] The society's office-bearers had already heard of the bloody deeds of the Queensland Native Police, their attention having been drawn to them 'more times than we care to count up'. But the Miner's letter was such a graphic eyewitness account of atrocity that the society's secretary F. W. Cheeson sent a copy to the Secretary of State for the Colonies accompanied by a powerful letter which read in part:

> The Committee regret to state that barbarous outrages of this kind are of frequent occurrence in the pastoral districts of the above colony; and they have reason to fear that the local Government is not sufficiently alive to the duty of protecting the natives.
>
> The Society's correspondents in Queensland are of the opinion that the Native Mounted Police Force, as at present constituted, is an unmitigated source of evil, and that, whenever let loose, it makes no distinction between the innocent and the guilty.[24]

The Colonial Office answered the letter promptly promising to draw the matter to the attention of Queensland's new governor.

The British Society received most of its intelligence about Queensland from their 'excellent correspondent' in Brisbane, Alfred Davidson, who dispatched 36 letters on a regular basis to London between September 1869 and his death in 1881. He was a persistent and passionate advocate for justice for the Aborigines, an unrelenting opponent of the Pacific Island labour trade. Like many other colonial humanitarians he felt isolated and greatly valued the connection with the Aborigines Protection Society through which he could exert a degree of influence impossible to achieve by action within Queensland itself. Even so he was a highly industrious advocate, wiring to the society in 1869 that 'one does not like speaking of oneself but during the last two years I have struggled much'.[25] He scanned the colonial newspapers, wrote letters to them himself as well as to the government, lobbied politicians and governors. He was forever frustrated, fobbed off, rebuffed. But as he explained to the Protection Society, 'I still continue to watch every thing and it is known that I do'.[26]

But he was realistic about the forces arraigned against the humanitarians' lobby. 'A few of us have endeavoured to do our best under many disadvantages', he wrote in 1870, but he believed that public opinion was weaker in the colony than in England. The employers, he explained, had a 'clear hold on the newspapers: the claims of capital are felt'.[27] He was deeply concerned about the Torres Strait Islanders who came under Queensland sovereignty in 1879 as the colonial border was pushed north to within a short distance of the Papuan mainland and wrote to the government on behalf of the society. 'I do not *expect* any support from that quarter', he subsequently explained, 'and altho' they will ignore it *yet* they will have heard what had to be said. I had no reply at which I am not surprised.'[28]

Davidson had no illusions about the chance of changing policy towards the Aborigines. 'I am trying to do something for the Aborigines', he informed the Protection Society in 1871, but it was a 'very difficult and discouraging subject'.[29] He explained that members of

parliament openly admitted shooting blacks while object-
ing to any attempts to ameliorate their condition. The
murders of these men, he pointed out, are 'publicly
avowed and admitted'.[30] He was convinced that it had
been a mistake to give Queensland 'or any other colony'
a constitution without insisting on an 'Efficient Native
department' to govern and protect the Aborigines. He
related that he was

> telling one of the last Executive Ministry of an act of
> Native Police oppression and he replied nothing will
> ever be done for our Aborigines until the Imperial
> Government does it [sic] he has been in a position to
> know the feelings of the leading men of Queensland.
> I believe he is right.[31]

Davidson's passionate denunciations of Queensland
policies were largely ignored in the colony. The prominent local politician John Douglas explained to the
Protection Society that their correspondent was 'a very
excellent man' but that he was isolated and powerless.[32]
But the society was persuaded that Queensland was
profoundly at fault and condemned the colony in language rarely used in the regular surveys of conditions in
all parts of the Empire. The strongest denunciation came
in 1874 when the society accused Queensland of
pursuing

> in various disguises, the wholesale extermination of
> the helpless race from whom all has been taken. The
> extermination goes on day after day, and goes on
> without any attempt at conciliation, without an effort
> at civilization, without a pang of remorse, without a
> feeling of Christian zeal to convert or save.[33]

Davidson was joined in his lonely crusade in 1875 by the Scottish Roman Catholic priest Duncan McNab who arrived in the colony with a long-frustrated ambition to work with the Aborigines. He threw himself into the task, urging bishops and politicians to become engaged in the cause and irritating those he met with his single-minded urgency. Like many humanitarians before and after him McNab was confronted by colonial attitudes and frontier traditions. He was told when he arrived in Queensland that any attempt to 'improve' the Aborigines would fail because they were 'the lowest of the human race' and certain soon to die out. McNab ignored the gratuitous advice which failed to shake his conviction that they had been 'created by God for the same end as other men'.[34]

McNab travelled widely in the colony and soon learnt of the brutality of the frontier, the marauding Native Police Force and the despair of life in squalid fringe camps. He compared the situation of the dispossessed with that of slaves who were, he believed, 'better fed, clad and housed than our blacks'. They were also protected from 'foreign violence and extermination'[35] whereas the natives had been too frequently and still were subjected to an indiscriminate slaughter of the guilty and the innocent. McNab heard many stories about the violent onslaughts of the Native Police Force which could be used to

> great advantage, were it only used in necessary self-defence and with proper moderation; and were it to hinder the killing of the natives with impunity by private individuals.[36]

As it was, hundreds had fallen to Native Police rifles.

McNab appreciated that land was the central issue because the colonists had occupied it without consent, without any compensation or any adequate provision being made for the maintenance of the dispossessed who were not allowed to possess 'in their own right one foot of land in the Colony'.[37] To remedy the situation McNab demanded that the government allow Aborigines to select land in order to become independent farmers. He urged Aborigines to select blocks of land in their own country because until 'instructed' they had no idea they could become 'possessed' of property like the whites. Many natives, he argued,

> would occupy homesteads who would not live on a reserve . . . It may be said that the natives never had a home. That is true in the sense of a fixed abode, but they had a territory which was their own, on which they had a right to reside and did so and used it for their maintenance to the exclusion of all other.[38]

The missionary had come to appreciate that Aborigines remained attached to their land and wanted to live on it. But he believed that this could only be achieved if they became farmers in their own right. Now that the circumstances of their country were rapidly changing they 'must live differently mainly by pasturage and tillage'.[39]

At least some Aborigines were interested in McNab's plan. He recorded in his diary the case of one man who walked eighteen miles to learn from the missionary how he could get land 'then went off to work by which he could earn enough to secure it'.[40] But McNab's zeal met government indifference and refusal to adopt any initiative which would ameliorate the condition of the

Aborigines. He left the colony in 1879 and took his crusade to Europe where he lobbied both the Vatican and the Colonial Office for action to help bring about change in Queensland. In a letter to the Secretary of State for the Colonies, the Earl of Kimberley, McNab denounced the colonial politicians for condoning extermination. He believed responsibility reached to the apex of Queensland society. He related an incident which had been reported to him by a member of the Legislative Council who had attended the Governor's Christmas banquet in honour of a visiting English duke. The discourse 'turned on' the treatment of the Aborigines and the conclusion arrived at was that there was 'nothing for them but extermination'. It was a claim which the Governor rejected.[41] But McNab had enclosed in his letter to the Secretary of State powerful supporting evidence in the form of a pamphlet entitled *The Way We Civilize* which was published in Brisbane in 1880, the impact of which will now be considered.

VI

THE CRUSADE OF THE
QUEENSLANDER, 1880–90

The most powerful attack on the Native Police came
not from professed humanitarians like Davidson but from
the leading weekly newspaper, the *Queenslander*
—commissioned, but not written, by editor-owner
Gresley Lukin. Under the heading *The Way We Civilize*
the paper ran thirteen editorials between 1 May and
17 July 1880 and opened up the columns to
contributors, 27 of whose letters were published between
May and September. The whole collection was then
issued as a pamphlet and distributed widely. In this
second form *The Way We Civilize* became one of the
most influential political tracts in Australian history.[1] The
anonymous author of the editorials subsequently
explained that both he and Lukin acted in the hope of
arousing the conscience of the Queensland public to
'induce them to adopt a more humane method of
behaviour with the Aborigines'. They sought to force
the government into calling a Royal Commission into
the Native Police. Every statement made was rigorously
tested to ensure its accuracy and the cases chosen to
illustrate the state of race relations were selected because

they were thought to be supportable before the hoped-for commission. The author himself had no illusions. Eleven years in Queensland as a journalist allowed him to know as well as he knew his 'own existence, that murder, rape and violence of all sort are habitually committed by the whites of the frontier district on the blacks'. The Native Police existed to repress the natives, to 'scourge the blacks by wholesale and indiscriminate slaughter into passive submission'.

Lukin and his journalist knew they would enrage many of the country readers of the *Queenslander*. While the perpetrators of brutal acts were a minority public opinion in the outback was 'feeble in its condemnation of these deeds, and strong in its condemnation of the idea of punishing them'. The attempt to force the government to a Royal Commission failed. Writing two years after the crusade the journalist 'despaired of doing much good for the blacks' while he had incurred great 'personal ill-will . . . by writing on their behalf' during his residence in Queensland.[2]

The campaign opened with a reference to the 'brutal war of races' that was being fought in the outlying regions of the colony and a hope that the government would at last adopt policies which reflected less disgrace on the community. Following that prelude the *Queenslander* spoke with a fierce honesty:

> It is necessary, in order to make the majority of the community understand the urgent necessity for reform, to dispense with apologetic paraphrases. This, in plain language, is how we deal with the aborigines: On occupying new territory the aboriginal inhabitants are treated in exactly the same way as the wild beasts

or birds the settlers may find there. Their lives and
their property, the nets, canoes, and weapons which
represent as much labor to them as the stock and
buildings of the white settler, are held by the
Europeans as being at their absolute disposal. Their
goods are taken, their children forcibly stolen, their
women carried away, entirely at the caprice of the
white men. The least show of resistance is answered
by a rifle bullet; in fact, the first introduction between
blacks and whites is often marked by the unprovoked
murder of some of the former—in order to make a
commencement of the work of 'civilising' them. Little
difference is made between the treatment of blacks at
first disposed to be friendly and those who from the
very outset assume a hostile attitude. As a rule the
blacks have been friendly at first, and the longer they
have endured provocation without retaliating the
worse they have fared, for the more ferocious savages
have inspired some fear, and have therefore been
comparatively unmolested.[3]

The editorial then changed direction to consider the
reaction of the community to these awful events and
argued that the majority of settlers had been apparently
influenced by the same sort of feeling as 'that which
guides men in their treatment of the brute creation'.
Many, perhaps the majority,

have stood aside in silent disgust whilst these things
were being done, actuated by the same motives that
keep humane men from shooting or molesting animals
which neither annoy nor are of service to them; and
a few have always protested in the name of humanity
against such treatment of human beings, however
degraded. But the protests of the minority have been

disregarded by the people of the settled districts; the
majority of outsiders who take no part in the outrages
have been either apathetic or inclined to shield their
companions, and the white brutes who fancied the
amusement, have murdered, ravished, and robbed the
blacks without let or hindrance. Not only have they
been unchecked, but the Government of the colony
has been always at hand to save them from the
consequences of their crime.[4]

When the Aborigines resisted, as they currently were
doing on Cape York the Native Police was dispatched
to disperse them. What that term meant, the anonymous
writer observed, was well enough known having been

adopted into bush slang as a convenient euphuism for
wholesale massacre. Of this force we have already said
that it is impossible to write about it with patience.
It is enough to say of it that this body, organised and
paid by us, is sent to do work which its officers are
forbidden to report in detail, and that a true record
of its proceedings would shame us before our fellow-
countrymen in every part of the British Empire.

When the police have entered on the scene, then
the conflict goes on apace. It is a fitful war of
extermination waged upon the blacks, something after
the fashion in which other settlers wage war upon
noxious wild beasts, the process differing only in so
far as the victims, being human, are capable of a wider
variety of suffering than brutes. The savages, hunted
from the places where they had been accustomed to
find food, driven into barren ranges, shot like wild
dogs at sight, retaliate when and how they can. They
spear the white man's cattle and horses, and if by
chance they succeed in overpowering an unhappy
European they exhaust their savage ingenuity in

wreaking their vengeance upon him, even mutilating the senseless body out of which they have pounded the last breath of life. Murder and counter murder, outrage repaid by violence, theft by robbery, so the dreary tale continues, till at last the blacks, starved, cowed, and broken-hearted, their numbers thinned, their courage overcome, submit to their fate, and disease and liquor finish the work which we pay our native police to begin.[5]

It was tough, challenging journalism. It was very brave and enormously provocative in the circumstances stripping away euphemism, breaking complicit silences, savaging the romantic image of the white pioneer.

To back up the original editorials, the paper then published over seven weeks a series of stories about white brutality, providing detailed information about atrocities, citing time, place and participants whose names were omitted.

But the *Queenslander* did not rest with attacking the marauding frontiersmen. Those who passively tolerated cruelty and murder condoned the crime. Even the Brisbane resident who failed as a citizen and voter to 'wipe out the stain' disfiguring the whole colony shared the disgrace of it.[6]

The debate of 1880 was different to the one of 50 years before. A much changed intellectual climate and two generations of common experience of colonisation had brought the two sides closer together. There was almost no assertion of racial equality based on the Biblical notion of shared descent and common blood. Practically all discussants in 1880 took it for granted that the Aborigines were members of an inferior race, one with

unique and unfortunate characteristics. Many assumed
that they were more primitive than the white race and
would eventually die out. There was much less reference
than in the 1830s to civilisation, evangelisation and the
saving of souls. The idea of a displeased and vengeful
God had receded. The settlers may have to contend with
disapproval from overseas and especially from Britain.
They might fear the stern gaze of Mother England but
not the judgemental eye of an all-seeing deity. The
editorial writer of the *Queenslander* hoped and believed
his fellow colonists would have 'some regard for the
good name of the colony', some desire to see it 'stand
well in the estimation of their countrymen in the mother
country'.[7] The horror of shedding blood, so pronounced
among humanitarians in the 1830s, had moderated.
Murder might be morally wrong, or bad in principle,
but many people had come to see it as a regrettable but
unavoidable accompaniment to colonisation. In the
1880s few public figures referred to Aboriginal ownership of land or of a debt owing to the displaced tribes.
The idea of an 'equivalence', so common in the 1830s,
had all but gone. Development had become justification
in itself. In the process the pioneer had acquired
immense moral authority as the creator of wealth and
industry. Colonial society of 1880 was far more assertive
about its achievements. It was taken for granted that the
frontier settler would displace the 'savage' and that the
displacement was both inevitable and for the better. The
Queenslander's controversialist questioned the practice of
colonisation, not the principle, arguing that:

> There is nothing of which any people need be
> ashamed in taking possession of a country like

Australia, occupied only by a few thinly-scattered hordes of savages without even the smallest rudiments of civilization. That they must suffer is certainly an 'inevitable consequence'. They must be subdued. It is the law of the whole world that the inferior race must submit to the stronger. We inflict death and pain on the whole animal creation to provide ourselves with the food we eat. But we hold the man guilty of a shameful crime who in the exercise of his lawful mastery over the brutes inflicts on them unnecessary pain and suffering. And if we, by common consent, punish those who torture an animal, what plea have we to urge for the horrible brutality with which we assert our mastery over creatures lower in the scale of humanity than ourselves, but still men and women able to feel and suffer in the same manner as we do? In the form that our cruelty assumes, in our vices, we acknowledge their humanity, and yet we deny to them the plea for immunity from unnecessary suffering which we admit on behalf of the brutes. That immunity is the first claim we make on behalf of the blacks. We have argued, and our opponents have admitted, that our system of dealing with them leads to abuses of which the degree may be questioned but the existence cannot be denied. We ask for a reform, we are prepared to show that reform is possible, and there are witnesses coming forward in all parts of the colony to maintain the need for it and uphold its practicability. Is our demand an unreasonable one?[8]

Many Queenslanders thought so and soon hit back. A week after the initial crusading editorial appeared the first of many letters was published from a correspondent calling himself *Never Never* who had lived for sixteen

years 'in outside country always'. He was, he openly
confided, a murderer because he had dispersed and
assisted to disperse Aborigines on a number of occasions.
It was all very well, the bushman argued, to complain
about the treatment of the blacks. The fundamental
question was:

> What lives are to be sacrificed—black or white? Are
> we to protect the black or protect the white? Shirk
> it as we will, this is the question. So long as we have
> country to settle, so long as men have to trust to their
> own right hand, so long shall we come in contact
> with the natives, and aggressions and reprisals will take
> place.[9]

Never Never didn't relent. He plunged straight on,
expressing views which would have shocked humanitarians while confirming their worst fears about the
corrupting influence of frontier violence. But there was
a hard-bitten realism that must have disturbed many
readers. He conceded that, in common with other
bushmen, he was 'regretfully compelled to admit that
the deeds of blood curdling atrocity' had been committed by white men. But that was really beside the point
which was:

> Is there room for both of us here? No. Then the
> sooner the weaker is wiped out the better, as we may
> save some valuable lives by the process. If the black-
> fellow is right in murdering white men for invading
> and taking possession of his country, then every white
> man, woman, and child who sits at home at ease in
> our towns and townships is a murderer, for if they
> had the courage of their opinions they would not
> stop on in a colony built up on bloodshed and rapine.

Do they do this? Do our black protectors—our philanthropists of to-day—go out and enquire into the
truth of the many stories that are brought in from the
back country, or do they rather sit in the high places,
and partake of the corn and oil, leaving it to the sinful
to go out and bear the heat and burden of the day?
I rather think they do the last.

Hide it as you will, our policy towards the black
is bad, but it is only the game we played all over the
world; and it starts with the original occupation of
the country, and any other policy would be equally
outrageous that entailed the taking of the land from
the blacks. Say that we make reserves, and put the
natives on them—have them guarded, and watched,
and cared for—is not that just as arbitrary and high
handed as shooting them? Would *we* recognise the
justice of a superior race coming here, curtailing our
boundaries, picking out our best country for their
own use, and instituting a fresh code of religion, law,
and morality for our benefit? Would we submit
tamely, or prefer a quick and easy death to it? By its
very presence and publication here the *Queenslander*
recognises the utility, to put it mildly, of dispossessing
the blacks, and until it takes its departure to another
country, and there preaches its sermon, its voice has
a very hypocritical ring about it. We all want to get
on here, and we all want to get somebody else to do
the work needful; and if there is any dirty work
necessary we are the first to cry out against it—when
we are in a position to do so. This is the black
question, as put forward by the protectors of the poor
savage. I know full well that I shall hear of atrocities,
of barbarities, and other disgraceful proceedings committed by the whites; but that does not touch the
point at issue.

The unanswerable fact remains that by overrunning this or any other country we expose the natives to the chances of suffering the rigors of guerilla warfare—always the cruellest and worst—and, knowing that, we come here and take up our quarters with our eyes open; by our very presence in the land justifying the act of every white ruffian in the outside country. We are all savages; look beneath the thin veneer of our civilisation and we are very identical with the blacks; but we have this one thing not in common—we, the invading race, have a principle hard to define, and harder to name; it is innate in us, and it is the restlessness of culture, if I dare call it so. The higher we get in the educated scale, the more we find this faculty; and if we do not show it in one shape we do in another. We work for posterity, we have a history, and we have been surrounded by its tales and legends since infancy. We look upon the heroes of this history as familiar friends, and in all our breasts there is a whisper that we too by some strange chance may be known to posterity. This brings us here to wrest the lands of a weaker race from their feeble grasp and build up a country that our children shall inherit; and this feeling is unknown to the native of Australia. He has a short history, but it is more a matter of gossip than anything else, and only goes back one generation. He has no thought of the future, because he never knew of anyone being remembered more than a lifetime, therefore he has no interest but to pass through life as easily as possible, and he never seeks to improve land for those who will come after him. This justifies our presence here; this is the only plea we have in justification of it, and having once admitted it we must go the whole length, and say that the sooner we clear the weak useless race away the better. And being a useless race, what does it matter what they suffer any more than the distinguished philanthropist, who writes in his behalf, care for the wounded half-dead pigeon he tortures at his shooting matches. We are pursuing the same policy in Zululand and Afghanistan, and, I suppose, on a more barbarous scale; the recital of all the atrocities going, of all the shooting and slaying by the Native Police, never alters the fact that, once we are here, we are committed as accessories, and that to prove the fidelity of our opinions we should leave the country.[10]

The paper responded savagely to *Never Never* arguing that they would no more expect a bushman accustomed to dispersals to understand the 'feeling with which the deed is regarded by most civilized men' than they would look for an expression of pity 'from a terrier engaged in torturing a wounded rat'. Such men had lost the great lesson of civilisation which taught that there was 'some other law than that of brute force' and that the weakness of any race did not justify dealing with them as the mere caprice of the moment dictated. The tone of *Never Never*'s letter indicated how the ordinary white man's conscience could be 'seared and his nature hardened by familiarity with scenes of bloodshed in the bush'.[11]

But the most effective response came from a correspondent using the nom de plume *Outis* and who could also speak from experience in the bush:

Sir,—In the *Queenslander* of the 8th instant is a letter signed 'Never Never' in which the writer endeavours to justify the system upon which our Native Police force is conducted. I should be very sorry to believe that the writer actually believes one half of what he has written, for if he does he ought to be locked up as a would-be murderer of the dangerous description . . . And yet, sir, the most distressing fact is that 'Never Never's' letter very fairly embodies the spirit and sentiment of a large number of those who take active part in pioneer settlement. Even presuming the blacks have committed every enormity that is possible, is it not horrible and monstrous that the shedding of human blood should come to be regarded so lightly? Like 'Never Never' I, too, have lived among blacks in a newly-settled district, and my experience is that blacks, like whites, have among them both good and bad, and that any wholesale massacre of them such as is daily perpetrated is as unjust as it is horrible in the sight of God and man. Are there ten men in Brisbane who really understand the working of our Native Police? How many among us understand the euphemistic word 'dispersal?' Can they know that it means this?—A white man, 'an officer and a gentleman,' at the head of some half-dozen black murderers, watches a camp of blacks all night. The cool dawn of the morning comes, and the slender smoke circles up among the trees by the waterhole as the unsuspecting blacks wake to prepare their morning meal. Suddenly a shrill whistle, then the sharp rattle of Sniders, shriek on shriek, rushing to and fro: then, ammunition gone, the struggle at close quarters, and well-fed lusty savages, drunk with carnage, hewing down men, women, and children before them. How long shall these things be? for that they exist no dweller in outside country can deny. Are they not the theme of discussion by every camp fire in the Western land? And though much must be deducted for exaggeration, 'where there is smoke there is fire.' Why do the Native Police never take white men with them who might afterwards appear as witnesses against them? Surely this one fact should show that their deeds are evil. Is there a record in the Chief Commissioner's office in which any sub-inspector boldly says that he and his 'boys' deliberately shot a certain number of blacks? Why, if all is right, should the truth not be openly stated? Why should we be unable to learn from official records what the public servants are doing? If it is advisable that, as a colony, we should indulge in wholesale murder of the race we are dispossessing, let us have the courage of our opinions and murder openly and deliberately—calling it *murder*, not 'dispersal.' I hope I have said enough to attract attention to the loathsome and horrible system of dealing with our blacks that we as a colony have hitherto sanctioned. I have known gentlewomen in the bush who refused to allow officers of the Native Police to enter their doors, or share the generous hospitality accorded to every deserving wayfarer. Surely, sir, when a pure-minded gentlewoman need shudder to let herself or her children come in contact with a police officer there must be something particularly disgusting in his usual avocation. How is it that our police hardly ever bring to justice white men who offend against blacks? Do those of us who have lived in outside districts know of no outrages committed by whites? No black boys (servants who get no wages) brutally flogged and ill-used? No young women forcibly abducted from the tribe for purposes I dare not mention here? When I think of the nameless deeds of horror that I have heard discussed openly by many a camp fire, I can scarcely control my indignation and write calmly. How long shall the present state of things exist; how long shall we, the people of Queensland, have men in our employ carrying out our orders for extermination—'Slay, and spare not'—against our dark-skinned and weaker brethren?[12]

The controversy initiated by the *Queenslander* was carried into the parliament where a group of progressive members led by John Douglas endeavoured to force the government to set up a Royal Commission to investigate all aspects of the Native Police Force. But after two long debates the attempt was rebuffed by a substantial majority in the House of Assembly. Members put on the record a fascinating discussion about the relations between Aborigines and settlers.

The reformers were modest in demand and cautious in approach. They conceded that a war of races was inevitable and that the weaker race would be defeated. John Douglas agreed with opponents that they must look forward to 'the eventual extinction of the weaker race'. 'That might be admitted on all lands', he added.[13] Critics of the police were careful not to offend outback settlers. Mr Rutledge did not wish to say a word in deprecation of the energy of those men who had 'gone out to every point of the compass and subdued the wilderness and colonised the interior'. 'All honour to those pioneers!', he declared.[14] The principal concern of those pressing for an inquiry was the bad reputation of the colony and the demoralising effect of frontier violence. Douglas believed that brutalities and murders had been over and over again committed in the north and they had become so common that 'the European nature was in danger of demoralization'.[15] The way in which the blacks had been dealt with had caused the Europeans to become 'terribly callous, and they had almost lost sight of the fact that murder of this kind was unjustifiable'.[16] The young Brisbane lawyer Samuel Griffith voted with Douglas but he felt that punitive expeditions were sometimes justified. He did not think that 'all cases of reprisals should be treated as murders' because there were many situations in which 'recourse could only be had to the tribal law and in which it would be absurd to allow the offence to go unanswered'.[17]

The defenders of the Native Police bestrode the moral high ground. They spoke for the pioneer, contemptuously dismissing critics who had not actually lived in the outback. The Colonial Secretary A. H. Palmer ridiculed Douglas as knowing nothing of the blacks and taunted: let him try 'a few months on the frontier, and camp out for a few months with only a black boy with him'.[18] Then he would change his views. His namesake H. W. Palmer thought it ridiculous of members 'who were never 40 miles outside civilization in their lives to tell them how they were to treat the blacks'.[19] The deep antagonism between frontier settlers and urban based humanitarians was manifest. B. D. Morehead angrily declared:

> If the black attacked the white he suffered ten fold, but he would not be molested if he kept quiet. It was all very well for quasi-humanitarians, while they sat at ease in their armchairs to say it was a shame. They did not consider that men had to deal with the blacks in a rough-and-ready way . . . Those hon. Members [critics of the Police] could afford to philosophise and moralise and be very good. They could be like the Pharisee looking up to heaven and thanking God they were not as other men were. The men in the outlying districts had to fight their way and

hold their own; and, because they did that, they who to a great extent made the colony were to be held up to contempt and scorn by the hon. members opposite who were reaping the benefit of their trials and sufferings.[20]

And bush-wise politicians were quite clear about the Aborigines. They knew the black, they declared. Colonial Secretary Palmer explained that 'the nature of the blacks' was so treacherous that they were only guided by fear. They could only be controlled by 'brute force and by showing him you are his master'. He warmed to his subject and later in the same speech announced:

> They knew that the native black of Australia was essentially a treacherous animal—that he would spare neither man, woman, nor child, cattle, sheep, horses nor pigs—that the only way to keep him down was by using a firm hand, and that the only way to ensure that firm hand was to show them that the whites were superior animals and could beat them down.[21]

Most members who spoke in the debates believed that the settlers were engaged in warfare with the Aboriginal tribes. Douglas referred to the Native Police as being quartered in 'an enemies country'.[22] Mr King argued that much of the problem arose because the law assumed the Aborigines to be British subjects whilst in point of fact 'they were not British subjects but our enemies'.[23] The colonists, Mr Morehead explained, 'had come there as white men and were going to put the black man out'.[24] Loyalty to race overrode every other consideration. It was the responsibility of every man to care for his own family and race. It was the duty of the colony 'first of all to protect the whites and afterwards the blacks'.[25] Running through many of the speeches was the powerful current of popular social Darwinism. It was a trite saying, but true, Morehead argued, that where the white man appeared the black man disappeared. They all knew that the black man 'had to disappear off the face of the earth before the tide of advancing European civilization'.[26] Attempts to ameliorate the condition of the Aborigines were actually 'fighting against nature'.[27] In the conflict of races 'that must take place in every newly settled country'[28] it was clearly the duty of the government to protect its own people and preserve the white race.

Queensland's political leaders rebuffed the parliamentary attack on the Native Police Force and denounced the campaign by the *Queenslander* as a spurious agitation based on sensational articles written by a highly imaginative reporter.[29] But the pamphlet *The Way We Civilize* was widely distributed and taken very seriously outside the colony, confirming the view that Queensland had developed an ethos of racial intolerance and casual brutality. The very confidence with which Queenslanders affirmed their views condemned them in the eyes of humanitarian outsiders. A Royal Navy officer wrote to the Aborigines Protection Society in 1883 referring to his experience while serving on the Queensland coast. He had been horrified to read an editorial in a Townsville newspaper in 1881 which declared that the sooner the Aborigines were exterminated the better. But what provoked him to write to the society two years later was the reaction of the locals. To his surprise the well-educated men he consulted about the matter said that they agreed with the sentiment.[30] A far more senior

British official, Sir Arthur Gordon, reacted in a similar way to his experiences while visiting Queensland during the time when he was Governor of Fiji, South Pacific High Commissioner and Governor of New Zealand. In a letter to his close personal friend, the British Prime Minister William Gladstone, Gordon denounced the Queenslanders:

> The habit of regarding natives as vermin, to be cleared off the face of the earth gives to the average Queenslander a tone of brutality and cruelty in dealings with 'blacks' which is very difficult for anyone who does not *know* it, as I do, to realize. I have heard men of culture and refinement, of the greatest humanity and kindness to their fellow whites, and who when you meet them at home you would pronounce them to be incapable of such deeds, talk, not only of the *wholesale* butchery . . . but of the *individual* murder of natives, exactly as they would talk of a day's sport, or having to kill some troublesome animal.[31]

The Way We Civilize was particularly useful for the humanitarian bodies and individuals who acted to thwart Queensland's ambitions to extend its control over Papua which eventually led to the colony attempting to unilaterally annex the territory in April 1883. By then British humanitarians, led by the Aborigines Protection Society, had begun to regard the Queenslanders 'with a suspicion hitherto largely reserved for the Boers of South Africa'.[32] In May 1883 the society wrote to Lord Derby, the Secretary of State for the Colonies, strongly opposing Queensland's attempted annexation both because of the colony's involvement in the Pacific Island labour trade but also because of its record in regard to the Aborigines.

Central to the society's case was an enclosed copy of *The Way We Civilize* accompanied by the following explanation:

> We beg further to remind your Lordship that Queensland has laboured for many years past under the imputation of having failed to take proper steps for the protection of her own aborigines. The Committee desire me to forward, for your Lordship's information, a copy of a pamphlet on the native police in Queensland, published in Brisbane three years ago. We abstain from referring to such outrages as, unfortunately, too often take place in the remoter districts of a newly settled country, and which are to a large extent due to sheer inability on the part of the Executive to restrain the elements of disorder; but it is obvious that the native police is a force for whose conduct the Queensland Government is necessarily responsible. Your Lordship will perceive that the enclosed pamphlet consists of articles and letters which appeared in the 'Queenslander', a Colonial journal of high character. They are manifestly written in good faith, and, representing, as they do, both sides of the question, contain materials for enabling the reader to form an impartial judgment. We understand that the compiler of the pamphlet is willing to make himself responsible, in his own name, for the charges he has brought against the native police, and to place the Government in the way of obtaining trustworthy evidence on the subject, in the event of an official inquiry being made.
>
> We beg respectfully to urge that until such an inquiry has been made as should vindicate the good name of the Colony, it is most undesirable that Her Majesty's Government should be a party to any

arrangement which would place a great native population, of the estimated number of three or four millions under the authority of the Queensland Ministry. We regret to be compelled to make this remark, but the published details justify the fear that in too many instances the operations of the native police have been conducted with wanton cruelty; that revolting outrages have been committed upon native women; that unoffending blacks have frequently been murdered in cold blood; and that sometimes, even when the guilty have suffered punishment, the work of repression has degenerated into a massacre. Moreover, the secrecy with which the doings of the native police are surrounded, one evidence of which is the non-publication of the reports of their officers, is calculated to strengthen the belief that too little official supervision is exercised over the proceedings of the force.

It would have been comparatively easy for the Colonial Government to ascertain the truth or otherwise of the grave accusations to which we have referred by appointing a Royal Commission to inquire into the whole subject. This they were invited to do by the Hon. John Douglas, ex-premier and formerly Agent General for the Colony in England; but his proposal was not entertained, and Bishop Hale, Chairman of the Aborigines Commission, was equally unsuccessful in his efforts to induce the Government to take some action in the case of an alleged massacre of blacks to which he called their attention. They will perhaps allege that the charges made are either untrue or greatly exaggerated, but it would manifestly be unsafe for Her Majesty's Government to take this for granted in the absence of inquiry, and in the teeth of the strong testimony to the contrary which has been given by a number of respectable Colonists and never disproved.[33]

It was an acute and comprehensive attack on Queensland's record. But while the Aborigines Protection Society was a powerful opponent of Queensland's imperial ambitions, Sir Arthur Gordon was an even more formidable one. Gordon had received a copy of *The Way We Civilize* while Governor of New Zealand from the Russian scientist-explorer Baron N. De Miklouho-Maclay and wrote back to the savant asking to be put in touch with 'anyone who could enable me to verify and authenticate the shocking particulars there related'.[34] Maclay obliged and arranged for at least two important letters, one from the anonymous author of *The Way We Civilize* and the other a copy of a letter written to him in 1880 by the prominent and respected Police Magistrate F. B. Sheridan. Sheridan's letter was the more shocking. He began by recalling the Native Police raid in Maryborough in 1860 when 'five thoroughly innocent men paid the penalty with their lives and no inquiry was ever made into the action of the Police'. He recalled that on many occasions wounded Aborigines would rush into his father's house seeking protection, 'it being the custom of the Police to fire on the camp and shoot the men, women or children indiscriminately' on the pretence of arresting some offender. After detailing further gross atrocities Sheridan observed: 'Such matters as these I have heard Native Police officers make a subject boast to an admiring audience'. He admitted that:

> To a great extent we have to depend on rumor for the acts of cruelty committed against the aboriginals but if one tithe of the murders and rapes be true (and

of that I am sorry there can be little doubt) then our legislators have brought a lasting disgrace on the colony by their legalising wholesale crime.[35]

The author of *The Way We Civilize* wrote to Gordon to assure him that the articles were carefully researched and that the newspaper had only used material that the editorial staff felt could be substantiated before an official inquiry. He explained that initially he had doubts about whether he should write to Gordon at all given the controversy surrounding the *Queenslander's* crusade and the hostility he had encountered. But he decided that 'it would be cowardly to hold back now' and gave Gordon the right to use the letter in any way he wished. Gordon sent a copy to the Aborigines Protection Society which allowed the office-bearers to send *The Way We Civilize* with great confidence to the Colonial Office. It is not clear if the author was ever aware of the widespread impact of his pamphlet.[36]

Armed with the brutal intelligence about Queensland conditions Gordon was implacably opposed to the colony's annexation of New Guinea which occurred when he was on leave in England. Four days after news of the annexation reached Britain he wrote a long letter to Prime Minister Gladstone. He began by excusing himself for taking advantage of the privilege of being able to write privately to the great man but was moved by a 'most earnest hope' that he would not be 'induced without very careful consideration to consent to the suggested appropriation of New Guinea' to Queensland because he could 'hardly conceive any government more unfit for such a task'. He did not think that any large native population could safely be entrusted to a 'small, for the most part ignorant, and selfish oligarchy, of another race, having interests directly opposed to those of the natives themselves'. Beyond that there was 'a special unfitness in the case of Queensland'.

He drew Gladstone's attention to the fact that an expansion of the boundaries of Queensland would entail an extension of colonial law which was based on the principle of *terra nullius*. 'No right in the soil is recognized in the native', he explained. This would have serious consequences in New Guinea. He noted that in 1879 Queensland had 'almost silently' annexed the islands of the northern Torres Strait including the Murray Islands which had a pattern of land-use and tenure similar to Papua. But the first act of the government was to advertise the islands for sale at five shillings an acre regardless of the fact that they were 'the homes and property of many hundreds of natives'. Gordon concluded his appeal to Gladstone with a sweeping rhetorical flourish:

> You are engaged at this moment in the endeavour— and it is an endeavour which commands my heartiest & most thorough sympathy—to extend local self government in India—you are full of a generous sense of what we are bound to do for the people of Egypt. Will the same hands that are busied about such tasks, deliberately make over the millions of New Guinea, I will not exactly say to slavery, for that sounds rhetorical, but to the absolute control of those who will despise—use—and destroy them?
>
> I do not know that I have ever felt more strongly, or more deeply, on any question, and, whether I think of you as the foremost statesman of the time, or simply as a friend whom I love and venerate, I am

equally anxious that the consummation of what seems
to me an iniquity should not be associated with your
honoured name.[37]

Gordon followed up his letter to Gladstone with an
anonymous article in *The Times* in the middle of May
which covered much the same ground. But he returned
to the question of white–Aboriginal relations which had
not been such as to 'promote sympathy or kindly feeling
on either side'. While there might be exaggeration in
many of the stories of atrocity in Queensland it was
impossible to converse with any average colonist, to read
local newspapers, to listen to speeches in parliament
without perceiving that the native was 'regarded as
simply an encumbrance on the soil', as being destitute
of rights and existing 'only on sufferance, for which he
should be grateful'. To allow Queensland to gain control
of New Guinea would 'incur grave moral guilt'.[38]

Four days after Gordon's article appeared, Gladstone
wrote to his Secretary of State for the Colonies expressing the hope that the government would find itself 'in
a condition utterly to quash this annexation effected by
Queensland on her sole authority, for I suppose her to
be untrustworthy as well as unauthorised'.[39] Many forces
were at play but it seems that Gordon's views had 'great
influence' on Gladstone when he frustrated Queensland's
ambition to have its own tropical colony.[40] The Secretary of State, the Earl of Derby, wrote to the
Administrator of Queensland, Sir Arthur Palmer, on 11
July repudiating the colonial initiative. The language was
official and restrained. But the condemnation was clear.
Derby pointed out that the Queensland government had
proceeded without authority. There was no evident

foreign threat and the New Guineans had given no
indication of courting the annexation. Even if the extension of British sovereignty had been desirable or
necessary the involvement of Queensland would be open
to strong objection both because of the enormous size
of the existing colony and the fact that it was

> government by a Parliament which represents the
> white population, whose interests are altogether dif-
> ferent from those of the coloured races, aboriginal and
> imported, within the Colony: and while I am aware
> of the difficulties with which the Colonial govern-
> ment has had to contend in connexion with the
> labour traffic and other questions affecting native
> interests, the fact that those difficulties have not in all
> cases been satisfactorily dealt with cannot be disputed,
> and has often of late been the subject of much
> comment.[41]

The Way We Civilize found other appreciative readers
outside Queensland. It influenced the historian G. W.
Rusden who used it while writing his three-volume
History of Australia published in 1883. It provided the
major weapon in Rusden's passionate assault on Queensland for its treatment of the Aborigines. 'How does the
heart ache', he declared, to think of the Aborigines 'done
to death, and left mangled and stark on the soil of
Queensland'.[42] He suspected that the northern colonists
were trying to throw a veil over the history of atrocity
in the hope that it would 'wither out of men's knowledge unexposed'.[43] But they had been thwarted by the
'gallant conduct', the 'manly conduct' of the *Queenslander*
which enabled the historian to read the words of eye-
witnesses and actors. And use them Rusden did—across

twenty pages of fierce denunciation. 'The air of Queensland' he thundered, 'so reeks with atrocities committed
and condoned' that the few who pleaded for 'justice and
mercy' deserved more praise. Even the government
statistician fell in with 'the prevailing vice'. The registrar
general, Rusden observed, found no place for the Aborigines and in his table of causes of death in Queensland
he 'omitted the rifle'.[44]

But the historian saved his most angry rhetoric for
the contributors to the *Queenslander* who had defended
current practices and especially *Never Never* who tried to
justify 'the loathsome conduct' of the Native Police.[45]
The defence of atrocity was 'almost as nefarious as the
atrocities themselves'.[46] Rusden thought that out of
consideration for any reputable relations of *Never Never*
he should not be named although in the colony the
'sincerity of the writer was known, and he was not
without admirers'. After quoting a long passage from the
offending letter Rusden wrote in disgust:

> Who shall say that Swift's description of his country-
> men, as a pernicious race of odious vermin suffered
> to crawl upon the surface of the earth, would have
> been hyperbolic if they were as worthy of it as the
> *Queenslander*'s correspondent?[47]

Writing to the Aborigines Protection Society just
prior to publication of his history Rusden said that he
expected 'a howl from some of the Queenslanders' about
the way in which he had been compelled to show 'how
the natives have been treated'.[48] But he did not relent
and issued dire warnings to the colonists:

The subject is not inviting. The dead or dying bodies of black brethren are passed by on the other side, while petty local claims or amusements engross attention. And yet unless, as a people, the colonists recognize a duty in the matter, for all these things a reckoning will be made. If the community suffer in no other manner, the demoralization engendered by their own acts must corrupt the body politic, and wring from future generations an expiation for past crimes.[49]

Eight years after Rusden provoked a howl from the Queenslanders, the young New Zealand graphic artist and journalist A. J. Vogan published *The Black Police*, a novel based on his experiences in outback Queensland. Like Rusden he told a story of great brutality but his book probably reached a wider audience than the historian's earnest three-volume work. The novel depicted the experiences of Jolly, 'a new chum' who is confronted with the casual acceptance of violence in the outback. The young Englishman gets into an argument about the Aborigines but is interrupted by the young hostess:

Swinging round on her chair at the piano, the pretty, little, fragile hostess, who is a young woman of twenty, but who looks at least twenty-five years old, eyes the debaters with an amused and rather satirical face.

'Well', she says, interrupting the somewhat heated conversation, making a pretty little *moue*, 'what's the good of talking about those horrid blacks? Augh! I hate them. And I ought to know, for I'm a squatter's daughter; and my father had to shoot more niggers when he first took up the Whangaboora country than any man in Queensland has.'

The young black-coated philaboriginist turns his head, and looks with mute wonder at the fair young advocate of human slaughter.

'What's wanted here is a Black war like they had in Tasmania,' continues the fair pianist. 'Wait till you've been amongst our squatters awhile, and you won't think more of shooting a nigger than of eating your tucker.' The speaker laughs a silvery little laugh, and all her audience, save one, smile in acquiescence. 'What are the blacks? They're only horrid thieves, and worse than wild animals, . . .'[50]

The conversation turned to a recent murder of a stockman and the resulting punitive expedition:

'Did they send the "boys" out?' drawls out a languid youth, who has been silent so far.

'Yes, rather!' answers the bright little hostess, with a curious steely gleam in her grey eyes, clasping her tiny hands together on her lap, as a child does when excited with delight or anticipated pleasure. 'Yes, rather! Inspector Puttis, my cousin, you know, was at Gilbey's station at the time when the news came in. And you bet he gave them a lesson they won't forget in a hurry.'

'Did he catch the murderers?' asks the unfortunate Mr. Jolly innocently, immediately wishing, on noticing the half-hidden sneer on all the faces present, that he had kept quiet.

'Catch the murderers?' the little lady in white repeats, with a grin that spoils for the instant her pretty face. 'No, indeed. We don't go hunting round with sleepy Bobbies here, and summonses and such rubbish.' A murmur of applause rises from the cigar-holding lips of the auditors. 'No! Cousin Jack I guess cleared off every nigger from the face of the earth within forty miles of the place. At least, if he didn't, he ought to. They're a horrid nuisance, and besides, it's a long time since they've given the "boys" a chance of doing anything.'[51]

After blundering on for a few minutes Jolly was given a friendly warning about his behaviour.

A grave-looking young man, who has sat in silence watching the face of the heretical new chum, expounder of the doctrine of Mercy, now leans forward and touches his shoulder.

'It won't do, Jolly,' he says, in a half whisper, 'you really mustn't express your ideas upon this subject. It isn't business-like to speak of your opinion against that expressed by a possible customer. You'll have to get case-hardened, like I had to. We ain't in England now, and you'll have to close your eyes and ears to much out here. A new chum is especially the object of suspicion and dislike to many of the older colonists. "He's come out to reap the harvests we have sown in labour and danger." They say; and consequently the figurative "new chum" is hated. You can ask as many questions as you like, but don't air your opinions on such subjects as you've broached tonight. You'll find the colonists hospitable if you wink at their pet vices and sins, but act otherwise, and,—they're the very devil. Now I've told you the square facts, and don't you forget it.'[52]

Vogan himself found that the colonists were 'the very devil' when they read or read about his novel. In a letter to the Aborigines Protection Society in September 1891 he explained that he had become a 'marked man'. He had made 'numberless enemies' as a consequence of publishing the novel and his 'old profession of special reporter' was closed to him in Australia.[53] Things had not improved fifteen months later and he wrote again to the Protection Society soliciting their help in finding him a position in East Africa. He explained that:

> My book 'Black Police' has virtually closed my news-paper life in Australia, I wrote upon the unpleasant subject, out of a sense of duty I owed to my fellow countrymen . . . But it has done me such harm here—this meddling with the pet national sin of Australia that I am forced to seek fresh pastures.[54]

Queenslanders did not take kindly to critics of their behaviour. Nor did their contemporaries in the other frontier colony, Western Australia, as the missionary John Gribble discovered when he sailed from the eastern colonies early in 1886.

VII

JOHN GRIBBLE GOES WEST, 1885–87

In August 1885 the 37-year-old John Gribble arrived in Western Australia to take up the position of Anglican missionary in the remote north-west of the sprawling colony. He had worked as a parish priest in rural Victoria and then established an Aboriginal mission over the border in New South Wales at Warrangesda on the Murrumbidgee. A year before he sailed for Fremantle his book *Black by Comely: Aboriginal Life in Australia* was published in London.[1] There was much in the book which helped explain the extraordinary impact which Gribble had on Western Australia and his departure as a social pariah less than two years after he disembarked in Fremantle.

Gribble related how, as a child, he had become lost and was temporarily cared for in the local Aboriginal camp. His feeling of pity for Aborigines had, he wrote, grown with his growth and strengthened with his strength as year after year he had been 'confronted with the terrible wrongs to which they [had] been subjected'. He confessed that while he had life and strength his only ambition would be 'to befriend the black population' of Australia.[2]

His positive childhood experience notwithstanding Gribble had little contact with Aborigines until he set out on a trip around the pastoral stations of the Riverina where he eventually visited poverty-stricken fringe camps which he found in a condition 'most shocking to contemplate'.[3] Having been particularly disturbed by one such visit he discussed the situation with a station owner's wife who confirmed all his fears about the position of Aborigines in the pastoral districts. In *Black by Comely* he described his distress and how having gone to his bedroom he was 'filled to overflowing with the wants and woes of this unhappy people'. He fell on his knees and 'wept before God'.[4] But it was still some time before he was willing to commit himself to the precarious, demanding life of a missionary. For six months he experienced a severe struggle between flesh and spirit:

> The flesh said—'Stay where you are; why impoverish your wife and family and isolate them from all society?' But the spirit said—'Go and rescue the perishing! Go and build them a home in the wilderness'.[5]

The spirit won and in March 1880 the Gribble family, their sparse possessions and a handful of Aboriginal retainers, straggled out of Jerilderie and away from the comfortable life it provided. The townspeople thought that Parson Gribble had developed 'Blacks on the Brain'.[6]

By the time he came to write his book Gribble had a clear picture about the history of relations between Aborigines and settlers. From the earliest days of settlement, the 'native tribes' had been most 'wrongly treated by the white man'. The Europeans had also maligned them declaring them to be 'dull senseless clods, with but little brain, and entirely destitute of human soul'. Acting on these erroneous conceptions the Europeans had made the blacks the victims of their 'carnal and cruel passions'. They were regarded as so many wild beasts to be dispersed.[7] The missionary was undoubtedly aware that such views were unpopular. He conceded that many observations in his book would sound 'harsh and severe, especially to the ear of Australian colonists'.[8] But Gribble was not one to trim his sails to catch the winds of popular approval. Facts, he wrote,

> are stubborn things, and certain facts are very unpleas-
> ant to hear. And if the terrible gaping wound exists,
> is it right to keep it concealed?[9]

Gribble, too, was stubborn—and self-righteous, out-spoken, tactless, humourless, obsessive and enormously courageous. An incident which occurred when his ship called at Bunbury foreshadowed much of Gribble's trou-bles in the west. An Aboriginal prisoner was brought on board, chained around the neck. Gribble wrote in his diary that he 'truly pitied the poor fellow'. A fellow passenger declared that the Aborigines were little better than monkeys. Gribble replied that if that was the case then the passenger himself was 'not much superior than a monkey'. The man responded hotly. Gribble noted that he 'grew wroth [sic] and threatened me grievous bodily harm. But I held to my opinion his threat notwithstanding'.[10]

When he arrived in Perth a few days later Gribble was well received by the leading colonists—the Anglican Bishop, the Governor, the Colonial Secretary—and was pleased at their professions of support for the 'good work on behalf of the blacks'. It was, he thought, 'a most hopeful feature'.[11] But when Gribble preached in the cathedral some people began to have second thoughts. The morning after his sermon, the Dean told him that 'certain parties' had taken offence at what he had said. Gribble responded by pointing out that he had not referred to Western Australia at all. 'And furthermore', he reported in his diary:

> I told him that I had not come to please man but to do *God's* work and that I could not help the obtuseness of unreasonable men.[12]

Gribble sailed for Carnarvon a few days later. The editor of the conservative *West Australian* observed that to succeed in the north the missionary would require a practical and unprejudiced understanding of the 'relative position of white and black'.[13]

In fact Gribble probably had little understanding of the situation in the north. His experience in Victoria and New South Wales would have done little to prepare him for the nature of race relations on the frontier where small numbers of Europeans—and predominantly men— were outnumbered by the indigenous population, many of whom had experienced only limited contact with the whites. Gribble was entering a harsh, brutal and unaccustomed world. In 1885 Western Australia was a Crown colony, ultimate governmental responsibility residing in London rather than Perth. Policy was still made in the Colonial Office and overseen by the local governor. The violence, so characteristic of Queensland settlement, was consequently more restrained. The Imperial authorities had resisted attempts to establish a para-military force similar to the Native Mounted Police. But the West Australian settlers were far more dependent on Aboriginal labour than their Queensland counterparts. Indigenous workers were the mainstay of both major northern industries—pastoralism and pearling. They were frequently recruited at the point of a gun, were ruled by fear, flogged, underfed and unpaid. Aboriginal women were universally taken by white men either for casual sex or for longer relationships in which they provided both sexual comfort and unrewarded labour. Critics who questioned the system threatened not only the self-esteem and moral standing of frontier settlers but their economic survival as well.

Gribble's reaction to the physical environment around Carnarvon did not augur well for the success of his venture. On 28 August he sighted the 'low and very uninteresting coastline' where the Gascoyne River entered the Indian Ocean. Nothing, he wrote in his journal, could be more depressing to the spirit of a stranger than the first sight of this part of the coast:

> No headlands. No grass, nor trees and no sign of habitation or animal life of any kind.[14]

But he was initially pleased with the response of the townspeople who he found 'very kind and obliging'.[15]

Their goodwill did not last long. Northerners knew a troublemaker when they saw one. Within a few hours of his arrival Gribble visited the blacks' camp on the sandhills at the back of the town. The residents were in 'a wretched state', burrowing in the sand 'just like so many wild animals'.[16] But Gribble's induction into the ways of the north had only just begun. More shocks were in store for him on that memorable first day. As he walked through town he saw an Aboriginal girl of about thirteen in the company of a 'great rough looking bush man' who had arrived with a dray load of wool from a station 120 miles up river. He confronted the fellow and asked him if the girl was travelling with him on her own. To Gribble's amazement the teamster replied that it was the custom in the north for everyone to have a black girl and that girls were better than boys because they didn't run away. A station manager later confirmed Gribble's fears about his new environment, telling him that it was 'quite the order of things in this district for white men to do as they pleased with the black women and girls'. Truly, Gribble confided in his diary, there 'is monstrous iniquity to be grappled with and purged out in these parts'. 'God help me do it', he wrote beseechingly.[17]

Within a few days the missionary left Carnarvon for a tour of the surrounding stations where he was deeply disturbed by the squalor in which many of the white men lived. He was censorious and unsympathetic, not understanding how men could live 'disorderly and in dirt'.[18] Gribble undoubtedly told his various hosts of his disapproval. He also lectured all and sundry on the evils of promiscuous sex with the Aboriginal women. He was amazed to see on one station a stockman 'debauching' a young woman on a verandah in full view of anyone who passed. 'I was horrified', he later wrote,

and I asked him how he dared do such a thing. He was astonished at the inquiry, and with the most unblushing effrontery said 'She has been assigned to me by the police for six months, and I can do what I like with her'.[19]

Gribble was disturbed by other aspects of frontier life. At a small police station he discovered six Aboriginal men and one woman chained to each other 'like so many dogs' where they were to be held for weeks until the magistrate from Carnarvon arrived.[20] He quickly appreciated the critical importance of Aboriginal workers but thought it a pity that those who reaped the benefit from their toil could not be persuaded to treat them in a manner 'commensurate with such benefit'. He drew one station manager's attention to the neglected appearance of the local Aborigines and was told in reply,

> that the treatment was quite good enough for the 'niggers'. And that it was absurd to think that they should have tea, sugar, etc., etc. And mark—these same natives I found were saving this very station hundreds of pounds per annum.[21]

By the time Gribble arrived back in Carnarvon the bush telegraph had done its work. The missionary was a dangerous man. A public meeting was called which denounced Gribble and a petition was drawn up asking the Bishop to withdraw him from the district. The settlers, Gribble realised, had found that he was not a suitable man for them. He observed that:

> I had, while up-country, seen wrongs and abuses to which I had conscientiously drawn their attention. I learned not to 'call a spade a spade'. I simply said that certain things ought not so to be; and because of my honesty of speech, I found three months subsequently that the whole district was confederate against me.[22]

At a later public meeting the missionary said he knew that he was not liked, declaring that because he did not drink and play billiards, adhered to Christianity and did not 'bring himself down to the level of the district, a dislike was taken at once to him'.[23]

Gribble was characteristically defiant, even excited by the prospect of confrontation. 'I like a healthy opposition', he noted in his diary. It gave one a 'greater intensity of zeal and a greater determination to do and dare for God and oppressed human beings'.[24] Hostility from those around him increased his conviction that his course was righteous. It was a sure sign that his work was 'of God'. The craft of evil men, and the work of Satan were in danger, hence his opponents 'stir and rage'.[25] But Gribble felt his isolation and supposed that the local settlers thought him merely 'a mad enthusiast'. It was a characterisation he didn't entirely reject. After all, he recalled, Saint Paul himself had spoken of the desirability of being 'fools for Christ's sake'.[26]

But the Governor, the Bishop and his other patrons in Perth were of more immediate use and Gribble sailed south to secure their support and explain his side of the story. He received a new mandate from the church and returned to Carnarvon. But the support of influential southerners meant little in the north and by the time the missionary returned he found that his enemies were 'enraged against him'.[27] They attempted to prevent him from landing his building supplies from the ship. Shopkeepers refused to serve him, butchers to supply him with meat. Those who gave Gribble any support were boycotted in turn and suffered from a decline in trade. When he attended a prize-giving evening at the local school he was 'generally shunned'. Those who would be well disposed to him were 'afraid to show [him] any countenance'.[28] Overnight his allies placed a large placard between two hotels bearing the slogan: 'No boycotting in Carnarvon let everyone have fair play'. It was torn down the following morning and replaced with another banner reading: 'Down with Gribble and his supporters and confusion to all sneakers'.[29] When Gribble visited the local hall he discovered a placard with the doggerel verse,

> Old [Bishop] Parry sent a parson here
> His name is J. B. Gribble
> Poor silly wretch he damned himself
> To save the Lord the trouble[30]

Townspeople were called together again to denounce Gribble. They were deeply offended by reports of a lecture the missionary gave about the north-west when he was in Perth. Gribble attended and demanded the right to speak despite the anger of the audience. Battling against continued interruption which 'at times rose to uproar', he spoke for an hour. He was both exhilarated and threatened, telling his hostile listeners that he well knew that he was 'fighting a great fight single handed'. In his journal he observed that his opponents were 'just like a pack of hungry wolves hounding me down'.[31] A few days later Gribble decided to go to Perth again in an attempt to strengthen his position. 'I must get special protection and authority to carry on this mission', he wrote, 'or its enemies will destroy it which is their fixed determination'.[32] But he made a second and more portentous decision as a result of the hostility of the public meeting. He shouted at his tormentors that if they would not hear him directly they would do so indirectly.[33] He decided to use the press to publicise his cause, beginning

with articles and letters in the Perth papers *Inquirer* and
Daily News, then in the press in the other colonies and
eventually in England. A collection of his articles was
published as a pamphlet, *Dark Deeds in a Sunny Land*.[34]
At the same time he began writing regularly to the
Aborigines Protection Society in London. In justifying
his decision to seek wide exposure for his crusade
Gribble explained:

> I would, however, have it to be distinctly understood
> that my journal and articles were published after, and
> not before, all the barbarous tactics of the settlers to
> get rid of me. It is a fact that none can contradict,
> that for five months I endured every kind of cruelty
> at the hands of the Gascoyners, without publishing a
> thing against them, either in this colony or in any
> other, and it was only when they hounded me down
> at the second public meeting in Carnarvon, that I
> resolved to adopt the only course open to me, viz:
> the columns of a free press . . . [35]

Gribble's sense of being a marked man was accen-
tuated by his experiences on board the SS *Natal* as it
steamed from Carnarvon to Fremantle in February 1886.
Many northern settlers were on board and the missionary
quickly realised that the feeling was 'very strong' against
him.[36] With the ship lying at anchor in Champion Bay
off Geraldton and most of the crew ashore, Gribble was
attacked by a group of men who eventually besieged
him in his cabin. He barricaded his door and held his
attackers at bay for an hour and a half. In his report of
the incident to the Bishop Gribble described the scene:

> During the period of the siege I received the most
> violent threats; they said if they could only get me

for ten minutes they would 'do for me', and one man said he would shoot Gribble 'the devil', and they taunted me by saying I had come from New South Wales to interfere with their natives, but they would not let me live to reach Fremantle. Language was also used which was too disgusting to repeat, as to their intentions.[37]

Gribble's attempts to bring charges of assault over the incident were continually frustrated although he appealed for assistance to the Bishop, the Governor, the Chief Justice and the Colonial Office. The matter never came to trial.

As soon as he arrived in Perth Gribble realised that the publication of extracts of his journal had aroused great hostility. He noted in his diary that 'a strong feeling exists against me'.[38] Gribble as an irascible missionary was one thing. As a high-profile public figure he was altogether more troublesome. He became the focus of intense controversy, winning both new friends and new enemies. He was concerned that his family was being boycotted in Perth. He had difficulty in getting a solicitor to take up his case against his shipboard assailants. Of the many clergymen he wrote to, only a few replied.[39] It was hard to get doctors to attend his three very ill children. He pleaded and stressed the seriousness of their condition. The doctor so addressed said he would rather not attend the family but reluctantly did so. Mrs Gribble, recently arrived from the coast, 'felt her isolated position very much'.[40] But things got even worse. On 24 February the family experienced two shattering blows. Livingstone, their 3-year-old boy, died and the bank which held their only savings closed its doors leaving them penniless.[41]

The church authorities were deeply disturbed by Gribble's capacity to attract publicity. The Committee of the Board of Missions declared that Gribble's decision to publish material in the popular press met with their 'unqualified condemnation'.[42] The Bishop sought the right to censor any material that Gribble had prepared for publication, a demand refused on both ecclesiastical and political grounds. If he accepted the curtailment of his right to appeal to the public it would mean 'the wrapping up of the instincts of true Christian manhood' and committing them to the perpetual safe-keeping of ecclesiastical superiors.[43]

Gribble told the Bishop that while he was willing to show him any material he intended publishing, he would never give up the 'right of private judgement and liberty of conscience' which he believed were his 'birth-right as an Englishman'.[44] In his letter to the Bishop, Gribble insisted on his right to reserve to himself 'liberty of conscience and the right of private judgement' especially in relation 'to cases of wrong and cruelty to the natives'.[45] The Bishop was also concerned about Gribble writing to the Aborigines Protection Society in London. In fact he 'emphatically vetoed' any such correspondence. Gribble recorded his response in his diary:

> I told him . . . I would not sell the birthright of my freedom of conscience. And I would not submit to the unholy prohibition. I told him that I felt that a crisis was reached in my history as a missionary. I was willing to obey him in all things lawful and right but to sign away my liberty, I could not especially when

the object was to *keep covered* the wrong doings of white men in relation to the natives.[46]

Gribble continued to write regularly to the Protection Society, his letters playing an important part in informing British humanitarians of conditions on the West Australian frontier. The Bishop, needless to say, felt quite free to write to the society himself and explain the reasons for his difficulties with Gribble, who, he thought, judged the settlers hastily and unfairly and 'acted too injudiciously in proclaiming at once open war against the whites'. The missionary behaved in a very impetuous and unwise manner 'calculated to invite hostility and opposition'. Gribble, the Bishop believed, was 'an earnest good man' with his whole heart in his work but he had none of the 'wisdom or patience needful to the prosecution of such work as has been entrusted to him'.[47] While not mentioning it to the Protection Society, the Bishop was undoubtedly also concerned about alienating the church's powerful and wealthy patrons.

Ernest Gribble was told 40 years later by the retired editor of Perth's *Daily News*, and the only living survivor with a knowledge of the Gribble affair, that his father had been sacrificed by the church in order to appease wealthy patrons. 'Your father was sacrificed to build the Cathedral', he said, 'we were raising money for it at the time'.[48]

Gribble's inimitable capacity to ruffle fine feathers was illustrated by his relations with the Governor, Sir Napier Broome. In March 1886 after his troubled journey south from Carnarvon he was invited to have lunch with the vice-regal couple at their summer residence on Rottnest Island. Quite gratuitously he offended Lady

Broome by belittling her pet project, the construction of Perth's Anglican Cathedral. He reflected on the incident in his diary, observing that in polite society one must be prepared to offer 'a most emphatic affirmation' to every question 'no matter what one's own opinion may be'—a course of action which 'to JBG is simply abominable. I believe in saying what I think of persons and things.'[49] But at other times JBG realised that he had a real problem with his outspokenness and lack of tact. 'I must keep my mouth with a bridle', he wrote in his diary but then added: 'How difficult it is at times to do so'.[50]

Gribble's disillusionment with the Governor grew rapidly during the weeks after their lunch together on Rottnest Island. Frustrated with his inability to get his assailants into court, he wrote an angry letter to Broome concluding with the flourish:

> If I am obliged to abandon this case through the force of circumstances, I shall most certainly lay the blame at the door of the Government of this Colony . . . I shall not keep anything back from the sister Colonies, nor from the authorities, civil and ecclesiastical in England; I shall make it my mission to reveal to the Christian world the wrongs obtaining under the British flag in Western Australia.[51]

The Governor declined to answer the letter but complained about Gribble to the Missionary Committee which in turn sternly rebuked their troublesome employee for the 'insolent tone' of his letter. The Archdeacon explained to Gribble that it was not creditable to his profession as a clergyman to address the Governor in such a manner and to have forgotten his duty as a British subject and a Christian minister.[52] Gribble replied that in writing to the Governor he simply did that which his conscience dictated in 'the interests of common justice'. As a missionary to the Aborigines he could do nothing nor could he say anything 'contrary to the truth in relation to them'.[53] But the church was not finished. The Dean issued instructions that Gribble was neither to preach nor lecture in any church in the diocese.

Far from being humbled the missionary was good to his word. He sent a formal complaint to the Colonial Office about the Governor's failure to deliver justice to him and on 26 June sailed from Fremantle to lay his case before both the general public and the church authorities in the eastern colonies. When the boat reached Adelaide he received a telegram dismissing him from his post of missionary. By the time he disembarked in Melbourne, Gribble was ready to carry out his threat to expose Western Australia's abuses to the wider world. Soon after his arrival he was interviewed by a reporter from the *Daily Telegraph* which resulted in long articles on 6 and 9 July. The material was controversial enough; the headlines were sensational. 'Slavery in Western Australia!' they screamed, 'Horrible Cruelties!', they declared.

The missionary explained for the benefit of his Victorian readers the nature of what he called the assignment system of black labour, which, while it had no foundation in law, allowed the settlers to make Aboriginal men and women 'perpetual slaves of the white man'. No register of servants was kept and the Aborigines never knew when their time of service had expired. Gribble observed that he had been told that the settlers could keep their servants as long as they liked. The system survived because the government of the colony was in the hands of a few families who had direct interests in both pastoral and pearling industries. The police magistrates in the remote areas were hand in glove with the settlers whose benefit was their sole concern. But as well as these familiar arguments the paper highlighted Gribble's claim that the 'white masters of the slaves' gave orders that any children born of sexual relations between Aboriginal women and white men were to be killed. The bodies, he claimed, were then eaten by the Aborigines.[54]

Reports of the Melbourne articles whipped up a storm in Perth. The reaction was initiated in the Legislative Council. In a debate on 'Libellous Statements Published by The Rev. J. B. Gribble' members poured out their anger which was hardly surprising given the missionary's attacks on them as being interested in 'settlement and pearling' and therefore determined that nothing should be done to protect the Aborigines. But Gribble went further, telling his Victorian audience that there were men in the council who had been charged with murdering blacks but had been acquitted.

Councillors believed that Gribble had betrayed the whole community. He had 'traduced and maligned the settlers of Western Australia in the eyes of the world'. The whole colony was 'held up to execration', it had been 'insulted and degraded before the whole world'. Gribble was urged on by nothing other than

> a vindictive feeling towards those who have given
> him a cordial welcome to their homes and extended

to him the right hand of fellowship, this man now never lost an occasion to malign them, and to tell the most atrocious lies about them—lies, which, if there was any foundation for them, would hold up the people of Western Australia, and deservedly, to the execration of the civilized world.[55]

The editors of the conservative *West Australian* were no less affronted than council members but took the calculated risk of attacking Gribble without the protection of parliamentary privilege. The missionary, they declared, was a 'lying, canting humbug'.[56] Gribble grabbed the bait and sued for libel claiming damages of £10 000 even though the paper printed an apology the following day. It was nine months before the case came to trial.

They were nine hard months for the Gribble family. Their savings were gone. There was no reliable income. The churches were shut against JBG and he had little scope to earn a reliable living. He preached in the open air and in working men's halls; he ran a Sunday school and launched a temperance crusade. The older children did odd-jobs; friends and supporters sent food and money. In May the Bishop told Gribble to leave the diocese because there was no prospect of his ever being offered work in the colony.[57] His moods swung violently. At times he reported in his diary 'loss of self control and extreme nervous excitement' and on other occasions he longed for peace. 'Rather restless and excited', he wrote in October 1886, 'oh for the calmness and perfect rest in God at all times'. But then depression descended. In November he recorded: 'rather despondent, and very much like giving up the struggle of right against might'.[58]

The case of *Gribble v. Harper and Hackett* opened on 16 May and ran through until 10 June. Gribble himself spent eight days in the witness box. Much of the evidence supported his account of race relations in the north-west. Chief Justice Onslow expressed both understanding of and sympathy for Gribble's crusade and he had done so, privately, before the libel suit was initiated. He observed that the missionary had been the subject of a grievous outrage on board the SS *Natal* and he had been prevented from bringing his assailants to trial. It was, Onslow declared, a 'most unfortunate miscarriage of justice'.[59] Despite that the missionary was

> called insolent by his fellow-clergymen for attempting to obtain redress for that outrage, and when broad hints were made that his real object was to make money out of his grievances. I cannot but think, and I feel constrained to express my opinions, that Mr Gribble was not at that time treated with the consideration which he had every right to expect. He undoubtedly had much to say which called loudly for a patient hearing, for it is now admitted that the charges made by Mr Gribble have been productive of much good.[60]

But judicial sympathy did not save Gribble. Onslow believed that in his interviews and lectures in the east Gribble showed a 'wilful disregard for the truth' which justified the defendants' epithets 'lying, canting humbug'.[61] And so the case was lost. The impoverished Gribble was ordered to pay costs. He wrote in his diary:

> Judgement given in the libel case . . . I am beaten but not conquered. 'The Lord reigneth'. Were it not

for my dear wife and children would be willing to
go through all again for the oppressed natives.[62]

His supporters rallied around, gave him a purse of
sovereigns and smuggled him aboard a steamer in
Fremantle where he hid in a cabin for five nights until
clear of Western Australia. The past bore down on him
but the future beckoned. He noted in his diary: 'I need
rest from the injustice and oppression of men'.[63] He
dreamed he was on a new mission station 'on some
distant river'. It had 'seemed very real'.[64] Gribble
emerged from his cabin as the ship left Albany. 'Great
was my joy', he wrote, 'when the ship left King George's
Sound'.[65]

Great too was the joy of Gribble's opponents when
they heard that he had quitted the colony. The editors
of the *West Australian* believed that the colony had been
cleared of wrongdoing, its name and reputation were
restored. Every genuine son of Western Australia would
rejoice that the missionary's 'foul career of slander' had
been brought to an end by the 'unanswerable command
of the Supreme Court'.[66] But controversy and conflict
did not depart with Gribble. The opposition paper, the
Inquirer cried:

> let the Squattocracry say the colony is cleared! But of
> what! Not of anything Mr Gribble has said respecting
> their cruelties towards the 'niggers', but cleared of a
> Mission any effort that would have made the colony
> what a vigorous Church and good Government
> should strive to make it—one in which our black
> brethren would be elevated and protected, instead of
> ill treated and demoralized.[67]

Gribble worked for several years in rural parishes in New South Wales. But his dream of a 'new station' was prophetic. In 1892 he established Yarrabah on Cape Grafton just south of Cairns. He died of the combined effects of malaria, dengue fever and tuberculosis in June 1893. He was only 45. He had left the mission in the hands of his son Ernest. His tombstone in Sydney's Waverley cemetery describes him as the 'Black Fellow's Friend'.[68]

Gribble's brief, stormy sojourn in Western Australia was not forgotten. The Roth Royal Commission of 1905 into the condition of the Aborigines bore out many of Gribble's observations about race relations in the north. Public meetings in Perth and Fremantle, called to demand reform, passed motions retrospectively applauding Gribble's hard-fought crusade. A large and influential meeting in Fremantle on 9 March 1905 passed a resolution to express its condolence with the widow and family of the late Rev. John Gribble 'in the loss that they and the cause of justice and humanity have sustained by his undeserved fate and untimely death'. The resolution was accepted with 'earnest unanimity'. In a letter to Mrs Gribble the meeting organiser, F. L. Weiss, explained the tributes paid to her husband by the mover and seconder of the resolutions were received with 'many manifestations of intense approval'. Weiss concluded his letter with the hope that

> the awakening of the national conscience, and expression of the People's sorrow for a great wrong done, voiced in the preceding Resolution, would not only do an all too long delayed act of justice, and entirely clear your respected Husband's name; but will also

afford some sad consolation to the Widow and family of a good and brave Gentleman—martyred in the noblest of all causes, those of Justice and Humanity.

The letter was sent with a cover-page carrying the message:

Vindication
of
The late Rev. J. B. Gribble
February 24th 1905

JBG's eldest son Ernest wrote on the bottom of the page:

My father died June 3rd 1893
His 'vindication' 12 years too late.[69]

VIII

TWO UNLIKELY AGITATORS:
ANGELO AND CARLEY,
1880–90

Gribble's criticism of attitudes and policies towards the Aborigines was clearly more acceptable in 1905 than it had been twenty years before. But he had not been alone even then. He had been encouraged by many supporters and well-wishers including those who saw the missionary as the persecuted opponent of an unpopular ruling oligarchy. There were also others who fought for a better deal for the Aborigines including two men from the opposite ends of the social spectrum—the ex-convict David Carley and Lieutenant Colonel E. F. Angelo. Both took up the Aboriginal cause; both suffered as a consequence.

Angelo had devoted his life to the military. In his youth he had fought in the Crimean War and subsequently served in India. He took up the position of commander of the voluntary army reserve, first in Tasmania and then in Western Australia, until he was appointed to the position of Government Resident for the northern districts stationed at Roebourne, arriving in the small outpost late in 1885.

Angelo travelled north at much the same time as

Gribble and like the missionary was deeply shocked by what he saw, writing to Governor Broome in April 1886 that the method of labour recruitment practised locally was 'a disguised but unquestionable system of slavery'.[1] He was distressed by the systematic brutality of the white employers, their disregard for the welfare of their workers and the arrogant self-confidence of the settlers. He informed the Governor about the activities of two well-known 'nigger catchers', who 'publicly advertised themselves to procure and put niggers on board [pearling luggers] at £5 a head for anybody, or shoot them for the government at half a crown a piece'.[2]

The Colonel found that there was little he could do to change the way things were done in the north given the complicity of the leading men in business, the professions and the magistracy and the tight bonds of small community camaraderie. In a report to the Governor in April 1886 he explained:

> I have been warned repeatedly by persons of all classes
> of the community *not* to *touch* the 'Native Question'
> but to take matters at the 'North-West' as I find
> them.[3]

Such was the opposition to Angelo's zeal for reform that he felt under siege and thought that attempts would be made on his life, informing Colonial Office officials that they could expect at any moment 'to hear of my being got rid of some way or another'.[4] By the end of 1886 he had seen enough of the north and applied for a transfer on the grounds that he could not serve in a colony where he was obliged to 'wink at a system of organized slavery'.[5]

While the Governor and his officials in Perth and

their superiors in London found Angelo's dispatches disturbing they concluded that he had damaged a hitherto unblemished record by becoming too emotionally involved in the Aboriginal cause and could, therefore, not be promoted or transferred. He was discussed in a series of intra-office memos in the Colonial Office.

When the Permanent Under-Secretary, Sir Robert Herbert, read copies of the letters that Angelo had written to Governor Broome he wrote a brief, damning comment: 'This man is, I fear, mad'. Three months later the verdict was that Angelo had ruined his career by showing himself to have 'much heart but little head'.[6] Unaware of the judgements being made about him in London, Angelo kept applying for transfer or promotion. His case was discussed at greater length in 1888. The Colonial Office's Australian expert, Thomas Fuller, wrote a long minute on the matter to Robert Herbert:

> He has been a constant applicant for promotion, & up to the date of those minutes [about the Aborigines] was thought worthy of all recommendations.
>
> Afterwards as you know, he lost his head over the native question & placed himself in violent opposition to the Government.
>
> There was nothing disgraceful in anything that he did except once perhaps when he brought a lot of wild accusations against those whom he called bad people in the colony.
>
> He would not be fit for any position of great responsibility as he cannot keep his head cool, & I fear it might be difficult to find him an appointment without responsibility having a salary attached to it at all approaching that which he draws at present.[7]

Having read the memo the Under-Secretary commented that he feared that Fuller's view was correct and that there was little probability of being able to offer Angelo a better appointment. He noted that a previous governor of Western Australia had spoken well of him and that since then he had continued to receive commendation for 'energy and painstaking work'. But 'he lost his head over the native question'.[8]

Angelo eventually escaped his purgatory in the north and was appointed to the position of Government Resident in Bunbury. He ended his career as governor of the Aboriginal prison on Rottnest Island.

Lieutenant Colonel Angelo was an unlikely person to 'lose his head' over the native question. So too was the ex-convict David Carley whose crusade for justice outlasted those of both Angelo and Gribble. When the 42-year-old Carley arrived in Western Australia in May 1863 he had spent a good deal of his adult life in prison. He was twice sentenced for being a 'rogue and vagabond' in 1851 and 1852 and for an unspecified misdemeanour in 1852. He was sentenced to a six-year gaol term in 1855 and for a further ten years in 1861. On his arrival in Western Australia his record described him as 'middling stout' and of middling stature. He had light hair, grey eyes and red whiskers. He was married, but childless; a Roman Catholic who could both read and write. His occupation was described as labourer but in the colony he took up a number of semi-skilled occupations—chairmaker, jeweller, repairer of umbrellas and watches. Apart from a few minor offences Carley passed through the penal system in Western Australia receiving his ticket of leave in 1865, conditional pardon in 1869 and full pardon three years later when he moved north to the small northern outposts of Roebourne and Cossack.

Like Gribble and Angelo after him Carley was shocked by the treatment of the Aborigines and began to compile a dossier of atrocities which he had witnessed or heard about on good authority. In January 1884 he bundled up a parcel of documents and sent them to the Aborigines Protection Society in London including '58 Pieces relative to the Slavery Rapine and Murders at the Nor West Coast of Australia'.[9] Carley's carefully documented list of atrocities played a major part in the growing movement for reform and was similar in its impact to the compendium of brutal incidents published by the *Queenslander* in 1880.

Gribble met Carley for the first time in Perth on 4 March 1886 having just come from a long meeting with Bishop Parry who had pressed him to pursue a policy 'contrary to right in relation to the settlers and the natives'. The meeting with the old lag could not have been more different. Gribble noted in his diary that Carley had,

> for years lived in the North West and witnessed most horrible cruelties committed on the natives. Some of the cases cited by him were blood curdling. I am almost driven to desperation when I contemplate doings in this Colony and the very worst feature of the subject is that no redress can be secured. Those in high places are so mixed up with those who are guilty of wrong doing that it seems to be impossible to get justice meted out.[10]

Two days later Gribble himself wrote to the Protection Society, moved by the impact of Carley's passionate testimony.[11] He used Carley's evidence extensively in his own pamphlet *Dark Deeds in a Sunny Land* and in his numerous articles and speeches. They added greatly to the things he had seen and heard himself during his short sojourn in Carnarvon and helped explain the sense of outrage which motivated both Gribble and Carley in their confrontations with the rich and the powerful in the colony. Carley was quoted extensively in Gribble's infamous 1886 articles in Melbourne's *Daily Telegraph*.[12] As a resident of the north-west for eleven years he had in his possession, the missionary explained, tangible evidence of 'murders and cruelties and rapine of the grossest description' which included the following extensive 'catalogue of horrors':

It is very well known by all who knock about Nickol Bay and the 'Flying Foam passage,' that in one day there was quite sixty natives, men, women and children shot dead. The natives themselves have shown him one of the skulls of fifteen who were shot. Three of the skulls were those of children, and two of the small skulls had bullet holes through them. I have seen many natives shot in the back for no other reason that that of running away from their cruel slavemasters. I saw at 'Flying Foam' passage no less than twenty-four natives handcuffed together, and then conveyed to Delambre Island, and there detained until they were required for pearl diving, their only food being a little flour.

In September, 1878, I was inside my house at Cossack, when I heard a native woman calling out to me to save her boy from a man who was kidnapping him. I went out, and saw the woman struggling with a white man for her boy. I did not interfere, as it was useless, knowing that the man's brother was a M.P., whom I had seen sign away numbers of kidnapped natives. The man tore the boy from his mother, and took him to a store close by and got him assigned. The next day the boy was put on board a cutter in spite of the screams and struggles of his poor mother. I drew the attention of a constable to the case, and he said he could not interfere. I have seen hundreds of children brought into Cossack who have been torn away from their mothers, and yet it is said that where the British flag flies slavery cannot exist. In October, 1880, two white men came to Cossack, having on board their cutter ten kidnapped natives. They were sold to — for £20 cash and a debt of £35. I saw the money paid.

In September, 1880, I saw at Roebourne a police constable pass on his way to Cossack. He had in charge a native man, who had a chain locked around his waist, and then attached to the saddle of his horse. Soon after I started for Cossack myself, and when about five miles along the road I saw the constable cantering his horse, and the native was running to keep up. I saw him fall down from sheer exhaustion, and he was then dragged along the ground for a considerable distance. I galloped up and said to the constable, 'I have seen what you have done, and I know that is no use reporting you, but I warn you not to do it again.' Soon after I reached Cossack the trooper and the native arrived; the unfortunate being could scarcely crawl, and he had a terrible blood-stain right around his waist, caused by the friction of the chain, and blood was flowing from both of his shoulders. A friend of mine, as he beheld the sight, exclaimed, 'What would they say in England if they knew this?' In the year 1874, when at Cossack, I saw two dead native women; they had died through eating poisoned flour which they got from a station near the George River, and I was told by natives that three others had died from the same cause. The owner of that self-same station afterwards poisoned himself, as commonly reported. In May, 1883, three men, well armed and mounted, left Cossack for the purpose of kidnapping on the Fitzroy River. I reported the circumstance to the authorities, and was told to mind my own business. In October of the same year these men returned to Cossack with twenty natives; some of them made their escape, but they were pursued and recaptured. I may state that during my sojourn in the North-West it was quite a common practice to sell cutters for a considerable sum over their real value, because of the number of natives they had attached to them. I have been sworn in Perth to this fact, and it has been allowed to die out in order, I suppose, to prevent exposure. In the same year I saw for several days in succession large numbers of natives who had recently returned from the pearling grounds, assigned as general servants by a drunken J.P., in a public-house at Cossack. Some of the natives told me that they did not want to sign, but they were forced to do so. I have seen numbers of natives brought in from the interior, and some of them had never before seen the face of a white man, and they were compelled to put their hand to a pen and make a cross, which they never could understand, and having done this they were then slaves for life, or as long as they were good for pearl diving. Their rations consist only of a little flour when they are engaged in pearling.[13]

Though a victim of the penal system, and exiled from his homeland, Carley had great faith in English justice and an entrenched belief that slavery could never flourish under the British flag. To begin with he sought to achieve justice for the Aborigines by appeals to the local police and magistrates. He got nowhere for his trouble and was severely beaten up by two police officers. He appealed to the Anglican bishop when he visited the north and was fobbed off. He moved to Perth where he attempted, unsuccessfully, to take legal action against the pearlers who openly bought and sold Aboriginal divers and labourers. By the time he met Gribble he had concluded that to attain his ends it was necessary to appeal to opinion-makers in Britain, first to the Aborigines Protection Society, then to the Colonial Office and eventually to the Secretary of State himself. In May 1886 Carley told Gribble that he was sure 'nothing could be done here but that the Imperial government should be made acquainted with all the injustice and wrong doing in the Colony'.[14] He had earlier written to the Aborigines Protection Society observing that he had been trying to call attention to conditions in the north since 1872 and that

I have Continued doing the same to the present date, and no notice of this was sent home till I wrote to your Society then they was forced to send Home knowing that you would call the attention of the Home Government to these Facts . . . [15]

In an early letter to the Protection Society, Carley apologised for not being able to get anyone to 'write' for him because they wanted to charge him for the service. 'I have not the Means of paying for this writing being done', he explained, 'I know no one who will do it without pay'.[16] So he wrote in his own clumsy, awkward hand every now and then blotting and smudging the page, presumably not having the money to buy more paper. His letters were full of grammatical errors and spelling mistakes and were virtually without punctuation. The gentlemen-reformers of the Protection Society must have immediately realised that their informant from Perth was a man of little education and humble origins. But the moral conviction shone through. The Secretary of the society wrote to the Secretary of State in February 1886 explaining that Carley had been in the habit of writing to them for 'several years past' and that they had given 'wide publicity to some of his allegations without them having received any contradictions'.[17] Ten months later when told of Carley's criminal history the Secretary said that they were still convinced that their informant 'acted in good faith'.[18]

In two letters of January 1884 Carley referred to the 'Horrid Crimes' which he had seen and known in the north and how men and boys were torn from their homes to be made slaves to dive for pearls and shell. He explained that he had done all he could for eleven years to expose the crimes of the northern settlers but that he had never yet succeeded in bringing any case to a fair trial. He feared his story might appear overdrawn but he had 'commonly stated many crimes', more than he had described to the society, and would do so again:

When I can be Defensered by a Lawyer but I am allone with out Money or Friends and I am to Old to Commence again [sic].[19]

He returned to the same theme in a letter of 26 May 1884 explaining that he had tried for more than eleven years to stop the 'Foul Stain on the Flag of our Country'[20] but the only good he had done was to ruin himself.

Carley continued to write letters and send newspaper cuttings to the Protection Society during 1884 but he was a man in a hurry and was frustrated at the slow response to his correspondence. On 24 August he complained:

> I have wrote a large number of letters but have not received any answer all I require is to know if you have received them . . . nothing more [sic].[21]

By 1886 Carley had decided that his only option was to approach the Secretary of State. He wrote to the Protection Society informing them:

> I think my memorial to the Secretary of State is very plain and Bold when I inform him that one of Englands Coloinis is Steeped to its Neck in Rapine and Slavery and Murder and as I have defended these murdered slaves to the best of my ability for 13 years and to my Complete ruin so I will defend them to the Last as I have long since given up all hope of aid from any quarter. Forty eight years ago I lived in New Orleans and I have seen American Slavery which is White as Snow when compared with the Murders and Cruelty done in this Country Under the British Flag [sic].[22]

As a postscript he provided the information that gold had been found in the Kimberley districts. 'God help the Natives', he added.[23]

169

In his address to the Secretary of State Carley declared:

> No doubt you will be told that the natives get every justice; if so those who say that are wicked liars they get as much Justice as a hungry wolf does to a sheep from the needy wretches of this colony they are despoiled of all their land their women and children their liberty and their lives and yet this Governor dare say that the natives are well treated and those who speak the truth are prosecuted to death.[24]

Carley and Gribble were right in their assessment that they would achieve more by directing protest and appeal to London than by confining their activity within the colonial boundaries. The Aborigines Protection Society pressed the Colonial Office and asked for answers to the accusations of illegality and atrocity. The Colonial Office in turn demanded answers from the Governor of Western Australia who indirectly had to respond to the two outcasts Carley and Gribble and take their charges seriously, whereas in the colony itself he could treat them with contempt or indifference. The Colonial Office was extremely sensitive to inquiries emanating from the Protection Society, being aware of its moral stature, social connections and political influence which was illustrated by the fact that the statements of Gribble and Carley were raised in the House of Commons by Mr W. Channing on 2 September 1886. He asked the Under-Secretary of State for the Colonies, Mr E. Stanhope, whether his attention had been called to the recently published statements of the two men 'as to the practical enslavement of the Natives in Western Australia' and:

Whether he will cause inquiry to be made into the truth of the allegations that Natives were compelled by fraudulent indentures to sign agreements to enter the service of white settlers for specified periods; that they are frequently kidnapped with a view to being thus 'assigned' to settlers; that this 'assignment system' is used for obtaining Native women for immoral purposes; that the Natives thus assigned are frequently chained, hand cuffed and subjected to other cruelties, and in many instances have been shot, on attempting to escape from the masters to whom they have been fraudulently assigned.[25]

It was an admirable synthesis of what Gribble and Carley had been telling the Protection Society. In reply Stanhope admitted that the government was aware of outrages by the settlers but that they were exceptional cases and not part of systematic oppressions. The Under-Secretary announced that the Governor had introduced new legislation to establish an Aboriginal Board and a system of protectors. With a dramatic flourish he announced—to shouts of Hear! Hear! from behind him—that just five minutes before he had received a telegram informing him that the bill had become law.[26]

Bad publicity in London, questions in the Commons—these were things dreaded by colonial governors and by colonial politicians alike. They undermined the good name of the colony and aggravated the touchy and often precarious pride of small striving societies. The critics had to be discredited. Carley was the most vulnerable and bore the brunt of the attack. His 'antecedents' were raised in the Legislative Council in July 1886.[27] Three days later the Governor denounced Carley in a dispatch to the Secretary of State.

Broome began by outlining Carley's criminal record and then provided a series of unsubstantiated claims about him. The police 'suspected' him of being a receiver of stolen property. During his residence in the north he was 'reputed' to be a thief, a receiver of stolen property, a pearl shell stealer and it was stated that 'he lived in debauchery with several native girls of tender age' and that he was a 'sly grog' seller to the natives. The Governor explained that he felt it was important to outline Carley's 'antecedents' because they had a bearing upon the value of the general and unproved portion of the statements he had made. The Governor's objective mask slipped progressively as the dispatch continued. Carley's claims were 'simply preposterous nonsense' but it must not be forgotten that he was 'a very disreputable person'. As for Gribble, his association with Carley had helped bring him down. The conclusion was that no importance should be attached to the statements made by either man.[28] The Permanent Under-Secretary of the Colonial Office, Sir Robert Herbert, sent copies of Broome's dispatches to the Aborigines Protection Society with the advice that attention should be given to the passages dealing with Carley's 'antecedents'.[29]

But while the Imperial officials did their best to discredit the messengers they clearly accepted the message of Gribble, Carley and Angelo that there were serious problems in the northern districts of Western Australia. That message had significant impact because it arrived at the time when the Colonial Office was considering the advance of Western Australia towards the self-government accorded the eastern colonies

30 years before. When Angelo's accusations arrived in the Colonial Office towards the end of 1886 they appeared to affirm what Carley and Gribble had been saying. He was the only one in Western Australia of those who had taken up the 'native cause' as against the government whose antecedents were 'above suspicion'.[30] The Colonial Office's Australian expert, Thomas Fuller, noted in an internal memo that whereas they were about to issue a parliamentary paper, the effect of which 'would have been to whitewash everybody connected with native affairs', the question would have to be reconsidered.[31]

The reports of Angelo, Gribble and Carley confirmed the Colonial Office officials in their view that the northern districts of Western Australia would have to be separated from a self-governing colony in the south. In January 1887 Robert Herbert noted that Governor Broome had already been told that if responsible government were granted the northern part 'might or would have to be separated'.[32] But during the first half of 1887 the perceived practical difficulties of separating the north overwhelmed the desire to do so. Herbert also doubted whether it would be expedient to enter into inevitable conflict with the colony. But even so it would be necessary to devise means to protect 'the Natives in the north'. The Secretary of State agreed with Herbert about the difficulties of trying to govern a Crown colony in the north but he was more emphatic than his permanent head about the need to make 'special arrangements . . . to ensure the protection and good treatment of the Native population'.[33]

Governor Broome brought forward a solution to the

problems in July 1887 when he suggested that authority over the Aborigines should remain an Imperial responsibility supervised by a Protection Board responsible to the governor and funded by a compulsory levy on the colonial revenue.[34] These proposals were eventually embodied in section 70 of the West Australian Constitution. Broome informed the Colonial Office that the local legislature would agree with him that some special arrangements should be made 'to ensure the protection and good treatment of the northern Native population'.[35] The Governor was over-optimistic. The colonists reluctantly accepted the provisions of section 70 because they knew that it was an inescapable condition of the grant of responsible government. Premier John Forrest observed in 1892 that there was much dissatisfaction about the special provisions regarding Aborigines but realising that the Imperial government would insist on their acceptance before granting responsible government 'no opposition was offered'.[36]

No opposition, that is, until power passed from London to Perth. Once that was achieved the colonial politicians felt free to vent their outrage at the measures which had far too much of Gribble, Carley and Angelo in them for their liking. The critics of the colony had helped persuade influential British officials, politicians and humanitarians that the settlers could not be trusted to administer the Aborigines. It was a humiliating message broadcast to all the world. Unlike fellow colonists in the rest of Australia and New Zealand, the West Australians were uniquely unfitted to deal with native people. In an angry letter to Governor W. C. F.

Robinson in November 1892, Premier Forrest explained that:

> The feeling that this Board is not only inefficient and unnecessary, but that its existence is a grave reflection on the honour and integrity of the people of the Colony to do what is just and right to the aboriginal population, is unanimous throughout the colony and we shall never be satisfied until this unjust stigma is removed.
>
> The existence of the Board is a proclamation to the world that notwithstanding the Government of Western Australia is entrusted with the entire control of $\frac{1}{3}$ of the Australian continent and the lives of Her Majesty's white subjects, the people of this Colony are not to be trusted to do justice and distribute relief to the poor aboriginal natives.[37]

After waging an unrelenting campaign against section 70 of the Constitution the West Australians persuaded the Colonial Office to give way and the local parliament assumed full responsibility for Aboriginal affairs in 1897.

David Carley was not impressed with the constitutional arrangements of 1890. He sent voluminous material to London to convince the Imperial government that injustice was still rampant. He had taken to writing directly to the Secretary of State for the Colonies, Lord Knutsford. They were not the polite, deferential notes expected in such correspondence. Carley hurled angry words at the distant Lord in frustration and in a mood of deep disappointment with the failure of British justice. He declared that Western Australia was up to its neck in 'Rapine Slavery Murder and Fraud' and that it was 'sanctioned by you Lord Knutsford and the Imperial

Government of Great Britain'.[38] 'Again I write to you', he informed Knutsford in November 1891,

> from the Land of Murder Slavery and Sin and you have upheld and protected those in this Colony that have committed far worse crimes than any done in Russia you have done this with a full knowledge of the terrible acts done to the Native slaves of W.A . . . The same atrocities are still sanctioned by you Lord Knutsford and your Government in this infamous Colony Western Australia.[39]

Carley was still fired with determination despite his advancing years, telling the Secretary of State that he would never rest till the murders, slavery, frauds and the 'filthy acts done to the native children and the women are brought to the knowledge of the world'.[40] The new colonial administration was even less patient with the irascible old man than the Imperial officials had been. In 1892 Premier Forrest declared that Carley was 'evidently deranged' and that his 'ravings need not be considered'.[41]

Despite his poverty, Carley continued to dream of a trip to London which would enable him to place his case before the British people. In a number of his letters to the Protection Society he referred to the action he would take, 'as soon as I can reach London'. In 1886 he declared that if his letter to the Secretary of State failed to obtain justice 'my next step will be at the door of the House of Commons where I will cry aloud of the Slavery of this infamous Country'.[42] But while Carley felt his letters failed to achieve the results he would have liked he realised that by writing to the Aborigines Protection Society early in 1884 he did ensure that the Colonial authorities were forced to respond to reports of atrocity and death. It was an achievement he was proud of. He wrote in February 1885: 'I am not likely to let anyone take that Honour from myself'.[43]

But Carley's achievements, his long crusade, were little appreciated by contemporaries and were soon forgotten, unlike those of his brother in arms John Gribble. When in 1905 a large Fremantle public meeting passed a vote of appreciation for the missionary's work for justice and humanity it is likely that few in the audience even knew of the equally significant contribution of David Carley.

West Australian dictionaries of biography, published over the last fourteen years, aren't even sure who Carley was and present a confusing picture of the man. In the 1984 *Dictionary of Western Australians*, David Carley died on 29 December 1884.[44] In the 1987 *Dictionary of Western Australia, 1829–88*, there were two David Carleys. One, an expiree, was born in 1823 and died in 1884. The second lived from 1826 to 1898.[45] In the 1994 *Dictionary of Western Australia*, vol. IX: *Convicts in Western Australia, 1850–1887* there was only one Carley who was born in 1821 and died in 1884. He went to Victoria in October 1882 but 'possibly returned'.[46]

IX

MODERN MASSACRE: FORREST RIVER AND CONISTON, 1926–28

In May 1926 William Hay, joint owner of Nulla Nulla station in the East Kimberley was speared to death by the Andedja elder Lumbulumbia. The spearing followed a period of increasing tension in the region as large bands of Aborigines moved over the country at the end of the wet season resulting in an increase of cattle killing still endemic in the Kimberley at the time. When he discovered his partner's body Leonard Overheu rode into Wyndham to notify the authorities and while there wrote a letter to his father in Perth in which he explained that he was going to 'pilot the police out' and assist them in every way he could so as to make the place safe for himself in the future. 'In officially reporting the matter to the police', he explained, 'I've asked for a strong force to go out, and also that the natives be dealt with drastically'.[1] Four days later Overheu accompanied the police party inland. It was made up of the two police constables, D. H. Regan and T. G. St Jack, two special constables, two civilians and seven Aboriginal trackers. The party had 42 horses and mules and carried 400 or 500 rounds of ammunition for their

Winchester rifles. As the party cantered out of Wyndham the onlookers shouted their encouragement, urging the police to teach the blacks a lesson they would never forget.[2] G. T. Wood, the Royal Commissioner who subsequently investigated the matter, concluded that the party was a very large one to effect the arrest of Hay's murderer and was 'certainly calculated to give rise to the thought that the expedition assumed the aspect more of a punitive expedition than one merely to effect the capture of a criminal native'.[3]

Lumbulumbia was quickly captured without violence and with the assistance of several men from the Forrest River mission which abutted Nulla Nulla station. But the police party assumed a wider brief. In time-honoured fashion members of the expedition combed the district shooting men, women and children, none of whom had any part in the white man's death. Commissioner Wood concluded that Aborigines had been killed at four sites and their bodies burnt in specially constructed pyres. He believed that as many as twenty people had been so disposed of.[4] The Forrest River missionaries believed the death toll may have been as high as 30, recording the names of Aborigines who were never seen again after the punitive expedition.[5] Aboriginal oral evidence recorded many years after the event suggested a much higher death toll, possibly amounting to a hundred and more.[6] In 1973 Grant Ngabidj talked to Bruce Shaw about those terrible events:

> Allabout go round this way some feller police there. Some feller police boy, policeman, all the boy . . . They bin roundins up . . . Put a chain along allabout now, puta chain allabout . . . black feller, lubra, lubra,

piccaninny . . . Travellin down the gully now. Tie em up allabout blackfeller, longa big tree. Nother lot tie em up longer nother big tree, tie em up nother longa big tree. This lot first time shooting that now . . . Might be more than a twenty. A'right. Go longa nother tree shootin that now. They pickim up old old women, piccaninny allabout that, make it a hundred.[7]

Whatever the death toll the impact on the local Andedja people was devastating. In 1961 the novelist Randolph Stow was told that they could still hear chains jingling, troopers' horses, babies screaming and ghosts crying in the night.[8]

The police did everything they could to keep secret their multiple assassinations. They burnt bodies, pulverised bones, buried charred remains, covered or scrubbed blood stains, silenced witnesses and retreated behind the solidarity of an approving, accommodating community. It had all been done successfully many times before. But the Superintendent of the Forrest River mission was Ernest Gribble, eldest son of J. B. Gribble. He could not be cajoled, coaxed or intimidated into complicit silence. Character, conviction and family history conspired to fire his determination to see the policemen brought to justice.

From early childhood the younger Gribble had been both victim of and coadjutor to his father's crusade. As a small child he travelled with him on his earliest excursions around the stations of the Riverina. He was taken away from school and friends in Jerilderie when the family moved to establish the mission station at Warrangesda. He had a few years away at school but his education was disrupted and uneven. At seventeen he was left in charge of the mission at Carnarvon while his father was away in Perth and the eastern colonies and had to deal with the hostility of the community. When the family was finally reunited in Perth, Ernest earned much of the income to fund his father's preaching and politicking. The move to the eastern colonies allowed him to achieve financial and emotional independence and for four or five years he worked as a stockman and drover in outback Queensland and New South Wales. He had seen enough of missionary work and vowed never to become involved. But in 1893 his father broke down and sent a peremptory telegram from the Cairns hospital demanding that he 'leave everything and come'. A mutually agreed six weeks at the struggling Yarrabah settlement had to be extended when John Gribble died in Sydney. Ernest remained at the mission for sixteen years. In 1914 he founded the Forrest River mission.[9]

John Gribble was a hard, exacting parent, as demanding of his children as he was of himself. Ernest's first memory of his father was of receiving a 'good whipping' at his hands.[10] But he was a conscientious acolyte adopting John's combination of steely puritanism and evangelical emotionalism. There was much of John in the son's personality. He was relentlessly self-centred, tactless, self-righteous, courageous. An affair with an Aboriginal woman at Yarrabah left him deeply troubled and at war with himself. He had periods of extreme emotional instability during which he became impossible to live and work with. He was experiencing one at the time of the Forrest River massacre. The Australian Board of Missions was deeply dissatisfied with mismanagement of the mission while his highly authoritarian, puritanical regime was the subject of growing criticism for being anachronistic and inappropriate. The anthropologist, A. P. Elkin, who visited Forrest River in 1928 wrote a damning report about Gribble who he described as 'an uncouth tyrant' who seemed to hate everyone and who had the 'unhappy knack of making himself disliked'. Elkin was scathing about the regime at Forrest River. There was too much repression and a 'little terrorising' in the attitude taken up towards the inmates.[11] Ernest was a very strict parent to 'his people'. Like many other missionaries at the time he separated children from parents and married them when in late adolescence paying no attention to traditional ties and obligations. Elkin's demolition of Gribble's reputation led to the decision of the Australian Board of Missions to dismiss him in September 1927.

Aborigines coming into the mission brought the first news of police mayhem. On 28 May the nursing sisters told Gribble that the parties passing the station were in a state of 'fear and fright'. Then the wounded began to appear—a man with buttocks full of buck-shot, another with a bullet wound in the leg.[12] An Aboriginal woman called Looabane arrived with her brother. She was wounded; the brother named six kin who had been shot and killed by police. Looabane told one of the nurses a truly terrible story. She explained that

> the police got all those Aborigines from the Kular tribe that lived from the coast to the mission . . . they put the men on one chain and the women with their children and their kids on another chain . . . they killed the men. They just lined them up and

shot them one by one . . . the women had to watch those men being shot . . . their husbands and brothers and relatives . . . the men had to collect fire wood first. They didn't know why they had to collect wood but they had to get a big pile of it . . . They lined them up and shot them . . . then they cut them into pieces, you know a leg, an arm, just like that and those bits of body were thrown on the wood . . . and burnt there.[13]

Gribble was profoundly shocked by massacre so close to the mission. But it provided a cause enabling him to redirect his turbulent soul and recapitulate his father's role of righteous martyr.

Rumour about massacre was one thing, actual proof quite another. That was eventually forthcoming towards the end of August. Gribble's educated Aboriginal assistant, James Noble, followed the tracks of the police party and found the place where an unknown number of Aborigines had been shot and their bodies burnt. He scooped up several shovelfuls of charred remains and returned to the mission. Armed with the first hard evidence Gribble and Noble went into Wyndham, handing the grisly parcel to the Government Medical Officer and sending telegrams to the Chief Protector of Aborigines, the Archbishop of Perth and the Chairman of the Australian Board of Missions in Sydney. In a letter to the same men Gribble declared:

It was a terrible affair. It has happened on the aborigines reserve in their own territory and in the name of the law. I sincerely hope that this awful tragedy of innocent men and women done to death in cold blood will lead to steps being taken to render such things impossible in the future.[14]

Both the local Inspector of Aborigines and the Inspector of Police visited the mission and were taken out to the site of massacre and incineration. Tracking and investigation disclosed three other places where the same desperate events had been enacted. Both inspectors, while sceptical at first, were convinced by the evidence. The first visitor, Aboriginal Inspector Mitchell was sickened by the gruesome discoveries and collected burnt pieces of bone, teeth and blood-stained stones. When he returned to Wyndham he cabled the Chief Protector Neville reporting the 'shocking revelations' and declaring that the police had been responsible.[15] Police Inspector Douglas was similarly persuaded by the evidence, kneeling in the ashes and vowing to bring the perpetrators to justice.[16] But Mitchell and Douglas were cautious men, appreciating the likely difficulties of protecting witnesses, gathering evidence and confronting a hostile local community.

Gribble was convinced that the two officials wanted to cover the atrocity up, or at best, to investigate it behind closed doors. He noted down a record of several relevant conversations with Douglas. After his visit to the mission the inspector talked with Gribble on the Wyndham jetty explaining how troubled he was about the massacre and that he realised that he only had two options—to press ahead with the investigation or to resign. He had decided that he must proceed. But a few weeks later, once again on the jetty, Douglas asked Gribble whether he would consider dropping the matter 'as nothing would come of it'. The missionary exploded with righteous indignation telling the inspector that if nothing came of it he would 'proclaim the matter throughout the states in pulpit and on platform'. Later as the two men sailed south to Perth Douglas tried again, suggesting that Gribble give up his crusade as 'nothing could be gained'. Gribble replied: 'What about Justice and Humanity?'[17]

Douglas knew how difficult the investigation was likely to be. In a letter to the Commissioner of Police he explained how hard it would be to prove anything 'with everyone in the district' except the missionaries up against him. Gribble was 'so cordially hated' that most of the locals would 'go to any measures to thwart his object'.[18] The community fell in behind the young constables. Aboriginal witnesses were sent 'out bush' and out of the reach of the Royal Commission. Commissioner G. T. Wood explained that three important witnesses, the trackers Sulieman, Windie and Frank, who accompanied the avenging party were held by the police on his explicit instructions. But a few days before the commission opening in Wyndham they were 'permitted to escape to the bush'.[19] The Commissioner demanded they attend and give evidence but the police declared they could not be found. Another important Aboriginal witness was almost certainly shot by the station owner Leopold Overheu. Potential European and Afghan witnesses refused to give evidence, leading Wood to observe that 'a conspiracy of silence existed throughout the locality'.[20]

Gribble was the focus of hostility. It was widely believed that the 'half-educated mission boys' were the source of all the trouble and the most persistent spearers of cattle. But his greatest crime in the eyes of the frontier settlers was that he treated the Aborigines 'as the equal of whites'.[21] Counsel for the police before the Royal Commission declared that:

> He continually puffs up blacks and has been a source of great mischief in the Wyndham district. That is why he is so cordially hated by those amongst whom he has lived for 13 years.[22]

Like his father before him Gribble was threatened and Douglas felt it necessary to give him police protection. The mission was boycotted by the townspeople; those who continued to deal with Gribble suffered as a consequence. One of the most poignant letters in Gribble's papers is a letter dated 6 February 1928, from the Chinese shopkeeper Lee Tong who explained:

> As there was so much loss caused to my business through your coming to my store at the time of the Enquiry and afterwards, I beg to state that when you return to Wyndham I shall be unable to let you use my house in the old way.[23]

Gribble had been dismissed from the mission five months before the worried shopkeeper took up his pen.

Despite the difficulties Commissioner G. T. Wood concluded that at least eleven Aborigines were murdered by the police party and 'most probably nine more', and that their bodies were subsequently burnt. He was damning in his comments on police practices, attitudes and evidence. He wrote:

> Taking all the evidence into consideration, I repeat that a bare denial or the extremely weak suggestions offered do not refute the very strong evidence on the

other side; nor do they account for the indications of intensely hot fires, burnt bones and human teeth that at intervals marked the trail of the police party almost from the start to finish through country scarcely visited by anyone but the blacks. Overheu wrote to his father that he had asked for a strong force to go out and also that the natives be dealt with drastically. I am firmly convinced that that spirit animated the police party throughout the expedition, that the natives were dealt with drastically by bullet and fire.[24]

It was the official condemnation of punitive expeditions that humanitarians had vainly sought for more than a hundred years. Ernest Gribble had every right to consider it both triumph and vindication. The realisation that he would certainly raise the issue throughout the country pushed a reluctant government into action. Gribble was keenly aware of the symbolic importance of Wood's judgement and of his personal thanks to the missionary for facilitating the inquiry. He read the report on 28 June; John Gribble had lost his libel case on 27 June forty years before. Ernest noted in his diary: 'Judgement given to-day in Royal Commission Whereby Son wins where the Father failed in 1887'.[25]

But the triumph was short-lived. Constables Regan and St Jack appeared before a magistrate three weeks later who concluded there was insufficient evidence to commit them to trial. The large crowd in the public gallery burst into applause and acclaimed the dismissal of charges. The two men were re-instated, transferred and promoted. Meanwhile conditions were still chaotic at Forrest River and on 29 September Gribble received notice of his dismissal. The same mail brought news of his mother's death. That evening he wrote in his diary:

News of Mother's death and my trial, condemnation
and dismissal without a hearing. That is all too hard
to bear. Self deeply wounded. Lord help me every
minute. Lord forgive my faltering faith. My time here
is now very short and the thought of my departure
hurts. 15 years of action, thought and prayer for my
people and the place.[26]

At the communion service before his departure Gribble
knelt before the memorial cross raised up in memory of
those killed in the police raids and cried out:

Yes, as a result of my being led by God to fight for
the cause of the Aborigines I am torn away from my
flock.[27]

Some time later Gribble returned to his triumphant diary
entry on 25 June 1927 and penned a bitter addendum:

Like my father I had no-one to see me off when I
left Western Australia a few months after the judgement.[28]

But no doubt departing the State unnoticed and friend-
less confirmed his comforting sense of lonely rectitude.

Meanwhile the report of the Royal Commission
sparked humanitarian concern in Western Australia and
elsewhere. Public meetings were held in Perth, letters
to the papers called for reform. In November 1926 a
group of urban Aborigines formed a new organisation
in order to obtain protection of the laws because they
were tired of being robbed, shot down and put into
miserable compounds.[29] Their spokesman William Harris
wrote to Perth's *Sunday Times* referring to the 'heaps of
human bones nicked with cartridge shells' which were
grim testimony to the reality of 'dispersion' which most

people had previously thought meant firing a few shots over the heads of Aboriginal parties to scatter them.[30] The Anglican *West Australian Church News* remarked that not only the State but the whole of Australia had been startled by the report of the Royal Commission. Up until then many people thought the whole affair seemed like the 'outpouring of a vivid imagination' influenced by the unreliable tales of natives. That Aborigines in police custody could be killed and their bodies burnt 'seemed beyond the bounds of possibility'. That such things,

> could happen within the British Empire which prides itself on justice to all, is bad enough; that they happen in our own State fills our heart with shame.[31]

Early in May 1927 the recently appointed federal Minister for Territories C. W. C. Marr received a large and influential delegation which included leading scientists, anthropologists, missionaries and churchmen. Members expressed grave concern about conditions in the north of Western Australia and urged the federal government to set up a Royal Commission into all aspects of Aboriginal affairs.[32] The new minister was impressed and promised to take action. Debate in the House of Representatives in October 1927 covered many aspects of Aboriginal policy and was clearly stimulated by published reports of evidence given before the Wood Royal Commission.[33] Senior government ministers were moved by the same material. The federal Attorney-General J. Latham told a meeting of the Armadale branch of the Australian Women's National League that:

THIS WHISPERING IN OUR HEARTS

He had recently read with feelings of shame what had been published as to the treatment of natives in the North-West by white men, who, if the allegations that were now subject to judicial investigation were true, were unworthy of belonging to our race. The reports of the royal commission on the subject would be taken all over the world . . . In his recollection, he thought there had hardly been an event which would so discredit the reputation of Australia generally.[34]

The Australian Board of Missions November meeting in Sydney sent a long telegram to the Premier of Western Australia observing that little had been done since the Royal Commission completed its work and that the two police officers were still employed in the State service. But their main concern was similar to that of Attorney-General Latham. The case involved the reputation of the Australian people throughout the world. Committee members observed that:

The circumstances have been widely commented upon in the Press of the Empire. It is no overstatement of the situation that the national character of the Australian people was brought to the bar of judgement of the civilized world.[35]

Leading humanitarians stressed how important the West Australian Royal Commission had been. The Chairman of the Australian Board of Missions, Rev. J. Needham, reported to a colleague in England in June 1929 that public opinion was being roused as never before. 'The conscience of the people', he explained, 'has been properly shocked' and the demand for the ending of the existing state of things was being heard on all sides.[36] The Secretary of the Sydney-based Association for the Protection of Native Races, the Rev. W. Morley, wrote to the Anti-Slavery Society in London observing that the Forrest River massacre had excited 'deep and painful interest' in the minds of the humane people in the community.[37] The Anti-Slavery Society took up a renewed interest in Australia which was maintained throughout the 1920s and 1930s. In December 1927 the society's office-bearers wrote to the Australian High Commissioner in London urging the need for reform of policy towards the Aborigines.[38] The world was paying renewed attention to the fate of Australia's indigenous people. But the interest and concern created by the Forrest River affairs was easily matched by public outrage about the Coniston massacre in Central Australia in 1928.

During 1928 Central Australia was suffering from prolonged drought. Competition between Aborigines and cattlemen intensified as the country dried out and bush tucker became harder to harvest. The Walpiri and Arrente clans clustered around scarce water sources. Cattle killing increased as hunger invaded the bush camps. Pastoralists demanded police protection as rumour of black vengeance passed back and forth among the scattered white station community. Randall Stafford, the manager of Coniston station, was warned that Aborigines were coming in from the desert to kill him. He asked the Alice Springs police to take decisive action.

But an already threatening atmosphere worsened dramatically when on 7 August the dingo trapper and local identity Fred Brooks was killed and his mutilated body thrust into an enlarged rabbit burrow. He had taken an Aboriginal woman from a camp beside a soak on Coniston station and had refused to return her or to supply the gifts expected as part of the exchange. But in the eyes of the white community nothing could excuse or extenuate the guilt which was not individual but collective. The cry went up, unanimous and ancestral—the blacks must be taught a lesson they will never forget. The scene was set for Australia's last official punitive expedition and one of its most brutal and unrestrained. It was led by Gallipoli veteran and hardened bushman Mounted Constable George Murray. He knew what was expected of him. But while anger welled in the settler community the news of the murder of Brooks alarmed the bush camps. White fella violence was bad at any time. When driven by vengeance and fierce racial solidarity it was awesome. The historians Peter and Jay Read, having listened to Walpiri recollections of the period, wrote:

> One can only guess at the fear that gripped the heart when a Walpiri or Arrente messenger, breathless and shaking, stumbled into the bush camps to cry out that the Whites had begun killing every Aborigine they found.[39]

Murray's party of eight well-armed horsemen left Coniston station on 16 August and returned to a hero's welcome in Alice Springs on 1 September. They brought two Aboriginal men, Padygar and Arkirka, with them, charged with the murder of Fred Brooks. Murray returned to the bush again for three weeks in late September and early October to take revenge for an attack on the legendary bushman Nuggett Morton. Murray eventually conceded that 31 Aborigines had been killed. It is likely that at least 100 died violently during that month of murder. Old Walpiri recorded in the 1970s were still haunted by childhood memories of atrocity:

> They yardem round, bringem to one mob, see, make
> it one heap
> And they shottit
> Two or three shotgun is goin', people is goin'
> . . .
> They comen there now, chasem round now, some
> all run away
> Right, prisonem whole lot, everyone
> Tiem up longa trees . . .
> And shootem whole lot, some feller, shootem,
> heapem up.[40]

The missionary Annie Lock provided evidence of the massacre in a letter written soon after the events to the Association for the Protection of Native Races. It was clearly written under stress. She insisted that it was confidential and that the association was not to speak about it 'until times when we are free to do so'. She told a terrible tale:

> The natives tell me that they simply shot them down like dogs and that they got the little children and hit them on the back of the neck and killed them.
>
> They rounded the natives up like mustering cattle and cleared or shot them out as they came to them. They had some prisoners and took the chain off them and told them to run away and as they were running they shot them.

Lock was aware she had to be very careful about accepting the 'native verdic' [*sic*] and that it was necessary to try and prove the accuracy of the account. She therefore questioned them in different ways and when they were least expecting it 'even to boys and girls' and they all said the same and 'instead of 34 it was over 70'.[41] But having convinced herself of the shocking details the missionary was so intimidated by the hostility she encountered in the Territory that she told the subsequent official inquiry that she didn't know of any cruelty by the whites to the blacks.[42]

Murray's reports to his superior officer in Alice Springs, Sergeant C. H. Noblett, were perfunctory and lacking in detail. He did not even provide a precise estimate of the number of people killed. Nor did Noblett convey that information in his report to the Commissioner of Police. As so often in the past the policemen thought that they could put all memory of the punitive expedition behind them. But the trial of the two Aborigines charged with the murder of Brooks in Darwin in November 1928 provided the opportunity for news of the massacre to reach a shocked public in both Australia and overseas. That process was facilitated by the Methodist minister Athol McGregor. He had heard rumours of the Coniston killings while visiting Alice Springs and had confronted the Government Resident of Central Australia, J. C. Carwood, who justified the massacre as necessary to maintain law and order. As McGregor rose to leave the Resident's office he was clearly not persuaded by what he had heard. Carwood said he hoped the clergyman was not going to go around causing an agitation about the matter. McGregor's answer was reminiscent of the response of many earlier humanitarians:

In God's eyes, the life of a black is as valuable as a
white's. I obey His law. I'll do what's right.[43]

A tense confrontation with Constable Murray in Kath-
erine increased McGregor's determination to travel to
Darwin to ensure that the forthcoming trial received
widespread publicity.

He began by giving several interviews to the *Northern
Territory Times* in which he declared that many settlers
preferred a dead black to a live one. The Coniston
killings revealed a state of mind which found acceptable
the fact that the Aborigine was 'regarded as dirt' who
could be 'shot wholesale on an unproven hypothesis'.
He spoke movingly both about those killed and the
survivors who had to deal with the practical and
emotional consequences of massacre.[44] McGregor's comments were published widely in the metropolitan press.
But as damaging for the local administration as were the
clergyman's revealing interviews they had nowhere near
the same impact as the frank, casual brutality of Constable Murray whose words were quoted throughout the
country and overseas as well. He readily admitted to the
fact that seventeen Aborigines, men and women, had
been killed. When asked why the party shot to kill the
constable answered:

What could I do with a wounded black fellow
hundreds of miles away from civilization.

Mr Justice Mallam then asked Murray how many he had
killed. Murray replied: 'Seventeen, Your Honour'. After
a long silence the judge remarked: 'You mowed them
down wholesale'.[45]

The Coniston killers made no attempt to hide their

involvement in massacre although they certainly under-
stated the scale of the killing. Unlike their Western
Australian colleagues at Forrest River they did not bother
about camping at the site of death and incinerating the
bodies, nor did they deny their blood-stained record. If
the State government had been forced into holding a
Royal Commission, the national one was obliged to
respond to the widespread protest and on 17 November
Prime Minister Bruce announced that an inquiry would
be held. But it lacked credibility from the start and
included on the three-man board, J. C. Carwood, who
as both Resident and Commissioner of Police had a very
obvious conflict of interest. The government refused
requests to include a representative of humanitarian or
mission organisations on the board. The report confirmed the widespread scepticism and determined that
the killing was fully justified. The result was so unsatis-
factory that it intensified the criticism of the federal
government both in Australia and overseas.

The report infuriated humanitarians in its assessment
of the reasons for the tension between Aborigines and
station owners. The three board members concluded
unanimously that no provocation had been given which
could account for Aboriginal attacks on the whites.
There was as well no evidence of starvation among the
tribes. What the board did point to was a series of issues
representing a compendium of frontier folklore—among
them were:

• unattached missionaries wandering from place to
  place, having no previous knowledge of blacks and
  their customs and preaching a doctrine of equality;

- inexperienced white settlers making free with the natives and treating them as equals;
- a woman missionary living amongst naked blacks thus lowering their respect for the whites;
- escaped prisoners from Darwin not being re-arrested—wandering about in their native country and causing unrest and preaching revolt against the whites.[46]

The report was tabled in federal parliament but was never printed. The government obviously saw it as an embarrassment. It illustrated the great gulf in sentiment between the outback and urban Australia which was beginning to show increased concern about the whole question of the future of the Aborigines.

The churches and mission organisations responded promptly to the trial in Darwin with its evidence of frontier brutality which many Australians thought a thing of the past. William Morley, secretary of the Association for the Protection of Native Races, wrote to a colleague in England, remarking that the Coniston affair was a 'very bad one'. It was typical of times 'we thought were entirely gone'.[47] Protest arose far more quickly and spread more widely than in the Forrest River case. Within four days of the first reports of the trial, the *Sydney Morning Herald* reported a general denunciation of police brutality. The case seemed all the more dis-creditable because the two Aborigines brought to trial for the dingo trapper's murder were judged to be innocent. Their capture was the ostensible reason for the police attacks in the first place. 'Press, pulpit and the general public unanimously agree with the jury's verdict', the *Herald*'s correspondent wrote, 'and are shocked by the candid admission by the police' that they shot to kill all the male Aborigines they came across.[48]

A week after the first reports from Darwin appeared in the metropolitan papers the major churches entered into the controversy. Meeting in Melbourne on 15 November the General Assembly of the Presbyterian Church of Victoria expressed indignation and horror at the shooting of seventeen Aborigines. A deputation was elected to wait on the Prime Minister S. M. Bruce and a resolution was drafted and adopted which urged that,

> those responsible for such wanton slaughter of human life be immediately suspended from duty, that a full inquiry be immediately made into the matter, and those responsible be brought to account for their actions, and that, in the light of previous reported massacres of Aborigines the Federal Government should adopt a definite humanitarian policy in regard to those whose protection and welfare are a sacred trust to the people of Australia.[49]

A week later the Australian Board of Missions, meeting in Sydney, expressed grave concern for the effect of the Coniston affair on the country's standing abroad. Reports of such atrocities caused 'untold damage to the good name of Australia throughout the world'.[50] The board foresaw questions in the House of Commons and adverse comment in the major British dailies. But they also feared wide circulation of reports in the vernacular press in Asia. In fact news of the Coniston affair, coming so soon after the Forrest River massacre, would arouse 'more widespread hostility throughout the world than most Australians realized'.[51]

The Times carried stories about the Coniston affair

on a number of occasions in September 1928. The Australian correspondent reported the claims by station owners that there was a general rising among the Aborigines and that the trouble was being caused by 'half-educated natives from the mission stations'. This was balanced by a comment from the celebrated scientist and politician, Dr Herbert Basedow, who attributed Aboriginal hostility to the fact that they considered the intrusion of settlers to be an invasion of the tribal country. The Australian correspondent informed British readers that references to police taking drastic measures meant that most of the blacks were shot on sight, something which happened nine times out of ten in similar circumstances. Aboriginal action should be seen as reprisal for earlier white violence rather than arising from criminal motives.[52]

The powerful and prestigious London-based Anti-Slavery Society wrote to Prime Minister Bruce in February 1929. The two influential office-bearers, Travers Buxton and Sir John Harris, explained that they had read reports of shooting of large numbers of men, women and children with 'painful surprise'. They focused on the issues which rendered the federal government most vulnerable to condemnation, observing that the killing was carried out by white police, in pursuance of official instruction. What was more, the shooting of at least 31 natives was 'deliberate and indiscriminate' and there was nothing to indicate that those who suffered had anything to do with the crime. The fact that the inquiry exonerated the police made matters worse. The evils of the existing system were even more evident because if the police were accustomed to treat the Aborigines in the manner publicly admitted 'under very slight provocation' what could be expected from the 'less responsible elements' of the community 'unrestrained by any force of law or public opinion'.[53] The Anti-Slavery Society continued to take a deep interest in Australia during the 1930s and established a special sub-committee to monitor developments. It was a step which annoyed and embarrassed many Australians. The clear implication was that the country could not be trusted to deal fairly with its indigenous people. For their part the humanitarian and missionary societies looked to England for support. The activist Mary Bennett wrote to the Anti-Slavery Society observing that the majority of people didn't care what happened to the Aborigines so that except for a 'very tiny devoted band here' the only help for 'our poor natives that there is comes from knowledge and public opinion in England. Australians are sensitive about that.'[54]

Concern about international opinion was one of the reasons why Coniston was the last official punitive expedition. Five years later the federal government was urged to send one into Arnhem Land to avenge the death of a policeman. But public opinion had changed to such an extent that a more peaceful path was chosen. After 138 years the age of the punitive expeditions came to an end.

X

THE CALEDON BAY
AFFAIR, 1932–34

On 17 September 1932 five Japanese trepang fishermen
were killed by the Yolngu Aborigines on the shore of
Caledon Bay in the north-east corner of Arnhem Land.
Six weeks later a police patrol visited the area but
returned without making contact with the local clans
which avoided the expedition. The police returned to
Darwin and a larger expedition was planned for the
following dry season. In June 1933 police parties
travelled to the region both by land and sea. On 31 July
on Woodah Island in Blue Mud Bay the 30-year-old
Constable Steward McColl was fatally speared. His
colleague Constable Jack Mahoney narrowly escaped the
same fate. Constable Vic Hall sailed immediately for the
mission station on Groote Eylandt to send telegrams to
the authorities in Darwin advising them of McColl's
death. Colonel Robert Weddell, the Administrator of
Northern Australia, informed Canberra on 11 August
and on 14 August the Minister for the Interior, T. A.
Perkins, informed the public of McColl's death.

Weddell advised the Minister that strong action was
required. A punitive expedition was needed. After a

conference with the Superintendent of Police and Constable Morey he sent a coded telegram to Canberra calling for a party of 24. 'Strong demonstrative force imperative', he declared,

> As natives numerous, hostile and cunning, many murders by them during the last sixteen years remaining unpunished. Stop. Consider Mission (ie. Groote Eylandt) in imminent danger if immediate action not taken. Stop. Propose arming party with twenty rifles and 2000 rounds of ammunition, twelve revolvers and 1000 rounds of ammunition and four shot guns and 300 cartridges . . .[1]

Weddell's sentiments reflected northern opinion. A correspondent wrote to Darwin's *Northern Standard* declaring that there was only one way to handle murderous blacks and that was the way 'the old pioneers' handled them.[2] The *Sun* reported that there was a strong feeling in the Territory that the Aborigines must be taught a severe lesson.[3] The Darwin correspondent of the *Sydney Morning Herald* observed that the murder of the policeman was regarded as a challenge to the white man's authority in the north.[4] Harold Nelson, member for the Northern Territory in the House of Representatives, told his colleagues that he had received telegrams from settlers in the Gulf of Carpentaria beseeching him to demand government action to save them from the Aborigines who were adopting a threatening attitude. He explained that the local tribes were a mixture of Japanese and Macassans, 'combining the cunning of the Japanese with the strength and barbaric savagery of the Macassan'. They had a fetish for murder and were seeking to exercise it far beyond their tribal boundaries.[5] On 2 September the Melbourne *Herald* reported that Darwin officials feared that there would be a general massacre of missionaries and other whites unless punitive action was taken. Only a display of force would avert catastrophe because the Arnhem Land tribes were 'vicious by instinct'. Killing was a part of their tribal code and they were inspired by an 'implacable hostility to white people'.[6]

The call for revenge came from influential figures in the federal bureaucracy and government as well. The Chief Clerk of the Department of the Interior, J. A. Carrodus, sent a note to the Departmental Secretary, H. C. Brown, at the end of August observing that the police party needed to be a large one because the Aborigines, having routed the first party, would be 'in high fettle' and would undoubtedly attack the second one. He insisted that the government 'must do something', otherwise the lives of all the whites in the north-east would be endangered.[7]

The Administrator of Northern Australia continued to pressure the government to act, assuring Minister Perkins that the white missionaries on Groote Eylandt were in danger. On 4 September the Canberra correspondent of the *Sydney Morning Herald* reported that it was almost certain that a punitive expedition would be dispatched before the end of the month, even though it was thought that bloodshed would be inevitable because the Aborigines had boasted that they would not allow white men to enter their territory. Perkins observed that while there was some opposition to the punitive expedition, the people with most experience of the Aborigines considered that it was absolutely necessary that strong action be taken to avoid further trouble in the future.[8] The Minister for Territories C. W. C. Marr said that in similar circumstances he would have no hesitation in sending an expedition against one of the New Guinea tribes. The *Herald* reported that Cabinet members with experience of native administration favoured the punitive expedition.[9]

The major metropolitan papers foreshadowed the imminent dispatch of the expedition. On 2 September the Melbourne *Herald* ran with the headlines:

GOVERNMENT PREPARES PUNITIVE EXPEDITION AGAINST BLACKS
EQUIPMENT TO BE RUSHED NORTH
MASSACRE OF WHITES IN ARNHEM LAND FEARED[10]

That evening the *Sun* was equally emphatic:

EXPEDITION READY TO PUNISH ABORIGINAL BLACKS
FIGHTING AND BLOODSHED FEARED[11]

The *Canberra Times* appeared with similar headlines:

TO PUNISH BLACKS, POLICE PARTIES READY TO GO
FIGHT FEARED

The paper's Darwin correspondent reported that all the local police were being held at headquarters and that the government boat *Maroubra* was ready to carry the avengers to Arnhem Land.[12] But by the end of the first week in September the government gave way before an unprecedented and unexpected torrent of protest from all over the country and from overseas as well. Almost as important as the volume of protest was that it was mobilised so quickly after the Minister's original statement which appeared in the press on 15 August. The term punitive expedition had taken on a sinister meaning. It had been stripped of ambiguity; it no longer worked as euphemism. It now meant massacre. After Forrest River and Coniston many Australians were determined that those awful and shameful events would not be repeated. They felt that the honour of the country was at stake.

Writing from London the Rev. C. E. C. Lefroy observed that

> 'Punitive' is a mild description. They might be called 'slaughtering expeditions'. They have long been the established custom—and it is only now, at long last that the Australian public has become conscious of their enormity.[13]

The campaign of protest began on 15 August. The Rev. W. Morley, Secretary of the Sydney-based Association for the Protection of Native Races (APNR), sent a lettergram to Prime Minister Lyons explaining that he had heard from Darwin that a punitive expedition was being prepared. He urged that the proposal be disallowed and that precautions be taken against the possibility of a repetition of the shooting that had accompanied similar expeditions in the past.[14] Two days later the left-wing League Against Imperialism called for a commission of inquiry and insisted that the police would not be allowed to kill 'whole tribes of innocent persons'.[15]

During the second half of August and the first week of September the clamour intensified. Telegrams poured into Canberra from the churches, missionary organisations, feminist groups, unions, Australian Labor Party (ALP) branches and pacifists. F. G. Bateman,

Secretary of International Labour Defence, explained that the wholesale slaughter at Coniston five years earlier was still fresh in the minds of many Australians and that police parties out in the bush were answerable to nobody.[16] Jean Daly, Secretary of the Women's Committee of the Victorian ALP, was equally concerned that police expeditions too often resulted in wholesale massacre.[17] Bernard Tuck, Secretary of the South Australian Council of Churches, telegraphed the government outlining a unanimous resolution to enter an emphatic protest against the proposed expedition. The council dreaded a wholesale massacre such as took place in 1928 when a 'large number of natives were ruthlessly slaughtered'.[18] At a public meeting in Bendigo the Rev. A. T. Holden told his audience that the relationship between Australia and the Aborigines was being judged by the world.[19]

Anthropologists added expert authority to the cause. The young research scholar W. E. H. Stanner wrote to the *Sydney Morning Herald* observing that many people were agitated and dismayed at the prospect of a punitive expedition which usually became an 'instrument of savage injustice' especially when public opinion was inflamed as it appeared to be in the north.[20] A. P. Elkin spoke out against the tradition of 'giving the natives a lesson'.[21] Olive Pink sent a telegram to the Prime Minister in the name of Australia and for the sake of ordinary humanity pleading against any decision to send an expedition into Arnhem Land.[22]

Even more authoritative figures joined the procession. Brisbane's Catholic Archbishop James Duhig demanded that peaceful and conciliatory means be adopted.[23] His Victorian colleague Archbishop Daniel Mannix sent a powerful message to Prime Minister Lyons. His telegram of 5 September read:

> With I hope a majority of Australians I would regard the punitive expedition with grave misgivings and the possible result with horror.[24]

By early September protest had spread to London. On the 5th, *The Times* printed a strong editorial headed 'Plea for a Remnant'. The phrase 'punitive expedition', the writer explained to his English audience, had an ominous sound which the past amply justified. Incidents like the present one had too often been made the pretext for the indiscriminate shooting of a people armed only with the boomerang.[25] The British Commonwealth League, the Anti-Slavery Society and the Society of Friends protested to S. M. Bruce, Australian High Commissioner in London. A worried Bruce telegraphed Prime Minister Lyons who replied on 5 September insisting that the government had not made any statement justifying assertions that a punitive expedition was under consideration. The phrase, he explained, had been invented by the press without any authority whatever.[26]

The telegram indicated that the government was in retreat. The *Sydney Morning Herald* of 5 September reported that a message had been received from Canberra to the effect that the dispatch of the expedition had been delayed in view of the protests.[27] The Prime Minister admitted that the government had been deluged with telegrams and observed that 'nothing even remotely resembling an organized massacre had ever been thought of seriously for a moment in cabinet'.[28] Minister Perkins explained that while he had decided that no expedition would be sent out with instructions 'indiscriminately to shoot natives as a lesson' something would clearly have to be done. Administrator Weddell continued to insist that the mission stations in the north were in grave danger of attack although the missionary organisations ridiculed the claim.[29]

The government sought means to meet the conflicting demands. Although force had been publicly ruled out, the equipment—revolvers, bandoliers, ammunition, binoculars and two-way radio—ordered by Weddell were shipped to Darwin on 9 September.[30] A party of four police were sent to Groote Eylandt with sufficient arms and ammunition to enable them to withstand a long siege.[31] Boredom proved to be their only adversary as they sun-baked, fished, swam and lounged around the island for six months. In response to the wave of protest the government took up the suggestion of the Church Missionary Society that a mission party travel to Arnhem Land in an endeavour to persuade the killers of the Japanese and Constable McColl to turn themselves in and travel to Darwin to stand trial. Sitting it out on Groote Eylandt Constable Ted Morey wrote that the honour of the Northern Territory Police would never recover from such an ignominy if the Caledon Bay operation was placed in the hands of missionaries.[32] But humanitarians throughout Australia applauded the decision, believing that the dispatch of the 'Peace Party' represented a turning point in the history of relations between European Australians and Aborigines.

If the ministers felt under siege during the first week of September they had even greater cause for concern up until the time when Minister Perkins announced acceptance of the mission party in October as the chorus of protest approached crescendo. Letters and telegrams came overwhelmingly from metropolitan Australia and mainly from Sydney, Melbourne and Adelaide. There were few from Perth or Brisbane. Three principle networks were activated to agitate the issue. The organised churches and the missionary organisations which had traditionally engaged in Aboriginal amelioration were joined by an assortment of feminist organisations and an array of left-wing bodies—ALP branches, unions, peace groups, unemployed worker collectives. A few individuals took up the cause like the Sydney man who sent a poem to Minister Perkins which read:

> When you and I behind the veil have past [*sic*]
> It will be known while this world shall last
> How Missions failed their purpose to fulfil
> Gunmen were sent Australia's blacks to kill.[33]

Many protest letters and telegrams concentrated on the most pressing matter, the punitive expedition, which members of the Punchbowl Unemployment and Distress Association believed would result in cold-blooded killing of many innocent natives.[34] The Australian Society of Patriots in Newcastle recalled the hundreds of similar cases which had occurred through the continent and insisted that the time had arrived when 'they should cease forever'.[35] The Committee of the Unemployed and Relief Workers of Rockdale believed that the Aborigines were entitled to the 'claim of nationality'.[36] To send armed forces against them would be nothing short of sacrilege and a disgrace to the administration.

William Morley of the APNR returned to the attack three weeks after his initial letter to the Prime Minister.

He deplored the projected action because it would be in direct conflict with the British principle of justice for all. It was inconsistent with professed care for subject races and represented a resort to primitive tribal vengeance. What is more, it would shock the civilised world.[37] The General Assembly of the Presbyterian Church in Victoria passed a strong and detailed motion in the middle of September 1933 placing on record

> its profound concern for the wellbeing of the tribes and races of the Aboriginal people of Australia. The Assembly notes with dismay the widespread opinion overseas that the Government and peoples of Australia have not done all they might and should have done to protect these natives from exploitation and from the cruelty and lust of the dominant white race . . .
>
> The Assembly believes the time is long overdue for the creation of a strong public opinion in every part of Australia as to our responsibility before God and the conscience of the world for the proper protection, food supplies and education of Australia's native races.[38]

Humanitarian opinion was buoyed by the decision to send the Peace Party on a mission to the Yolngu homeland. There was even greater applause when the missionaries brought five self-confessed killers to Darwin, including four men who had killed the Japanese and Dhakiyara Wirrpanda or Tuckiar who speared Constable McColl. But to the dismay of the missionaries the five men were arrested at the wharf in Darwin and thrown into prison to await trial. There was even greater concern when the men were found guilty and given heavy sentences. Mau, Natjelma and Narkaya were each sentenced to twenty years imprisonment for the murder of the Japanese fishermen. Tuckiar was sentenced to death. Although the evidence was fragmentary and contradictory, Judge T. R. Wells had no doubt about the appropriate sentence, declaring

> I take the view that this man, despite the fact that the evidence is very scanty, killed McColl in a deliberate and cunning way . . . I am certainly of the opinion that it should not be allowed to go out amongst the Aboriginal population that an Aboriginal can murder a policeman and get away with a few years imprisonment. The white population seems to be impressed with that fact. I cannot find any reason at all for doing other than pronounce sentence of death.[39]

The humanitarian movement responded instantly. On the night that sentence was passed a large meeting was held in Sydney bringing together the missionaries, clergymen and the radical left-wing organisation International Labour Defence. The meeting passed a motion to be sent to the Prime Minister and the Minister for the Interior which read:

> That this meeting consisting of workers and citizens of every shade of political thought, urges the Federal Government to adopt a more humane, scientific, and civilized policy towards the original inhabitants of Australia.
>
> By the release of all Aborigines now doing life sentences or condemned to death in the Northern Territory whose only crimes have been that they defended their women.[40]

The meeting also recommended that in future all such cases be tried at the scene of the crime and that the court have the assistance of a person who understood the local language and customs. More reserves were called for, as was the dismissal of Justice Wells who was 'unsuitable to try such cases'.[41] Faced with further criticism at home and abroad the government facilitated an appeal to the High Court which was heard between 29 October and 8 November 1934.

The court unanimously quashed the conviction adding southern insult to northern injury by declaring that a new trial under conditions fair to the accused would be impossible. The judges were highly critical of the conduct of the trial. The comments of Justice Wells were alone sufficient to 'render the conviction bad' while his charge to the jury made a fair trial even less likely. Tuckiar's counsel was also taken to task for failing to argue the case in favour of complete acquittal or conviction for manslaughter. Counsel was also guilty of grave mistakes in the conduct of the defence and in breaches of confidence.[42]

But the High Court's criticism reached beyond the conduct of the trial to the attitudes and behaviour common in the Territory and in other frontier districts where the judicial system had never been able to deal fairly with the Aborigines. Individuals were always treated as representatives of their race. They were not so much people as examples. Political points were more important than impartial justice. The courts were places to affirm white dominance and settler solidarity.

It was obvious that Justice Wells was determined to convict Tuckiar for murder. It was important that the blacks be given the lesson in court that interfering southerners had disallowed in the bush. For the sake of whites generally he must not be allowed to get away with killing a policeman. Honour, respect and security were all at stake. Justice Starke noted that the case against the prisoner was 'too forcibly stated' while aspects all-important to him were either overlooked or not presented with sufficient vigour.[43]

The defence of Tuckiar was compromised because it involved the reputation of the deceased constable. Third parties reported two confessions made by the defendant on the journey to Darwin. In one Tuckiar claimed that McColl had raped one of his wives. It was a story which provided both motive and some element of justification. But it also cast doubt on the character of the martyred policeman. Clearing his reputation became the principal objective of the trial. Justice Wells declared the story of the rape 'utterly ridiculous' and called a witness to attest to McColl's moral purity, evidence which the High Court determined was quite inadmissible. But the conspiracy to protect McColl was pervasive. After the preliminary coronial inquiry the coroner, defence and prosecution lawyers and Darwin's handful of journalists all agreed to suppress the story. The High Court found it necessary to remind the northern community that the purpose of the trial was not to 'vindicate the deceased constable, but to inquire into the guilt of the living Aborigine'.[44]

Justice Starke took the discussion farther than his colleagues and considered the impact on the Yolngu community of the entry into their country of a well-armed and aggressive police party which captured and handcuffed a group of women. He observed that the Aborigines may well have considered the police action as an attack on themselves and took up their spears in self-defence. Consequently a finding of not guilty or manslaughter was 'quite open to the jury on the evidence'. But Justice Wells was 'silent upon this important aspect of the case' and practically invited the jury to find a verdict of guilty.[45]

Humanitarians rejoiced at the verdict. The ethos of the frontier had been decisively repudiated. The activist Mary Bennett wrote enthusiastically to her friend Edith Jones in England proclaiming that the judgement marked 'a new and high level in the history of British justice in relation to subject races'.[46] Jones sent a cutting about the trial to the Anti-Slavery Society, of which she was a prominent member, and wrote:

> This is the biggest thing that has happened in the history of White v Black in Australia—can we do anything to mark our appreciation?[47]

Colleagues who knew the ways of the north had other concerns. Embarrassing Aboriginal witnesses or prisoners freed by the courts had often disappeared in the past. They feared for Tuckiar. William Morley of the APNR sent an urgent telegram to the Attorney-General Robert Menzies earnestly requesting the Commonwealth government

> to instruct immediate steps to be taken by Darwin authorities to find Tuckiar and protect him from dangers he is exposed to, and provide safe conduct for his return to his own country.[48]

Tuckiar was released from gaol and taken to the Kahlin Aboriginal Compound. A day later he disappeared and was never seen again. It was widely believed in Darwin that he was shot by the police and his body dumped in the harbour.[49]

But Mary Bennett and Edith Jones had a point. The fourteen months between August 1933 and October 1934 were a decisive moment in the history of Aboriginal–European relations. The High Court condemned frontier justice, the punitive expedition did not ride into Yolngu country and there had been an unprecedented outburst of public sentiment demanding a new deal for indigenous Australians.

XI

AGITATION AND REFORM, 1920–40

Late in August 1933 members of missionary organisations, clergymen and individuals of humanitarian
inclination met in Sydney to commemorate the
centenary of the abolition of slavery throughout the
British Empire. They saw themselves as the inheritors of
a long and honourable tradition which they shared with
fellow humanitarians in other parts of the world and
especially in Britain. William Morley who helped
organise the meeting believed that his Association for
the Protection of Native Races was furthering the work
of the great men of the movement, Buxton and
Wilberforce. He was also alive to the contemporary
importance of his own close links with the Anti-Slavery
Society in Britain.

Morley realised that the members of his and cognate
organisations were dealing with questions and grappling
with problems which had vexed and disturbed like-
minded people since the earliest years of Australian
settlement. At the same time he knew that the 1930s
presented opportunities for reform that had not been
available to his predecessors. Along with other colleagues

he saw great potential in the renewed and vigorous interest in Aborigines among the leaders of British humanitarian organisations and in the policies and activities of the League of Nations. In February 1934 he wrote:

> Recent events have shown that public opinion in Australia is stirred concerning this matter, and further, opinion abroad, especially in England is being brought to bear on it.
>
> Moreover as a member of the League of Nations we are morally bound to frame and work some policy designed to raise our Aboriginal race, and to solve by a well considered policy the problem of cultural and racial clash in northern and central Australia.[1]

Reform-minded Australians took comfort from the principles embodied in the Charter of the League and from the emphasis in League practice on the rights of minorities. They frequently drew attention to Articles 22 and 23 of the Charter. Under Article 23b signatories undertook to 'secure just treatment of the native inhabitants of territories under their control'.[2]

Article 22 dealt with colonies and territories inhabited by peoples 'not yet able to stand by themselves under the strenuous conditions of the modern world'. The wellbeing and development of such peoples was 'a sacred trust of civilisation' to be carried out by advanced nations which undertook the responsibility of becoming 'Mandatories on behalf of the League'.[3]

General principle became political reality when, in December 1920, Australia accepted the mandate for German New Guinea, assuming the right to exercise full power of administration as though the new territory was an integral part of the Commonwealth. Australia's interest was almost entirely strategic but the mandate committed the government to 'promote to the utmost the material and moral well being and the social progress of the inhabitants of the territory'.[4] Australia's performance was not particularly impressive but to humanitarians such a principled commitment could not be confined to New Guinea. If a trust existed there why should it not apply equally to indigenous Australians? Surely they had even more right to expect that their moral and material wellbeing would be promoted. Even more to the point was that mandatory powers had an obligation to report on their activities to the League. The welfare of native people was of concern to the world community which continued to have some responsibility for outcomes. To many humanitarians the system of mandates established a new benchmark from which the performance of governments would henceforth be measured. It was disingenuous of Australian governments to make the obvious legal distinction between the position of Aborigines and that of New Guineans. The feminist leader Bessie Rischbieth told Prime Minister Lyons in January 1934 that when signing the League of Nations Covenant, Australia undertook to look after all the native races under her care.[5] The Rev. C. E. C. Lefroy wrote to the *Contemporary Review* in 1929 calling on Australia to do 'for her own children what she does for adopted ones in Papua-New Guinea'.[6] In his influential 1933 article 'A Policy for the Aborigines', A. P. Elkin referred to the public outcry which had erupted in response to talk of punitive expeditions against Arnhem Land Aborigines. But of equal significance was the international response to the news from Australia. 'And what is more', he explained,

> the world abroad is interested in, and concerned about, the treatment meted out to a primitive race by a civilized nation, especially one represented on the League of Nations. In our control of Papua we show that we are trustees of the natives and seek their welfare and development; we are working along the same lines in the Mandated Territory of New Guinea, but we have not yet got to grips with our task in Australia, even though we have been faced with it for one hundred and forty-five years.[7]

Criticism of the Australian government moved from the general to the specific when it came to the question of slavery and forced labour. Under Article 23 of the Covenant members were committed to secure and maintain fair and humane conditions of labour for men, women and children, both in their own country and others with which they dealt. Under the New Guinea Mandate Australia had promised to see that no forced labour was permitted except for essential public works and then only for adequate remuneration. Australia subsequently ratified the Convention Against Slavery in 1926 and the Convention Against Forced Labour in 1930. Under Article 421 of the Treaty of Versailles Australia promised to apply conventions which had been ratified to colonies, protectorates and possessions which were not self-governing.[8]

It was inevitable that the critics would point to the sharp contradiction between Australia's international commitments and the situation faced by thousands of Aborigines working in the pastoral industry and who in most cases received no cash wages at all. Mary Bennett accused Australia of condoning slavery at a British Commonwealth League Conference in London in June 1930. Her allegations received wide publicity in Britain and Australia. She argued that Australia was breaking the slavery convention in three ways—employers were using forced labour on private property, they were refusing to pay wages to working Aborigines and they were removing people from their tribes and families.[9]

It was Bennett's first intervention in Australian politics. There were to be many more between 1930 and her death in 1961. Although little known today, she was probably the most important humanitarian activist of the 1930s and 1940s. The daughter of pioneer Queensland grazier Robert Christisson she had spent much of her adult life in England but returned to Australia in 1930 after the death of her husband. During the 1930s she was a highly successful and innovative teacher at the Mt Margaret Mission in Western Australia's eastern goldfields. She was also a skilful and determined lobbyist—always well informed, with a detailed knowledge of law and politics, of legislation and regulation. She had a flair for publicity and used the press with great effectiveness. Throughout her years as an activist she maintained a lively correspondence with a wide network of friends and allies both in Australia and overseas.

Two years after Bennett raised the question of slavery, the anthropologist Ralph Piddington returned from fieldwork in north Australia under the auspices of the Australian National Research Council and condemned existing conditions. His descriptions of Aboriginal suffering made sensational headlines. Under the banner:

'Aborigines on Cattle Stations in Slavery', *The World* reported that the anthropologist's observations revealed slavery, trafficking in lubras, and murdering and flogging of Aborigines by white men. 'The system of employing Aborigines on stations', he observed,

> virtually amounted to slavery. The only alternative that a native had to starving was to work for a white man at the white man's rates of pay, which consisted of food, a minimum of clothing and an occasional piece of tobacco.[10]

The sensational headlines notwithstanding the charges of forced labour and slavery were taken seriously by humanitarians, and government officials privately conceded that Australia had a problem on its hands.

The Chief Protector of Aborigines in the Northern Territory, Cecil Cook, warned the Administrator, R. H. Weddell, in July 1932 that Australia was in danger of being open to the charge of conniving at forced labour within its territories. Where there was any duress or coercion towards employment the conditions of service analogous to slavery could be said to exist. There was amongst employers an inclination towards 'the application of the principles of slavery' as evidenced by the fact that there was an unwritten law amongst pastoralists that they wouldn't employ an Aborigine 'belonging to' or resident upon any other station.[11] The Anti-Slavery Society gathered evidence about Aboriginal labour conditions and raised the matter on a number of occasions with the International Labour Organization in Geneva which while concerned felt it was unable to act against Australia. The Secretary of the society, Sir John Harris, wrote to Prime Minister Lyons in June 1935 urging the government to conform as nearly as possible to the obligations regarding conditions of labour laid down in the Treaty of Versailles.[12]

The Anti-Slavery Society and the Aborigines Protection Society merged in 1907. Between them they shared a tradition of involvement in Australia's affairs going back to the middle of the nineteenth century. The tradition was renewed in 1926 and continued with undiminished attention throughout the inter-war period. Society officials were swayed by the determined advocacy of Adelaide feminist Constance Cooke who was in London during 1927 and who related her own experiences in outback Australia. The Forrest River massacre and the consequent Royal Commission further galvanised the society which set up a permanent subcommittee to deal with Australian affairs. The committee was well served by two able and energetic members—Rev. C. E. C. Lefroy and Edith Jones—who had been involved in the Aboriginal cause in Australia. Australian correspondents supplied the committee with letters, reports, press clippings and advice with the result that the British-based reformers were usually very well briefed about developments in the Dominion. Two of the most valued and regular correspondents were the zealous and industrious pair William Morley and Mary Bennett.

The Anti-Slavery Society expressed 'grave disquiet' about the events disclosed by the Forrest River Royal Commission and took a delegation to interview the Australian High Commissioner in London, Sir Granville Ryrie, in December 1927.[13] This was followed up in March 1928 with a detailed memorandum urging the federal government to assume full responsibility for

Aboriginal affairs. Further letters of appeal and protest were sent to Australia in 1929 and 1930. In their public statements society officials were impeccably diplomatic, measured and restrained. Privately they were obviously outraged by Australia's treatment of the Aborigines. In a letter marked PRIVATE, to a Rev. C. Bosanquet in Cornwall, Sir John Harris remarked that many of the damaging claims being made in the press about Australia were true. The Aborigines had been 'robbed, outraged and murdered for years'.[14]

When news of the Coniston massacre reached Britain, society officials wrote to Prime Minister Bruce expressing 'painful surprise' at reports of the shooting of large numbers of Aborigines, including women and children. They noted that the action was carried out by white police in pursuance of official instruction and that the shooting of at least 31 Aborigines was 'deliberate and absolutely indiscriminate', there being nothing to indicate that those who suffered had anything to do with the crime. The fact that police were exonerated by the subsequent inquiry only made the evils of the present system more evident. And if the police were accustomed to treat the Aborigines in this way what could be expected from the 'less responsible elements of the community, unrestrained by any force of law or public opinion'. The letter concluded with an appeal to the Prime Minister to lift the question of the condition and treatment of the Aborigines to the 'higher level of true trusteeship'.[15]

In August 1932 the society addressed 'A Plea on Behalf of the Australian Aborigines' to the archbishops,

bishops, clergy, ministers and members of the Christian churches of Australia. It read in part:

> The Anti-Slavery and Aborigines Protection Society feel it their duty to make known to the members of the Christian Churches in Australia the fact that in quite recent years many appeals on behalf of the aborigines have been received by the Society from correspondents in various parts of Australia. These appeals have alleged cases not only of callous neglect of destitute and starving natives, and of positive cruelty and wrong-doing by low whites—but also of heartless and tyrannical conduct by the police in remote parts of the Commonwealth, and of miscarriage of justice where white and black are concerned; and such statements seem to be well authenticated. Indeed, reports appearing from time to time in the Australia public Press, and the results of official inquiries, fully corroborate in our judgement the information privately received. Those who have appealed have called upon our Society to use its influence, both in England and in Australia, to stop these evil practices and abuses, urging our help in securing a more humane and enlightened treatment of the aborigines—a treatment more in harmony with the ideas of the twentieth century, and the principles of humanity put forward by the League of Nations.

The plea continued with reference to the society's correspondence with the Australian government which appeared to be more amenable to reform than was previously the case. But alarming reports of injustice were still arriving in London, most recently those of the anthropologist Ralph Piddington. In a stirring peroration the plea concluded:

As a well-known Society, working for weak and oppressed races in all parts of the world, we now venture to appeal to the Christian leaders of Australia to make a united effort in this great cause, and to do all that is possible to sweep away old wrongs and injustices, to make generous reparations for the past, and to secure not only protection but also appropriate educational and moral uplift for the very considerable remnant of a race which is not only most ancient, but also endowed with remarkable and attractive qualities of mental and moral character. From every point of view the cause of the aborigines seems to us to be worthy of the closest attention of the Australian people.

Our Society will be very pleased to receive replies from any of those to whom this letter is addressed, and to assist the cause of the aborigines in any way that may be suggested, if it lies in the power of the Society to do so.

In conclusion, we cannot forbear a reference to the brave fight which the Christian Churches of South Africa are now putting up on behalf of the native inhabitants. In South Africa the problem is vaster and far more complicated than it is in Australia—and there, also, colour prejudice and racial jealousy are more bitter. If the Christian Churches in Australia will throw themselves into their corresponding struggle, the cause of all weak and depressed peoples throughout the world will receive fresh encouragement and reinforcement.[16]

The society returned to its more traditional approach of lobbying government and continued to urge reform on Prime Ministers Scullin and Lyons. In 1937 a submission to Lyons stressed the importance of land rights which were essential to any solution of the Aboriginal question. Society officials reminded the Australian leader that they spoke with experience gained as a result of 'long years of close association with aboriginal problems in all parts of the world'. They were unable to accept the view 'advanced in certain quarters' that there was a fundamental difference between Australian Aborigines and those of 'other hinterland territories'.[17]

The activities of the Anti-Slavery Society greatly encouraged Australian reformers. It had prestige, authority and social cachet. The board of management included lords of the realm and other notables. In 1933 William Morley wrote to London to report plans for the meeting to celebrate the centenary of the abolition of slavery. He wanted a gramophone record of encouraging words from one of the society's 'foremost men'. Such support from 'a very High Personage' would be of 'invaluable benefit'.[18] Mary Bennett was convinced of the enormous value of society support and encouragement and wrote to London explaining:

> Public opinion in Australia is very thin skinned about criticism from England, but does not care a jot about the minority who have struggled so long and so hard to get reform within States and Commonwealth. My desire is that you will realize the enormous value of Anti-Slavery's work in holding up a standard and shedding light on dark places.[19]

Writing from London to friends in Australia in June 1929 Bennett observed how much interest there was in 'native policies'. The subject, she explained, was 'in the air'.[20] The same phenomenon was noticed by Lucy Mair, the Lecturer in Colonial Administration at the London

School of Economics, who wrote in 1935 that the post-war era had seen a great increase in 'Empire consciousness'.[21] Colonial administration was the subject of extensive public debate stimulated by the activities of the League of Nations, the rise to prominence of social anthropology and the emergence of colonial nationalism to challenge Imperial policies and ambitions. Reform-minded Australians took an interest in colonial policy and attempted to apply the strategies and theories of Imperial administration to Australia. The country was, after all, part of the Empire. The Aborigines were 'native' people. If some humanitarians looked for inspiration to the mandated territory of New Guinea others turned to Britain's African colonies and the much publicised policies of indirect rule developed by Lord Lugard in Nigeria and Sir Donald Cameron in Tanganyika. The clearest example of this influence was the Aborigines State Movement launched in Adelaide by the Aborigines Protection League.

In February 1925 the local businessman Colonel J. C. Genders called a meeting of men and women interested in Aboriginal policy and suggested that a petition be presented to federal parliament praying for the creation of a 'separate State in Northern Australia' to be called 'the Australian Black State, the Australian Zion State, or some more appropriate name'.[22] Despite the radical agenda, prominent Adelaide citizens committed themselves to the cause including leading academics, politicians, scientists and feminists. The Aborigines Protection League (Native State) was set up in November 1926 under the chairmanship of prominent scientist Dr Herbert Basedow. A manifesto was prepared to accompany petition forms. It was announced at the November meeting that 1000 signatures had already been collected. When the petition was presented to parliament in October 1927 it was supported by 7113 signatures collected mainly in Adelaide, Melbourne and Sydney.

The text of the petition suggested that hitherto Australia had failed in its moral duty to the Aborigines and that as a race they were in danger of dying out. Remedial action was both desirable and urgent and could succeed,

> if we recognize their rights and do not treat them merely as chattels, if we assist them to accommodate their methods to new conditions, if we return to them areas of country on which they may work out their own salvation safeguarded from the envious eyes of encroaching white population we shall, at least have the satisfaction of knowing that even at the eleventh hour we shall have endeavoured to redeem any neglect, indifference or maladministration in the past and to do substantial justice.[23]

The central objective of the Protection League was to recognise Aboriginal land ownership and to hand land title back to those communities still living in their own country. While attending a national conference on Aboriginal policy in Melbourne in April 1929 league office-bearers Genders and Constance Cooke proposed and seconded a motion that 'to all nomadic tribes still with their tribal governments', land be allotted 'in perpetuity within traditional boundaries'. In moving the motion Genders argued that colonisation had meant that much land had been taken from the Aborigines but that now 'it is due to us to give them back some of it'.[24] In a letter to the Adelaide *Advertiser* in June 1930 he explained that it was 'coming to be recognized through-out the world' that non-Europeans should have the legal property in their land.[25] In discussions going on overseas about colonial policy, one principle predominated—the recognition that colonised people should have land in 'inalienable possession'.[26]

But land itself was not the full answer. Genders explained in a letter to the Anti-Slavery Society that the Protection League had been formed to advocate the return of land to the Aborigines 'to be governed by themselves'.[27] In the north government would be based on traditional law and custom with such 'assistance' from European advisers as was considered necessary. In a document entitled 'A Native Policy for Australia' an anonymous league member explained that:

> If the aboriginals are not to be destroyed, they should not be dispossessed nor subjected to a system that is alien to them, but they should be secured in all their tribal territories, and encouraged to adapt to new needs all that is best in their traditions under their own leaders, under the form of government that they understand, the direction of their day to day affairs by the tribal council of their own choosing.
>
> Recognized or not recognized, the principle stands: that dispossession and control of one race by another race are opposed to freedom and justice and perpetuate all the evils of slavery, that the only way to safeguard native tribes is to secure to them inde-feasible possession of their tribal territories where they can work out their own development with the help of white teachers.[28]

The league had initially focused attention on the traditional Aboriginal communities in the remote areas of Australia. But by 1928 it was suggested that a large area of land be set aside in the settled districts for a homeland for the 'detribalized and half-caste natives'. The administration of the native territory would be left as far as possible to the inhabitants themselves with the assistance of a government resident. No white man would be allowed into the territory without a passport which would only be issued to teachers, doctors and missionaries.[29]

League policy was reaching far beyond conventional policy making and foreshadowed radical constitutional change. It was proposed that Aborigines have their own representation on all boards, councils, commissions and inquiries, that the black 'states' should have representation in parliament. Genders looked forward to a situation in which the federal parliament could relate to Aboriginal communities in the same way in which it related to the States. He saw league policy as being one of indirect rule and therefore opposed to assimilation at least in the foreseeable future. Assimilation, he explained to the Anti-Slavery Society, could only be considered:

> When we have learnt not to discriminate between the colour of the skin (a very far cry) and when under . . . 'Indirect Rule' the Australian Aborigine has achieved national pride with his own Government, Chiefs, etc, has his own universities, colleges and Oxford and Cambridge men . . . then it will be time enough to talk of assimilation.[30]

Social anthropology was another influence on the humanitarian movement of the 1920s and 1930s in both

a direct and an indirect way. Individual anthropologists
became involved in the cause and participated in the
vigorous public debate of the period. Anthropological
theory and detailed ethnographic information began to
colour the thinking of educated Australians. Many leading humanitarians were obviously well versed in both
general anthropological literature and in contemporary
work on traditional Australian communities.

Like many urban men and women before them
anthropologists were often confronted by the traditions
of frontier Australia. They found it a harsh and forbid-
ding place. In a similar way to missionaries they were
there because of the Aborigines whose company they
needed and whose language and thoughts they sought
to understand. As a byproduct of their research they
came to know individuals, to understand their points of
view and problems and often to sympathise with their
suffering. Reminiscing about his first period of fieldwork
in north-west Australia W. E. H. Stanner recalled that
the Aborigines were looked on and used almost as free
goods of nature. They were only paid in kind. There
wasn't a single element in the whole system of life—land,
food, shelter, jobs, pay, the safety of women and children, even access to and protection by the law—in
which they were not 'at great disadvantage, and without
remedy'. The dominance of European interests was
'total, unquestioned, and inexpressibly self centred'.[31]

Stanner's more senior colleague, A. P. Elkin, also
carried out his fieldwork in the outback between 1927
and 1930. He went north having studied the literature
but his knowledge of individual Aborigines as persons
was, he revealed, 'almost nil'. He had 'no humanitarian

motive' nor was he concerned with the consequences of European settlement. His task was to study kinship, ritual and mythology and that was what he did. But almost unconsciously his mind stored observations of the relations between whites and Aborigines on stations, missions and around towns. He came to know and make friends with informants who did their best to explain their language and culture to him. Things he saw and discovered were disturbing—like the line of prisoners chained together and force-marched across the country. Even authentic research turned out to be shocking testimony. He discovered the gaps in genealogies on the Forrest River which represented the victims of the massacre of 1926. He was told by the local Protector of Aborigines that he had made a donation to finance the punitive expedition because the blacks must be taught a lesson from time to time. Everywhere he went frontier whites were suspicious and hostile sensing that the aloof scholar was an outsider who meant trouble.[32]

These were the sort of experiences that turned Elkin imperceptibly into an activist. In 1933 he became the president of the Association for the Protection of Native Races and found himself 'in the role of protagonist, and also adviser to humanitarian and missionary bodies'.[33] He had addressed the association's annual general meeting in 1932 and the resulting pamphlet *A Policy for Aborigines* had a powerful effect on contemporary thinking because he advocated the adoption of positive policies based on a 'scientific' analysis of the problems thrown up by the contact and clash of cultures.

Stanner recalled his response to the Elkin paper. Up until then he had taken for granted the conditions he had seen in the north. They were a 'natural and inevitable part of the Australian scene', which could be palliated but not ever changed in any fundamental way. He found Elkin's call for a positive policy 'radical and startling', because it both pointed the way to a better future and gave to the new 'scientific' experts a major role in the desired change.[34]

The anthropologist had replaced the frontiersman as the one who 'knew the native'. Long years on the frontier were no longer accepted as a necessary qualification for authoritative views on the Aborigines. Elkin's predecessor as Professor of Anthropology at the University of Sydney, A. R. Radcliffe-Brown, informed his colleagues at a congress in 1930 that the discovery of the social structure of tribal society was difficult and required skilled systematic investigation. One often found that people who had lived in daily contact with a native people for many years had no comprehension at all of the life of the people because 'they had never discovered the social structure by which that life is determined'.[35]

Anthropology seeped into the public discourse about Aborigines and helped challenge two of the ideas which had dominated debate in the 1880s—the certainty that the race was doomed to extinction and the conviction that it was a primitive and inferior survival from an earlier era. Both ideas were still widespread at the end of the 1930s but were being increasingly challenged although not all anthropologists were of one mind on the questions.

Stanner believed that what he called the 'anthropological principle' slowly permeated society. There was a growing awareness that there were no natural scales of better or worse on which it was possible to range the 'varieties of men, culture and society'. He detected evidence of a large swing from 'depreciation to appreciation'.[36] Leading humanitarians like Mary Bennett, Edith Jones, C. E. C. Lefroy, Charles Duguid and Herbert Basedow wrote letters, articles and speeches expressing their admiration for Aboriginal society and rejected the idea of an immutable racial hierarchy. Elkin confronted the belief that Aborigines were childlike in his speech to the public meeting in Sydney of 7 August 1934. He told his audience:

> The aborigine adults were adults as much as the adults here tonight (Cheers). They have gone through their initiation ceremonies, been instructed in the laws and tradition of their tribes, and accepted positions of responsibility. You are not up against child races, but against people who seem to be our equals in intelligence.[37]

The conviction that the Aborigines would die out was particularly destructive to plans for reform and regeneration. Stanner observed that while that belief prevailed anthropological knowledge could have only 'poignant relevance'.[38] When Elkin first spoke to the APNR he emphasised that a new approach to policy would only succeed if members adopted the view that the Aborigines were not going to die out.[39] Fellow reformers agreed, believing that there was nothing inevitable about the decline of Aboriginal populations, that the main problems were neglect, poverty, malnutrition and inadequate health care. Aborigines died because Europeans were unwilling to make the effort to keep them alive. The conviction that it was a matter amenable to human agency greatly stimulated humanitarian zeal. Thus, the Anti-Slavery Society officials wrote to the Australian High Commissioner in London in 1927 explaining the reason for their heightened interest in Aboriginal issues. They observed that:

> We understand that there is now good reason to say that it is not too late to save the aboriginal races of Australia from extinction. This theory hitherto held, as you are aware, was that these races were necessarily doomed; this seems to have been abandoned by large sections of public opinion in Australia.[40]

It is reasonable to assume that in colonial Australia women were as likely as men to have doubts about the morality of colonisation, to hear the whisper in the heart. But few women expressed their views in public. By the 1920s the situation had changed dramatically.[41] Women, and more particularly feminists, were a major force in the intense debate of the period. Feminist organisations took up and promoted the humanitarian cause including the Women's Service Guilds of Western Australia, the Women's Non-Party Association of South Australia, the Australian Federation of Women Voters, and the Victorian Women's Citizen Movement and the Women's Non-Party League of Tasmania. Overseas conferences provided Australian feminists with an international audience. The British Commonwealth League, in particular, was an effective platform which facilitated wide coverage in the English papers which in turn ensured extensive reporting in Australia.

Feminists shared many of the views of their male colleagues in the humanitarian and missionary organisations. They were confronted by injustice, were compassionate about suffering. Many women were practising Christians who derived a sense of mission from their faith. But the activists brought fresh perspectives and new priorities to the task of changing attitudes, behaviour and policy. Their commitment to women was ultimately a powerful counter to the concept of race although many women of the period continued to use language which cloaked the contradiction. Feminism had the capacity to develop lines of sentiment and solidarity across vertical biological divisions envisaged by racial theory. The things that women shared were often seen as being more important than those which divided them. Feminist activists understood that all Aboriginal people had experienced dispossession and injustice but black women had suffered in their own unique way which sympathetic white women could understand. In a paper on 'The Status of Aboriginal Women in Australia' Constance Cooke outlined the two great wrongs suffered by Aborigines. The first was when the original inhabitants were deprived of all their lands by the legal device of declaring them the property of the Crown. 'Women, as well as men, were relegated thus to the position of serfs.' But the second great wrong had been the 'interference of the white man with the native woman'.[42] Mary Bennett forcefully presented similar views demanding two things of government. The first was the provision of 'adequate territories for the natives and half-castes to develop themselves'. The second was for an affirmation of the right of Aboriginal women 'to the sanctity of her person' and for the implementation of reforms 'for her protection'. In Bennett's view

Aboriginal women suffered oppression from both white men and black.[43] Addressing the Conference on Aboriginal Welfare in Melbourne in April 1929, Edith Jones insisted that if a woman 'whether white or black has not the control of her body she is a slave'. Consequently many black women were slaves because their bodies were 'not subject to their own discretions'.[44]

Women activists believed that they had a double responsibility—to Aborigines in general and to Aboriginal women in particular. Edith Jones wished to awaken governments to the determination of women to 'secure their share in the righting of wrongs of Australian native women, probably the most wronged within the British Empire'.[45] Writing to the Anti-Slavery Society in October 1933 Mary Bennett thanked Sir John Harris for his encouragement in what they both saw as the arduous task of reform. She acknowledged the contribution of a 'very very few noble women' but believed that it was the 'business of Women's Societies to reform the conditions of Aboriginal and half-caste women in Australia'.[46] In her 1930 book *The Australian Aboriginal as a Human Being* she wrote:

> Faced with the suffering of our fellow women, with the suffering of children—is it beyond a woman's wit to find a way of helping them? A way to back up the work of women for them? Or is feminism a failure? Are we passing by on the other side?[47]

Bennett believed that it was essential for the women to be provided with the education and training that would enable them to achieve economic independence. Economic dependence, she told Bessie Rischbieth, 'is at the root of all evil'.[48] Along with a number of her colleagues she advocated the appointment of female protectors to assist Aboriginal women negotiate the difficult task of coming to terms with European society. But while Bennett wanted state officials to protect Aboriginal women she was vehemently opposed to the policy of removing children from their families. This brought her into sharp conflict with Western Australia's Chief Protector of Aborigines, A. O. Neville, which reached a climax when she gave evidence to the 1934 Royal Commission on the Condition and Treatment of the Aborigines. She passionately denounced the 'arbitrary deportation' of women and children which had caused more suffering and terror to the Aborigines than any other cause. Mothers with infants, individual children and sometimes families were 'mustered up like cattle' and deported to government settlements,

> there to drag out their days and years in exile, suffering all the miseries of transportation, for no fault but only because the white supplanters are too greedy and too mean to give them living areas in their own district.[49]

Bennett learnt much about the impact of government removals from observing her pupils at the Mount Margaret mission. Many of them had been hunted by the police for years and some still bore the marks of shock. A 'handsome lad' was haunted by fear and the terror that came into his eyes reminded her of shell-shock victims. Mothers went in fear of having their half-caste children taken away from them with the result that they reacted with 'terrified avoidance of all white people'.[50] Bennett was asked by Neville whether she considered it right to marry a half-caste girl to a full-blood native?

She replied that it was entirely a matter for the individuals to decide for themselves. The exchange continued:

Neville: You would not regard it from a ethnological point of view at all?

Bennett: We do not ask whites to marry ethnologically and why ask blacks? It is entirely a matter for the men and women concerned. Any interference would be against the liberty of the subject.[51]

When Bennett summed up her objection to the policy of removals she appealed to the Royal Commissioner:

I do most earnestly ask that the official smashing of native family life may be stopped, and that native families be permitted to live where they may wish within the law. The laws that are enough for the proper conduct of white communities should be enough for the proper conduct of native communities also.[52]

When Bennett told Sir John Harris that she thought the women's societies should push to reform the living conditions of Aboriginal women and children she added that she worried that they were too smug and self-seeking to attempt it. Like many other humanitarians Bennett was often depressed by the burden of the crusade and aware that change came very slowly. 'Yes, you are quite right', she wrote to Bessie Rischbieth in 1931, 'we struggle, seemingly, vainly, so long and so wearily'.[53] She realised that few of her contemporaries shared her passionate commitment to reform. She wrote to Buxton in October 1933 thanking him for his support and encouragement in the 'highly unpopular work' in which she was engaged.[54] Ten months later she wrote again to the Anti-Slavery Society exclaiming:

> But that I believe in God I should despair, not of the Aborigines who respond magnificently, but of the white people who are certainly not fit to rule over them.[55]

Herbert Basedow wrote to Buxton in similar vein explaining that the sympathy one received in relation to the work of ameliorating the 'unhappy lot' of the Aborigines was 'generally speaking, more of the exception than the rule'.[56] William Morley commiserated with Mary Bennett, writing to her in December 1931: 'It is very disheartening, but we must fight it out even if it seems a losing battle.'[57] Darwin humanitarian-businessman Fred Thompson wrote to Ernest Gribble explaining what a difficult task it was standing up for the blacks in the far north. 'To endeavour to protect the aboriginal', he explained, 'is like volunteering for a place in a forlorn hope party'.[58]

The humanitarians were often driven to despair about Australia, further compounding their sense of alienation. In 1928 Constance Cooke told the South Australian Minister for Public Works that she had been appalled by recent experiences in the north. What she had seen 'had made her feel ashamed of her own race'.[59] Mary Bennett became progressively more disenchanted during the 1930s. Nobody, she wrote in August 1936, could be more cruel, greedy, dishonourable and unjust in their dealings with the native races than the British Australians. 'We have a long way to go', she asserted, before human conditions will be obtained for this highly gifted and wickedly maligned race. The facts are at present they are being willed to death. The majority of Australians are still poisoned with strong anti-native bias—the criminal cannot forgive the victim he has wronged, and it serves no useful purpose to blink the facts.[60]

Many of her colleagues would have found Mary Bennett excessive in her righteous passion. Sir John Harris wrote to a friend in October 1933 that she was a lady of great zeal. She was 'glowing with indignation against the wrongs inflicted' on the Aborigines and her enthusiasm was inclined to carry her too far.[61] But many of those working in the field agreed with her about the damage that was being done to Australia's international reputation. Bennett wrote to Bessie Rischbieth in September 1933 referring to the 'extreme gravity of the pass to which we have brought Australia by our mishandling of our native race'.[62] J. S. Needham, Chairman of the Australian Board of Missions had similar concerns. He believed that Australia's professions of 'national righteousness' had been deeply 'jeopardised by the Forrest River Massacre' as was 'our public honour among the nations of the world'.[63] In the aftermath of the Coniston massacre the board was even more deeply concerned with the untold damage that was being done to the good name of Australia overseas. With their worldwide network of missionaries they realised, as few other Australians did, that such news items were widely reported in the 'vernacular papers' throughout Asia where they were 'often accompanied by bitter, and not always just or accurate comments'.[64]

Humanitarians were often in a dilemma as to whether they should carry their cause overseas. Many were comfortable appealing to the British public opinion and encouraged the Anti-Slavery Society to pursue the issue of justice for the Aborigines. They were greatly appreciative of the society's work and of the influence of British public opinion. The prominent Adelaide surgeon Charles Duguid wrote to the society in 1937 explaining that:

> The Governments of Australia—Federal and State—will not exert themselves on behalf of the natives until they realize that public opinion in England is determined. When the homeland recognizes those struggling to improve our good name among the nations we shall begin to move more quickly. The League of Nations knows that things happen today in Australia that could not under a mandate. I look forward to the day when as a nation we can hold up our head amongst the nations on the race problem.[65]

By the late 1930s Mary Bennett had attempted to take the Aboriginal cause to the Privy Council, the League of Nations and International Labour Organization. She had even considered raising the question in Japan. She looked forward to the day when all races whose lands were occupied by others could claim to be under special mandate from the League of Nations.[66] But there seemed to be no adequate way within Australia to achieve required reforms. 'If Australians are too mean', she wrote in March 1937,

> to feed their victims and educate their own children let them appeal for help to other nationals through the good offices of the League of Nations.

If the present wicked immoral traffic continues,
is allowed to continue, then Australia cannot last, and
it will be definitely to the good for Australia to
disappear.[67]

Early in January 1938 Bennett took the train from
Perth to Adelaide where she stayed with her friend and
fellow activist Constance Cooke. Addressing a gathering
of women called together by Cooke she denounced both
the federal and West Australian governments. Their
mutual aim, she declared, was to let the Aborigines die
out as quickly as possible.[68] Having infuriated her enemies in Perth by her views, which were widely reported
in the West Australian press, she moved on to Sydney
with the intention of attending the Aboriginal Day of
Mourning on January 26. It is not clear if she realised
it was a gathering for Aborigines only. She may have
found out when she arrived in Sydney. But perhaps she
set out to attend the function in Elizabeth Street and
was turned away at the door. So how did she spend that
day of public commemoration? Did she join the crowds
and help celebrate the arrival of Governor Phillip 150
years before and the great saga of settlement? Or was
she too alienated from mainstream Australia to share the
euphoria of the moment? Perhaps she spent the day alone
assessing what had been achieved in the previous ten
years of intense activism from the moment when, in
London, she committed herself to the Aboriginal amelioration and decided to return to Australia to throw
herself into the cause.

Bennett's disillusionment notwithstanding the
humanitarian movement had achieved a good deal in
the 1930s and certainly more than at any earlier time.

It was better organised than ever before with wider support and more effective networks. Leaders of the movement sensed that there was a significant shift in public opinion during the inter-war years which they both nurtured and exploited. They were effective in applying pressure to both State and federal governments and mobilising support from allied organisations overseas while stressing that Australia's international standing was 'intimately related' to the status and circumstances of her indigenous minorities. It was a lesson which was not forgotten. Activists of more recent times, often unknowingly, built on the achievements of their predecessors.

XII

CONCLUSION

They were with us from the start. They are with us still. The questions which concerned the Earl of Moreton in 1768 continue to trouble our moral sensibility. Were the Aborigines 'Lords of the Country' as Moreton believed? Were they in possession of the land? Did they exercise sovereignty over it? Was it legitimate—or even lawful—to annex Australia and expropriate their land? Was colonisation itself morally justified? If so how should the venture have been conducted? Should treaties have been negotiated, land purchased, compensation paid? Was violence inevitable or could it have been avoided or moderated? Was it necessary to spill so much blood?

These questions would matter less if they were not so intimately related to the stories which the colonists and their descendants have always liked to tell about themselves—those sagas of progress and burgeoning settlement, tales of triumph over adversity, of battlers making good in the new world and uniting in praise of equality and a fair go for all. The fate of the Aborigines casts long, deep shadows over those sunny narratives. Indeed the two stories are as closely interrelated as light and shade.

That was always understood by those who could hear the whisperings in the bottom of their hearts. And that is what made such people uncomfortable companions for their contemporaries who wanted to feel relaxed and comfortable about themselves and innocently proud of their history.

That is why the troubled words of 'A Letter from a Gentleman' have such contemporary resonance 170 years after they were written. The Gentleman's concerns remain relevant. His anguish is ageless. 'None can defend our conduct towards the New Hollanders', he wrote, 'let us not persist in it, and let them receive some reparation for the wrongs we have done to them'. His sense of debt was profound. 'Deeply then are we in arrears to these injured Beings', he insisted, 'at whose expense we live and prosper'. There could be no escape from the fact that settler prosperity was purchased with indigenous land and indigenous lives. That was the coinage of colonial success, the Gentleman observing that 'every new step which advances our interest is fatal to their existence'.[1]

Few humanitarians were opposed to settlement in itself. They did not advocate abandonment of the continent. Mary Bennett's belief that white Australia did not deserve to survive was exceptional. But what united a disparate group of reformers across generations was the conviction that colonisation need not be so brutal, so lacking in compassion, so drenched in blood. They thought the settlers could be fairer and more just, that Australia could do better. They believed that the treatment of the indigenous people mattered. That was what God, or history, or world opinion, or all three, would use to judge the nation in the long run, not acres cleared, sheep shorn, minerals unearthed or cities built.

Humanitarians of the 1830s like their counterparts 100 years later believed that a central and inescapable reality was that the Aborigines owned the land and that by denying this fact the British Australians jeopardised any chance for negotiation or reconciliation. Better educated colonists phrased the argument with greater facility but few got more directly to the point than John Cook, miner, who wrote to the Queensland government in 1891 arguing that:

> even if we are born in Australia we are only usurpers here for if we take away the people's property without paying for it it does not matter much how we beautifully try to cloak it it is and always must remain stolen land.[2]

Another unifying preoccupation was a rejection of the bloodshed which accompanied settlement from the 1780s until the 1920s. Humanitarians had a particular horror of the punitive expedition which, by its nature, was bloody, indiscriminate, disproportionate. Denunciation and exposure of violence motivated many humanitarians and earned them more obloquy and abuse than any other cause. Time and again the reformers declared that their fellow colonists were hellbent on extermination, that they literally wanted to clear the land of the indigenous people who reminded them of the manner in which the country was acquired, the uncertainty of the title and the dubious morality of the dispossession. Humanitarians rarely accused governments of complicity in extermination, although they had doubts about colonial Queensland. But they believed their fellows wished the Aborigines would disappear from the face of the earth. It was a harsh judgement but one for which there was ample justification. Colonists were not shy about confessing their genocide aspirations.

What in recent years has been pejoratively termed the 'black armband' version of Australian history is clearly not a recent creation but descends directly from the humanitarian tradition of doubt, dissent and disappointment. The much-criticised observation of High Court Justices Deane and Gaudron, in the Mabo case in 1992, that Australia has inherited a legacy of unutterable shame, recapitulates precisely the sentiments of humanitarian reformers from the 1820s onwards. Their views were never popular with the majority of their countrymen and women but they were as often as not the most courageous and morally scrupulous people of their generation. At other times and in different circumstances their public passion would have won applause, their principled stand earning admiration and emulation as true patriots who appealed to the heart of the people and to the honour of the nation.

The long history of humanitarian protest has received little recognition in Australia, either by contemporaries or in retrospect. Lone dissenters may have been unaware that their feelings were shared by others, that their chosen cause linked them with men and women separated from them by both time and space. With the humanitarian crusade woven into national historiography the story becomes richer, more complex, and, in many ways, more decent and easier to justify to the doubtful and suspicious both within the country and outside it. As we have shown there always were people who objected to the course of events, who stood out against conventional and accepted views and who proclaimed the cause of justice and equality, reparation and regret and who often paid a high price for their principled dissent.

But Australians of today who find comfort in the history of the humanitarian crusade should reflect that the protesters had little influence on events. Their assertions, however cogent, their moral appeal however persuasive, were largely ignored. Arguments forcefully put in the 1830s required restating in the 1930s. Many are still relevant today. What the humanitarian story shows is that an alternative agenda was aired, a more humane course projected, was listened to, understood and then comprehensively rejected, often with derision. The colonists were offered a choice and chose to continue in accustomed ways, preferring violent dispossession to purchase, treaty and negotiation; seeking for several generations to create a racially homogeneous nation which had no place for Aborigines who it was comfortably expected would 'die out' on cue.

A recurring humanitarian tactic was to appeal for justice outside Australia in despair at achieving it within. From the 1830s onwards activists believed, and not without reason, that they had a more sympathetic audience in Britain than in the colonies. Missionaries wrote to parent societies in London where key documents like 'A Letter from a Gentleman' still remain. Many reformers including Giustiniani, Lyon, Robinson, Gribble, Carley and McNab appealed to the Colonial Office which looked out on what was happening in the colonies after responsible government with detached disdain.

In both the nineteenth century and the twentieth

century humanitarians corresponded with the Aborigines Protection Society and the Anti-Slavery Society and found that avenue of protest far more effective than knocking on doors in Australia. Between the two world wars activists addressed their appeals to and projected their hopes onto the League of Nations and the International Labour Organization.

The tradition represented a vote of no confidence in Australia, in its institutions, laws and people. Each generation absorbed the same lesson. Australian neglect, injustice and indifference had to be fought outside Australia. Only there would sufficient sympathy be found and a sense of duty towards indigenous people which would embarrass Australia sufficiently to lift it out of inaction and inertia.

Agitation offshore further alienated humanitarians from their communities. At best they appeared to be unbalanced—self-righteous, obsessive and fanatical. At worst they seemed to be disloyal, unpatriotic, un-Australian in both their activities and their excessive fervour in a hopeless cause. But even when depressed and in despair, as they often were, the humanitarians believed that Australia was capable of improving its performance, that justice would eventually prevail. What they sought was what is currently known as reconciliation although neither supporters nor opponents of that cause appreciate how deep the roots of the movement strike in Australian experience. Detractors suppose it is a recent fad born of political correctness and fashionable feelings of guilt. On the other hand there appears to be little to suggest that supporters of reconciliation have any knowledge of the many people who since the early nineteenth century sought to ameliorate Aboriginal conditions and reform attitudes, policies and outcomes.

As a nation Australia should recognise the humanitarian crusade and accept that from the earliest years of settlement there were people who drew attention to moral, political and legal shortcomings of colonisation which have for generations earned the country a bad reputation overseas. The achievements of pioneering and nation-building have to be set against the costs, disproportionately borne by indigenous Australians. Light and shade have to be held as one.

It is just as important for indigenous Australians to appreciate that all Europeans were not hostile to their rights, that throughout the history of settlement there were people who stood up for justice and fairness and recognised Aboriginal rights to land. The humanitarians were often paternalistic/maternalistic and shared many of the ideas that were current in their generation. Some of them undoubtedly were racists in the way we understand that term now. They were people of their period. But if inquiry and understanding stops there we miss the passion for justice, the anger about cruelty and indifference which drove humanitarians along lonely, thankless and unpopular paths.

If true reconciliation is ever consummated in Australia and justice is not only done but seen to be done, the moment will without doubt be applauded from beyond the grave by all those men and women who hoped in their own time that such an outcome might eventually result from the European colonisation of the continent. And then, after 200 years, the whisper in the heart will be heard no more.

ENDNOTES

Some sources are referred to in abbreviated form in these endnotes and in the Select Guide to Reading and Research; a list of abbreviations follows.

AA	Australian Archives
ABM Papers	Australian Board of Missions Papers
AIATSIS	Australian Institute for Aboriginal & Torres Strait Islander Studies
AJCP	Australian Joint Copying Project
ANL	Australian National Library
ANU	Australian National University
APNR	Association for the Protection of Native Races
APS	Aborigines Protection Society
ASS	Anti-Slavery Society Papers
BPP	British Parliamentary Papers
CLR	*Commonwealth Law Reports*
CO	Colonial Office
GAR Papers	Papers of George Angustus Robertson
HRA	*Historical Records of Australia*
ML	Mitchell Library
Qld Col Sec	Queensland Colonial Secretary
QPD	Queensland Parliamentary Debates
QSA	Queensland State Archives
SMH	*Sydney Morning Herald*
SUA	Sydney University Archives
THRA	Tasmanian Historical Research Association, Papers and Proceedings
WALCPP	West Australian Legislative Council Papers & Proceedings
WAV&P	Western Australia Votes & Proceedings

INTRODUCTION

1. T.C. Beaglehole, *The Journals of Captain James Cook*, vol. 1, Cambridge University Press, Cambridge, 1955, p.514.
2. King to Bligh, King Papers, 2, ML. MSS. C/189.
3. 29 Sep. 1847.
4. C. Griffith, *The Present State and Prospects of the Port Phillip District*, Dublin, 1845, p.170.
5. 6 Aug. 1867.
6. *Southern Australian*, 8 May 1839.
7. 30 May 1842.
8. *United Australia*, 25 Oct. 1901, p.14.

CHAPTER I   THE CONCERNS OF GENTLEMEN

1. *Historical Records of Australia*, 1, 1, p.294; *Historical Records of New South Wales*, 1, part 2, pp.543–6.
2. Quoted by C. Turnbull, *Black War*, Cheshire, Melbourne, 1948, p.45.
3. ibid., p.47.
4. ibid., pp.57–8.
5. *Sydney Gazette*, 29 July 1824.
6. ibid., 5 Aug. 1824.
7. ibid., 26 Aug. 1824.
8. *Hobart Town Gazette*, 23 July 1824.
9. Letter . . . to a Friend, Oct. 1826, Methodist Mission Society, in Correspondence, Australia 1812–26, Folder 4, AJCP.
10. Thomas Bartlett, *New Holland*, etc, London, 1843, pp.65–66.
11. *Second Annual Report of Aborigines Protection Society*, London, 1839, p.14.
12. R. W. Newland to J. J. Freeman, 8 December 1840, Anti-Slavery Papers, Rhodes House, Oxford, MSS. S.18/C159, hereafter ASS.
13. G. A. Robinson, Journal, 18 Jan.–2 Feb. 1840, ML, MSS. A7036/1, p.64.
14. J. L. Stokes, *Discoveries in Australia*, 2 vols, London, 1846, 2, p.459.
15. J. Backhouse, *A Narrative of a Visit to the Australian Colonies*, London, 1843, p.558.
16. *The Colonist*, 17 Nov. 1838.
17. Stokes, op. cit., 2, p.259.
18. L. E. Threlkeld, Annual Report of the Mission to the Aborigines, 1838.
19. J. Dredge, *Brief Notices on the Aborigines of New South Wales*, Geelong, 1845, p.10.
20. Henry Mort to his mother and sister, 28 Jan. 1844 in M. E. McConnell, Journal, Oxley Library.

21. C. Griffith, *The Present State and Prospects of the Port Phillip District*, Dublin, 1845, pp.168–71.
22. A. Harris, *Settlers and Convicts*, 3rd ed., Melbourne University Press, Melbourne, 1953, p.222.
23. 8 May 1839.
24. Bartlett, op. cit., p.78.
25. E. W. Landor, *The Bushman*, London, 1847, pp.187–8.
26. 30 May 1842.
27. Aboriginal Protection Society Report, 5, 1839, p.137.
28. *Perth Gazette*, 27 July 1838.
29. ibid.
30. N. J. B. Plomley, ed., *Weep in Silence*, Blubberhead Press, Hobart, 1987, pp.595–6.
31. *The Colonist*, 27 Oct. 1838.
32. ibid.
33. R. Windeyer, On the Rights of the Aborigines of Australia, ML, MSS. 1400.

CHAPTER II   MISSIONARIES AND PROTECTORS

1. *Sydney Gazette*, 7 July 1810.
2. N. J. B. Plomley, ed., *Friendly Mission*, THRA, Hobart, 1966, p.276.
3. R. M. Lyon, Australia: *An Appeal to the World on Behalf of the Younger Branch of the Family of Shem*, Sydney, 1839, p.55.
4. Horton to Methodist Mission Society, 2 June 1823, Bonwick Transcripts, Box 52, ML.
5. J. C. Pritchard, *The Natural History of Man*, London, 1843, p.5.
6. R. M. Lyon, op. cit., p.xi.
7. Plomley, *Weep in Silence*, op. cit., p. 595.
8. *The Colonist*, 20 Oct. 1838.
9. W. Thomas diary as quoted in H. Reynolds, *Frontier*, Allen & Unwin, Sydney, 1987, p.94.
10. R. M. Lyon, op. cit., p.54.
11. Quoted by H. Reynolds, *Frontier*, op. cit., p.100.
12. H. Meyer, *Manners and Customs of the Aborigines of Encounter Bay*, Adelaide, 1846, p.1.
13. F. Tuckfield to Methodist Mission Society, 30 Sep. 1840, Bonwick Transcripts, Box 53, ML.
14. Threlkeld to Bannister, 27 Sep. 1825, ibid.
15. L. Threlkeld, *An Australian Language*, Sydney, 1892, p.88.
16. W. Watson, Journal, 4 Dec. 1832, Church Missionary Society, AJCP.
17. R. W. Newland, 8 December 1840, Anti-Slavery Papers, op. cit.
18. Plomley, *Friendly Mission*, op. cit., p.93.

19. ibid., p.276.

20. G. Robinson, Journal, 19 Feb. 1836, GAR Papers, vol.11, ML, MSS. A7032/3.

21. Dredge to Bunting, 10 May 1841, Dredge Notebook, La Trobe MS. 421959.

22. Tuckfield to Methodist Mission Society, 13 May 1839, Methodist Mission Papers, M.126, AJCP.

23. Plomley, *Friendly Mission*, op. cit., p.276.

24. Robinson Journal, 18 Jan.–2 Feb. 1840, ML. A7036/1, p.140.

25. J. Orton to Secretary Methodist Mission Society, Aug. 1836, Letterbook, ML, A1719.

26. Robinson to Hellyer, 25 Aug. 1832, GAR Papers, vol. 35, ML, MSS. A7056.

27. Threlkeld to London Missionary Society, 4 Sep. 1826, Bonwick Papers, 53, ML.

28. Gunther to Church Missionary Society, 30 Nov. 1838, CMS Papers C.N./047, AJCP.

29. *Extracts from the Letters of James Backhouse*, London, 1838, p.80.

30. Threlkeld to London Missionary Society, 10 Oct. 1825, Bonwick Papers, 53, ML.

31. Plomley, *Friendly Mission*, op. cit., p.202.

32. Walker to Watson, 5 Nov. 1821, 5 Dec. 1821, Bonwick Transcripts, Box 52.

33. J. Orton, Letterbook, op. cit., 28 Jan. 1842.

34. Tuckfield Journal, op. cit., p.176.

35. Gunther to Coates, 12 Dec. 1839, James Gunther Letters, Church Missionary Society, C.N./047, AJCP.

36. W. Watson, Journal, 29 June 1835, AJCP.

37. N. Gunson, ed., *Australian Reminiscences and Letters of L. E. Threlkeld*, 2 vols, AIATSIS, Canberra, 1974, 1, p.91.

38. Robinson Journal, April–July 1839, GAR Papers, vol. 14, ML. A7038.

39. Robinson to La Trobe, 14 Nov. 1840, GAR Papers, vol. 25, ML. A7046.

40. Robinson annual report, 1846, GAR Papers, vol. 61, ML. A7082.

41. *The Colonist*, 20 Oct. 1838.

42. Lyon, op. cit., p.xi.

43. ibid.

44. ibid.

45. 12 Dec. 1838.

46. ibid., 20 Oct. 1838.

47. Robinson to Whitcomb, 10 Aug. 1832, ibid.

48. ibid.

49. *The Colonist*, 20 Oct. 1838.

50. *Extracts from the letters of James Backhouse*, 3rd ed., London, 1838, p.80.
51. 12 Dec. 1838.
52. Lyon, op. cit., p.50.
53. W. Watson, Journal, op. cit., 29 June 1835.
54. *The Colonist*, 27 Oct. 1838.
55. 12 Dec. 1838.
56. Lyon, op. cit., p.x.
57. Dredge to Bunting, 10 May 1841, Dredge Notebook, op. cit.
58. Tuckfield to Methodist Mission Society, 13 May 1839, Methodist Mission Society, M.126, AJCP.
59. Lyon, op. cit., p.xiv.
60. ibid., p.xii.
61. 17, 20, 23 Oct. 1838.

CHAPTER III   A REASONABLE SHARE IN THE SOIL

1. See for instance—N. J. B. Plomley, *Friendly Mission*, op. cit.; *Weep in Silence*, op. cit.; V. R. Ellis, *Black Robinson*, Melbourne University Press, Melbourne, 1988; C. Pybus, *Community of Thieves*, Heinemann, Melbourne, 1991; L. Ryan, *The Aboriginal Tasmanians*, 2nd ed., Allen & Unwin, Sydney, 1996; H. Reynolds, *Fate of a Free People*, Penguin, Ringwood, 1996.
2. Reynolds, *Fate of a Free People*, op. cit., p.152.
3. ibid.
4. Plomley, *Weep in Silence*, op. cit., p.712.
5. Plomley, *Friendly Mission*, op. cit., p.733.
6. Robinson Journal, 21 Dec. 1835, GAR Papers, vol. 11, ML, MSS. A7032.
7. Robinson, Annual Report, 1848, GAR Papers, vol. 61, ML, MSS. A7082.
8. Robinson Journal, 3 May 1839, GAR Papers, vol. 14, ML, MSS. A7035.
9. Robinson Journal, 15 Jan. 1840, GAR Papers, vol. 14, ML, MSS. A7038.
10. ibid., vol. 15, ML, A7036, p.90.
11. Robinson Journal, 19 June 1841, GAR Papers, vol. 26, ML, MSS. A7047.
12. Report on an Expedition to the Aboriginal tribes in the Interior, Mar.–Aug. 1846, GAR Papers, vol. 29, ML, MSS. A7050.
13. Robinson Journal, 17 Sep. 1841, GAR Papers, vol. 26, ML, MSS. A7047.
14. Robinson, Report of a Visit to the Goulburn, Loddon and Mt Rouse Stations, 1847, GAR Papers, vol. 60, ML, MSS. A7081.

15. Robinson Journal, 3 May 1839, GAR Papers, vol. 14, ML, MSS. A7035.
16. Robinson to La Trobe, 12 Dec. 1839, GAR Papers, vol. 25, ML, MSS. A7046.
17. *Port Phillip Gazette*, 4 Dec. 1841.
18. Enclosure in Gipps to Stanley, 1 Apr. 1846, CO 201/366.
19. Enclosure in Fitzroy to Grey, 17 May 1847, CO 201/382.
20. ibid.
21. Robinson, Annual Report, 1848, GAR Papers, vol. 61, ML, MSS. 1, p.73.
22. ibid., pp.77–8.
23. ibid., pp.74–5.
24. ibid., p.86.
25. ibid., pp.73, 79.
26. Memos on dispatch Fitzroy to Grey, 17 May 1847, CO 201/382.
27. Grey to Fitzroy, 11 Feb. 1848, *HRA*, 1, vol. 26, p.226.
28. ibid.
29. Grey to Fitzroy, 6 Aug. 1849, dispatches to Governor, ML, MSS. A1308.
30. Memos by Mr Elliot on dispatch Fitzroy to Grey, 11 Oct. 1848, CO 201/400.
31. Gunson, op. cit., 1, p.91.
32. Threlkeld to Bunder, 2 Feb. 1825, Bonwick Papers, 53, ML.
33. Threlkeld Report, 21 June 1826, Bonwick Papers, 53, ML.
34. Threlkeld to Bunder, 4 Sep. 1826, Gunson, op. cit., 2, p.213.
35. Report to LMS, 1825, Gunson, op. cit., 2, p.194.
36. Threlkeld to Bunder, 13 Oct. 1825, Gunson, op. cit., 2, p.187.
37. Gunson, op. cit., 1, p.69.
38. R. Milliss, *Waterloo Creek*, McPhee Gribble, Ringwood, 1992, pp.259, 437.
39. *The Colonist*, 27 Oct. 1838.
40. Gunson, op. cit., 1, p.139.
41. ibid., 1, p.97.
42. ibid., p.146.
43. ibid., pp.146–7.
44. R. Milliss, op. cit., p.610.
45. ibid., p.714.
46. ibid.
47. ibid.
48. ibid.

CHAPTER IV   GREAT DISPLEASURE

1. Extracts from the Letters of James Backhouse, 2 vols, 3rd ed, London 1838, 2, part v, p.55.

2. ibid., p.8.
3. Western Australian Missionary Society, *Report of Inaugural Meetings*, London, 1836, p.4.
4. Lyon to Secretary of State, 1 Jan. 1833, CO 18/9.
5. R. M. Lyon, *Australia: An Appeal to the World on Behalf of the Younger Branch of the Family of Shem*, Sydney 1839 (hereafter *An Appeal*), pp.57–8.
6. A Glance at the Manners and Language of the Aboriginal Inhabitants of Western Australia, *Perth Gazette*, 30 Mar. 1833.
7. Lyon, *An Appeal*, op. cit., p.48.
8. Lyon to Secretary of State, op. cit.
9. ibid.
10. Lyon, *An Appeal*, op. cit., p.33.
11. Lyon to Secretary of State, op. cit.
12. Lyon, *An Appeal*, op. cit., p.56.
13. Lyon to Secretary of State, op. cit.
14. Lyon, *An Appeal*, op. cit., p.37.
15. ibid, p.35.
16. *Perth Gazette*, 9 Mar. 1833.
17. ibid., 6 Apr. 1833.
18. Lyon, *An Appeal*, op. cit., p.78.
19. ibid., p.79.
20. ibid., p.80.
21. ibid., p.82.
22. ibid., p.84.
23. ibid.
24. ibid., pp.86–88.
25. ibid., p.I.
26. ibid., p.XXII.
27. ibid.
28. ibid., p.VII.
29. ibid., p.XI.
30. ibid., p.XIII.
31. ibid., p.XVI.
32. ibid.
33. *Swan River Guardian*, 12 Jan. 1837.
34. ibid., 2 Mar. 1837.
35. ibid., 27 Apr. 1837.
36. ibid.
37. 4 May 1837.
38. *Perth Gazette*, 13 May 1837.
39. *Swan River Guardian*, 25 May 1837.
40. ibid., 8 June 1837.

41. ibid., 21 Sep. 1837.
42. Giustiniani to Colonial Secretary, 21 Aug. 1837, CSR, 55, 3335 of 1837.
43. 'Blood, and Innocent Blood Again', *Swan River Guardian*, 16 Nov. 1837.
44. ibid.
45. *Swan River Guardian*, 23 Nov. 1837.
46. ibid., 5 Oct. 1837.
47. ibid., 30 Nov., 1837.
48. ibid., 7 Dec. 1837.

CHAPTER V   AGITATION AGAINST ASSASSINATION

1. *North Australian*, 10 July 1860.
2. 'The Raid on the Aborigines', *Moreton Bay Free Press*, 15 Sep. 1859.
3. Reprinted in the *North Australian*, 19 Mar. 1861.
4. C.B. Dutton, to Colonial Secretary, 23 Mar. 1861, Queensland Col. Sec., 61/2545.
5. *North Australian*, 15 Nov. 1861.
6. ibid., 13 Dec. 1861.
7. 'Treatment of the Blacks in the Leichhardt District', *North Australian*, 21 Jan. 1862.
8. See J. Wright, *The Cry for the Dead*, OUP, Melbourne, 1981, pp.115–28.
9. G. S. Lang, *The Aborigines of Australia*, Melbourne, 1865, p.76.
10. ibid., p.77.
11. ibid., p.46.
12. ibid., p.47.
13. ibid., p.46.
14. ibid., p.51.
15. ibid., p.86.
16. Quoted by J. Wright, *The Cry for the Dead*, op. cit., pp. 125–6.
17. 'One Who Has Seen Too Much of the Native Police', Rockhampton Native Police, *Brisbane Courier*, 2 Apr. 1861.
18. *Rockhampton Bulletin*, 25 June 1867.
19. *North Australian*, 16 Apr. 1861.
20. 'Lieutenant Bligh's Sword', *Moreton Bay Courier*, 25 Apr. 1861.
21. ibid.
22. 'A Miner on Morinish', *Rockhampton Bulletin*, 18 June 1867.
23. 'The Native Police in Queensland', *The Colonial Intelligencer*, 1868, pp.44–6.
24. ibid.

25. Letters of A. Davidson to F. W. Chesson, ASS, Rhodes House, Oxford, MSS. British Empire S. 18/C132, 11 May 1869.
26. ibid., 4 Jan. 1876.
27. ibid., 1 Oct. 1870.
28. ibid., 16 June 1879.
29. ibid., 30 Aug. 1871.
30. ibid., 12 Aug. 1875.
31. ibid., 4 Jan. 1875.
32. ibid., 19 Dec. 1874.
33. *Transactions of the Aborigines Protection Society*, 1874–78, London, 1878, p.102.
34. M. Durack, *The Rock and the Sand*, Corgi, London, 1971, p.36.
35. Further letters from Rev. Duncan McNab, QSA, COL/A316, 2895 of 1881.
36. ibid.
37. ibid.
38. ibid.
39. ibid.
40. Quoted in P. F. Moran, *The History of the Catholic Church in Australasia*, Sydney, 1895, p.422.
41. Further letters from Rev Duncan McNab, op. cit.

CHAPTER VI   THE CRUSADER OF THE *QUEENSLANDER*

1. *The Way We Civilize*, Brisbane, 1880.
2. Anonymous letter to Sir Arthur Gordon, 23 Sep. 1882, ASS, S.22 op. cit., C 135/107.
3. *The Way We Civilize*, op. cit., p.3.
4. ibid., p.4.
5. ibid.
6. ibid., p.13.
7. ibid.
8. ibid., pp.12–13.
9. ibid., p.27.
10. ibid., p.28.
11. ibid., p.6.
12. ibid., pp.30–1.
13. Queensland Parliamentary Debates, *QPD*, XXXIII, 1880, p.669.
14. ibid., p.666.
15. ibid., p.676.
16. ibid.
17. ibid., p.675.
18. ibid., p.1136.

19. ibid., p.1142.
20. ibid., p.1141.
21. ibid., p.1138.
22. ibid., p.669.
23. ibid., p.673.
24. ibid., p.666.
25. ibid., p.666.
26. ibid.
27. ibid., p.1142.
28. ibid., p.1141.
29. ibid., p.665.
30. Maxwell to APS, 21 May 1883, ASS, S.22/142/181.
31. Gordon to Gladstone, 20 Apr. 1883, 'Sir Arthur Gordon on the New Guinea Question', 1883, *Historical Studies of Australia & New Zealand*, VII, no. 27, Nov. 1956, p.330.
32. P. Knaplund, *Gladstone's Foreign Policy*, Cass, London, 1970, p. 99.
33. Further Correspondence Respecting New Guinea, British Parliamentary Papers, C–3617, 1883, pp.140–1.
34. Gordon to Maclay, 13 Feb. 1882, Maclay Papers, 1, p. 132, ML mss A2889–1.
35. Sheridan to Maclay, 17 Sep. 1880, ibid.
36. Copy of letter to Gordon, 23 Sep. 1882, ASS, S.22, C 135/107.
37. Gordon to Gladstone, in P. Knaplund, Sir Arthur Gordon on the New Guinea Question, op. cit., pp.330–1.
38. *The Times*, 15 May 1883.
39. Knaplund, *Gladstone's Foreign Policy*, op. cit., p. 104.
40. ibid., p. 102.
41. Further correspondence respecting New Guinea, *BPP*, 1883, (C–3691), p.23.
42. G. W. Rusden, *History of Australia*, 3 vols, London 1883, 11, p.252.
43. ibid., p.249.
44. ibid., p.239.
45. ibid., p.244.
46. ibid., p.241.
47. ibid.
48. Rusden to APS, 5 Oct. 1883, ASS, S.22 C 146/17.
49. Rusden, *History of Australia*, op. cit., p.243.
50. A. T. Vogan, *The Black Police*, London 1890, p.42.
51. ibid., p.43.
52. ibid., p.45.
53. Vogan to APS, ASS, S.22, 4 Sep. 1891, 6.97.
54. Vogan to APS, ASS, S.22, 18 Dec. 1892, 6.97.

CHAPTER VII   JOHN GRIBBLE GOES WEST

1. Morgan & Scott, London, 1884.
2. ibid., p.17.
3. ibid., p.34.
4. ibid.
5. ibid., p.36.
6. M. McGrath, John Brown Gribble, B.Letters thesis, ANU, 1989, p.30.
7. *Black but Comely*, op. cit., p.14.
8. ibid., p.16.
9. ibid.
10. J. B. Gribble, Diary, 15 Aug. 1885, AIATSIS, Canberra.
11. ibid., 19 Aug. 1885.
12. ibid., 21 Aug. 1885.
13. ibid., 26 Aug. 1885.
14. ibid., 28 Aug. 1885.
15. ibid., 31 Aug. 1885.
16. ibid., 28 Aug. 1885.
17. ibid., 28 Aug. 1885.
18. ibid., 25 Sep. 1885.
19. *Daily Telegraph* (Melbourne), 9 July 1886.
20. J. B. Gribble, *Dark Deeds in a Sunny Land* (hereafter *Dark Deeds*), Perth, 1886, p.8.
21. ibid.
22. ibid., p.12.
23. *The West Australian*, 5 Jan. 1886.
24. Gribble, Diary, 31 Oct., 1885.
25. ibid.
26. ibid., 24 Oct. 1885.
27. ibid., 31 Oct. 1885.
28. ibid., 18 Jan. 1886.
29. ibid., 14 Jan. 1886.
30. Gribble, *Dark Deeds*, op. cit., p.13.
31. ibid., 28 Jan. 1886.
32. ibid., 31 Dec. 1885.
33. Administration of Justice, etc., *WALCPP*, 1889, 4, p.64.
34. Perth, 1886.
35. Gribble, *Dark Deeds*, op. cit., p.4.
36. Gribble, Diary, 6 Feb. 1886.
37. Gribble, *Dark Deeds*, op. cit., p.15.
38. Gribble, Diary, 10 Feb. 1886.
39. ibid., 20 Jan. 1886.
40. ibid., 20 Jan. 1886.

41. ibid., 24 Feb. 1886.
42. Gribble, *Dark Deeds*, op. cit., p.16.
43. ibid., p.17.
44. Gribble, Diary, 16 Jan. 1886.
45. Gribble to Parry, 15 Mar. 1886, Gribble Papers, AIATSIS, MSS. 1514/2–10.
46. Gribble, Diary, 10 Mar. 1886.
47. Parry to Aborigines Protection Society, 17 June, 17 July 1886, ASS, S.22/98, Gribble, 98.
48. ABM papers, ML, MSS. 4503/1822, Box 11.
49. Gribble, Diary, 12 Mar. 1886.
50. ibid., 17 May 1886.
51. Administration of Justice, *WALCPP* 1889, op. cit., p.54.
52. ibid.
53. Gribble to Brown, 24 May 1886, ABM Papers, ML, MSS. 1514/2, Box 10.
54. *Daily Telegraph*, 6 July 1886.
55. *Western Australia Parliamentary Debates*, 89, p.582.
56. *West Australian*, 24 Aug. 1886.
57. Gribble, Diary, 14 May 1887.
58. ibid., 4 Oct., 25 Nov., 29 Dec. 1886.
59. Administration of Justice, op. cit., p.54.
60. ibid., pp.63–4.
61. ibid., p.64.
62. Gribble, Diary, 27 June 1887.
63. ibid., 30 June 1887.
64. ibid., 2 July 1887.
65. ibid.
66. *West Australian*, 28 June 1887.
67. *Inquirer*, 29 June 1887.
68. S. J. Hunt, The Gribble Affair, B.A. Hons. Thesis, Murdoch, 1978, p.64.
69. Gribble Papers, AIATSIS, MSS. 1514/2–17.

CHAPTER VIII   TWO UNLIKELY AGITATORS

1. Quoted by Hunt, The Gribble Affair, op. cit., p.70.
2. ibid., p.71.
3. Angelo to Broome, 10 Apr. 1886, in Broome to Holland, 23 Oct. 1886, CO 18/207.
4. Quoted by Hunt, The Gribble Affair, op. cit., p.73.
5. Herbert, 28 Jan. 1887, comment on Broome to Holland, 23 Oct. 1886, CO 18/207.

6. Fuller, 22 Apr. 1887 on Broome to Holland, CO 18/208.
7. Fuller on Broome to Holland, CO 18/210.
8. ibid.
9. Carley to APS, 26 May 1884, ASP/6.98, Rhodes House, Oxford.
10. Gribble Diary, op. cit., 4 Mar. 1886.
11. ibid., 6 Mar. 1886.
12. 9 July 1886.
13. ibid.
14. Gribble Diary, 15 May 1886.
15. Carley to APS, 26 Jan. 1885, ASP, MS British Empire, 8.18, C128.
16. Carley to APS, 8 Oct. 1884, ASP, MS British Empire, 8.18, C128.
17. Chesson to Granville, 24 Feb. 1886, *Transactions of the APS*, 1883–89, p.315.
18. Chesson to Fuller, 14 Dec. 1886, CO 18/207 enclosed with Broome to CO, 16 Oct. 1886.
19. Carley to APS, 8 Jan. 1884, ASS, British Empire 8.18, C.128.
20. ibid., 26 May 1884.
21. ibid., 24 Aug. 1884.
22. ibid., 10 Apr. 1886.
23. ibid.
24. Enclosed in Broom to Holland, 28 Feb. 1888, CO 18/210.
25. Enclosed in W. Australia document no. 15753, CO 18/207.
26. ibid.
27. *West Australian*, 12 July 1886.
28. Broome to Granville, 12 July 1886, in ASS papers, MS. British Empire 8.18, C163/105.
29. Herbert to APS, 7 Sep. 1886, ASS papers, MS. British Empire, 8.18, C164/90.
30. Broome to Holland, 9 July 1889, no. 15992, CO 18/23.
31. Broome to Holland, 23 Oct. 1886, no. 22535, CO 18/207.
32. ibid.
33. Broome to Holland, 12 July 1887, no. 16795, CO 18/208.
34. ibid.
35. ibid.
36. Forrest to Onslow, 20 Apr. 1892, W. Australia, Correspondence Relating to the Proposed Abolition of the Aborigines Protection Board, *BPP*, C-8350, 1897, p.5.
37. ibid., p.18.
38. Carley to Knutsford, 3 Dec. 1891, ASS Papers, British Empire S.22, C128/94.
39. ibid., C128/95a, 18 Nov. 1891.
40. ibid.
41. Hunt, The Gribble Affair, op. cit., p.76.

42. Carley to APS, 11 Jan. 1886, ASS Papers, British Empire S.22, C128/90.
43. ibid., C128/87.
44. *Dictionary of Western Australians*, University of Western Australia Press, Perth, 1984.
45. *Dictionary of Western Australia, 1829–88*, University of Western Australia Press, Perth, 1987.
46. *Dictionary of Western Australia*, vol. IX: *Convicts in Western Australia, 1850–1887*, University of Western Australia Press, Perth, 1994.

CHAPTER IX   MODERN MASSACRE

1. *Daily News*, 8 July 1926.
2. C. Halse, The Rev. Ernest Gribble and Race Relations in North Australia, Ph.D. Thesis, University of Queensland, 1992.
3. Royal Commission of Inquiry into Alleged Killing and Burning of Bodies of Aborigines in East Kimberley (hereafter Royal Commission of Inquiry in Alleged Killing), *WAV&P*, 1, 1927, no. 3., p.vi.
4. ibid., p.xiii.
5. E. J. Gribble, *Forty Years with the Aborigines* (hereafter *Forty Years*), Angus & Robertson, Sydney, 1930, p.226.
6. R. Stow & D. Evans, 'The Umbali Massacre', *Bulletin*, 15 Feb. 1961, p.46; B. Shaw & Gribble. Ngabidj, *My Country of the Pelican Dreaming*, AIATSIS, Canberra, 1981, p.161.
7. ibid.
8. R. Stow & D. Evans, op. cit., p.46.
9. Gribble, *Forty Years*, op. cit., pp.7–56.
10. Halse, op. cit., p.33.
11. T. Wise, *The Self-Made Anthropologist*, Allen & Unwin, Sydney, 1985, pp.63–7.
12. . Royal Commission of Inquiry into Alleged Killing, op. cit., p.417.
13. Gribble Diary, 6 July 1926, quoted by Halse, op. cit., p.285
14. Royal Commission of Inquiry into Alleged Killing, op. cit., p.7.
15. Halse, op. cit., p.302.
16. ibid., p.304.
17. ABM Papers, ML, MSS. 4503/1822, Box 11, 15/7.
18. Halse, op. cit., p.304.
19. Royal Commission of Inquiry into Alleged Killing, op. cit., p.v.
20. ibid., p.vi.
21. ibid., p.21.
22. ibid.
23. ABM papers, op. cit., Box 11, 15/1.
24. Royal Commission of Inquiry into Alleged Killing, op. cit., p.xiii.

25. ABM papers, op. cit., Box 9, 12/2.
26. Quoted by N. Green, *The Forrest River Massacres*, Fremantle Arts Press, 1995, Fremantle, p.231.
27. ibid.
28. ABM papers, op. cit., Box 9, 12/2.
29. P. Biskup, *Not Slaves, Not Citizens*, University of Queensland Press, Brisbane, 1973, p.85.
30. A. Haebich, *For Their Own Good*, University of Western Australia Press, Perth, 1988, pp.271, 387.
31. *ABM Review*, 12 July 1927.
32. *Sydney Morning Herald*, 4 May 1927.
33. Commonwealth Parliamentary Debates, v. 116, 1927, pp.509–18.
34. ibid., p.509.
35. *ABM Review*, 12 Dec. 1927, p.163.
36. Needham to Lefroy, 2 June 1927, ASS, S.22/6.374.
37. Morley to ASS, 10 July 1928, ASS, S.22/6.374.
38. ASS, to Major General Ryrie, 2 Dec. 1927, ASS, S.22/6.374.
39. P. & J. Read, eds., *Long Time, Olden Time*, Institute of Aboriginal Development, Alice Springs, 1991, p.34. See also T. Cribbin, *The Killing Times*, Fontana, Sydney, 1984.
40. P. & J. Read, op. cit., pp.49–50; Cribbin, op. cit., p.164.
41. Lock to Gordon, 28–29, (no month/year on letter) APNR Correspondence, 1911–68, SUA, S.55 1/131.
42. Cribbin, op. cit. p.124.
43. Cribbin, op. cit., p.96.
44. *Northern Territory Times*, 9, 13 Nov. 1928.
45. Cribbin, op. cit., p.114.
46. ibid., pp.154–5.
47. Morley to Buxton, 29 Jan. 1929; ASS, S.22/6.374.
48. *Sydney Morning Herald*, 13 Nov. 1928.
49. ibid., 16 Nov. 1928.
50. *ABM Review*, 15 Dec. 1928, p.170.
51. ibid., p.175.
52. *The Times*, 5, 8, 11 Sep. 1928.
53. Buxton & Harris to Bruce, 13 Feb. 1929, Anti-Slavery and Aborigines Protection Society, AA, A431/48/273.
54. Bennett to Buxton, 10 Feb. 1934, ASS, S.22/6.382.

CHAPTER X   THE CALEDON BAY AFFAIR

1. Murder of Japanese, etc., AA: A431/1, 47/1434.
2. Letter from 'A Bagman', 25 Aug. 1933.
3. 11 Aug. 1933.

4. 15 Aug. 1933.
5. Charges by Mr Nelson, AA: A1 34/1141.
6. *The Herald* (Melbourne), 2 Sept. 1933.
7. Carrodus to Brown, 28 Aug. 1933, Murder of Japanese, etc., AA: A431/1, 47/1434.
8. *Sydney Morning Herald*, 4 Sept. 1933.
9. *The Herald* (Melbourne), 4 Sept. 1933.
10. ibid., 2 Sept. 1933.
11. *The Sun*, 2 Sept. 1933.
12. *Canberra Times*, 1 Sept. 1933.
13. *Anti-Slavery Reporter*, 18, no 1, 1927, p.7.
14. Morley to Lyons, 15 Aug. 1933, Murder of Japanese, etc., AA: 431/1, 47/1434.
15. ibid.
16. Caledon Bay Protests, AA: A1 1933/7632.
17. ibid.
18. ibid.
19. *The Herald*, (Melbourne) 5 Sept. 1933.
20. *Sydney Morning Herald*, 5 Sept. 1933.
21. Caledon Bay Protests, op. cit.
22. ibid.
23. *Canberra Times*, 6 Sept. 1933.
24. Caledon Bay Protests, op. cit.
25. *The Times*, 5 Sept. 1933.
26. Caledon Bay Protests, op. cit.
27. *Sydney Morning Herald*, 5 Sept. 1933.
28. *The Herald*, (Melbourne) 5 Sept. 1933.
29. ibid.
30. T. Egan, *Justice All Their Own*, Melbourne University Press, Melbourne, 1996, p.42.
31. *The Herald* (Melbourne), 12 Sept. 1933.
32. Egan, op. cit., p.44.
33. A. Wilson, 14 Sept. 1933, Caledon Bay Protests, op. cit.
34. Caledon Bay Protests, op. cit.
35. ibid.
36. ibid.
37. ibid.
38. *The Herald*, (Melbourne) 16 Sept. 1933.
39. Egan, op. cit., p.152.
40. *Sydney Morning Herald*, 7 Aug. 1934.
41. ibid.
42. Tuckiar and the King, 52 *CLR*, 1934, pp.335–6.
43. ibid., p.351.

44. ibid., p.345.
45. ibid., p.352.
46. Jones to Harris, 23 Jan. 1935, ASS, S.22/G.377.
47. Jones to Harris, 16 Nov. 1934, ibid.
48. Morley to Menzies, 2 Feb. 1934, Re Murder of Constable McColl, AA: 34/1437.
49. Egan, op. cit., p.192.

CHAPTER XI   AGITATION AND REFORM

1. Deputations, APNR, 1935, AA: A1 35/4116.
2. W. J. Hudson, *Australia and the League of Nations*, Sydney University Press, Sydney, 1980, p.212.
3. ibid., p.210.
4. ibid., p.200.
5. Rischbieth Papers, Rischbieth to Lyons, 19 Jan. 1934, ANL, 5/1623, 1a/58.
6. *Contemporary Review*, 135, p.223.
7. *The Morpeth Review*, 3, 25, October 1933, p.29.
8. A. Thomas, *The International Labour Organization*, Allen & Unwin, London, 1931, p.421.
9. Bennett to Nevenson, 7 June 1930, ASS, S.22/G.374.
10. *The World*, 14 Jan. 1932.
11. Cook to Weddell, 23 July 1932, Apprentices (Half Caste) Regulations, AA: A1 33/479.
12. Harris to Lyons, 21 June 1935, Anti-Slavery Society, AA: A1 48/273.
13. *Anti-Slavery Reporter*, 18, 1, 1927, p.7.
14. Harris to Bosanquet, 15 June 1934, ASS, S.22/G.376.
15. Buxton & Harris to Bruce, 13 Feb. 1929, Anti-Slavery Society, AA: A1 48/273.
16. *Anti-Slavery Reporter*, 22, 3, Oct. 1932, pp.95–7.
17. Buxton & Harris to Lyons, 10 Aug. 1937, Anti-Slavery Society, AA: A1 48/273.
18. Morley to Harris, 11 May 1933, ASS, S.22/G.374.
19. Bennett to Buxton, 18 Oct. 1933, ASS, S.22/G.377.
20. Bennett to Lees, 28 June 1929, North Queensland Collection, James Cook University.
21. L. Mair, *Native Policies in Africa*, Routledge, London, 1936, p.1.
22. *Daylight*, 28 Feb. 1925.
23. M. Roe, A Model Aboriginal State, *Aboriginal History*, 10, 1986, p.41.
24. Aboriginal Welfare Conference, AA: A659 44/1/3148.
25. *The Advertiser*, 21 June 1930.

26. Report on Welfare Conference; Aborigines Friends Association; Aborigines Protection League, AA: A1/1 32/4262.

27. Genders to ASS, n.d., ASS, S.22/G.378.

28. Aborigines Protection League, A Native Policy for Australia, AA: A/1/ 32/4262.

29. *SMH*, 28 Jan. 1928.

30. Genders to ASS, ASS, S.22/G.378.

31. W. E. H. Stanner, *After the Dreaming*, ABC, Sydney, 1969, pp.12–13.

32. A. P. Elkin, 'Australian Aboriginal and White Relations', *Journal Royal Australian Historical Society*, 48, 3, July 1952, pp.208–30. For an excellent survey of anthropological thinking in the period see R. Macgregor, *Imagined Destinies*, Melbourne University Press, Melbourne, 1997.

33. Elkin, op. cit., p.214.

34. Stanner, op. cit., p.15.

35. A. R. Radcliffe-Brown, *Applied Anthropology*, *Aus. Association for Advancement of Science Congress Proceedings*, 20, 1930, p.271.

36. Stanner, op. cit., p.39.

37. *SMH*, 7 Aug. 1934.

38. Stanner, op. cit., p.38.

39. A. P. Elkin, 'Australian Aboriginal and White Relations', op. cit., p.214.

40. Roberts, Buxton & Harris to Ryrie, 2 Dec. 1927, ASS, S.22/G.374.

41. For feminists politics generally see, P. Grimshaw et al., *Creating a Nation*, Penguin, Ringwood, 1994 and especially Ch. 9, 'Giving Birth to the New Nation' and Ch. 10, 'Depression Dreaming' by M. Lake. For feminist attitudes to race see F. Paisley, 'Feminist Challenges to White Australia', in D. Kirkby, ed., *Sex Power and Justice*, Oxford University Press, Melbourne, 1995, and her thesis, Ideas Have Wings, Ph.D, La Trobe, 1995. See also the articles by M. Lake, including: 'The Inviolable Woman', *Gender and History*, 8, 2, Aug. 1996, pp.197–211; 'Between Old World Barbarism and Stone Age Primitivism', in N. Grieve & A. Burns, eds., *Australian Women: Contemporary Feminist Thought*, Oxford University Press, Melbourne, 1994, pp.80–91; 'Colonised and Colonising: the White Australian Feminist Subject', *Women's History Review*, 2, 3, 1993.

42. ASS, S.22/G.382.

43. *Daily News*, 17 June 1933.

44. Aboriginal Welfare Conference, AA: A659 44/1/3148.

45. ibid.

46. Bennett to Buxton, 20 Oct. 1935, ASS, S.22/G.377.

47. Alston Rivers, London, 1930, p.127.

48. Bennett to Rischbieth, Rischbieth Papers, op. cit., 12/23.

49. Royal Commission Transcripts, WA Archives, AN537, ACC2922.
50. ibid., p.228.
51. ibid., p.300.
52. ibid., p.229.
53. Bennett to Rischbieth, 19 Dec. 1931, Rischbieth Papers, op. cit., 12/22.
54. Bennett to Buxton, 20 Oct. 1935, ASS, S.22/G.377.
55. Bennett to Buxton, 20 Aug. 1936, ASS, S.22/G.378.
56. Basedow to Harris, 26 April 1929, ASS, S.22/G.374.
57. 27 Dec. 1931, APNR, S.55 1/1/31, Series 7.
58. Thompson to Gribble, 8 Oct. 1929, APNR, SUA, S.55 1/131, Series 7.
59. *Advertiser*, 15 June 1928.
60. Bennett to Buxton, 22 Aug. 1936, ASS, S.22/G.378.
61. Harris to N. Buxton, 9 Oct. 1933, ASS, S.22/G.376.
62. Bennett to Rischbieth, 20 Sept. 1933, Rischbieth Papers, op. cit., 12/50.
63. *ABM Review*, Nov. 1928.
64. ibid., 15 Dec. 1928; 15 Sept. 1930.
65. Dugued to Harris, 1937, ASS, S.22/G.378.
66. Bennett to Buxton, 22 Aug. 1936, ASS, S.22/G.378.
67. ibid., 7 Mar. 1937.
68. Bennett to Buxton, 7 Mar. 1937, ASS S.22/G.378.

CHAPTER XII   CONCLUSION

1. 'Letter to a Friend', Oct. 1826, Methodist Missionary Society, in Correspondence, Australia 1812–26, Folder 4.
2. Cook to Griffith, 25 Aug. 1891, QSA Col. A674/1152 of 1891.

SELECT GUIDE TO READING
AND RESEARCH

Some of the humanitarians wrote books themselves. Others wrote journals and letters which have been published. See for instance, N. Gunson, ed., *Australian Reminiscences and Letters of L. E. Threlkeld*, 2 vols, AIATSIS, Canberra, 1974. Threlkeld's grammar was published in a number of places, but see *An Australian Language*, Sydney 1892. G. A. Robinson's Tasmanian journals and papers have been published in two large volumes edited by N. J. B. Plomley—*Friendly Mission*, THRA, Hobart 1966, and *Weep in Silence*, Blubber Head Press, Hobart 1987. Robert Lyon's book *Australia: An Appeal to the World on Behalf of the Younger Branch of the Family of Shem*, Sydney 1839 is a rarity. There is a copy in the Mitchell Library in Sydney and a photocopy in Perth's Battye Library.

The articles, editorials and letters which appeared in the *Queenslander* in 1880 were collected and published as a pamphlet, *The Way We Civilize*, Brisbane 1880. A. J. Vogan's novel *The Black Police* was published in London in 1890. John Gribble published two books *Black but Comely: Aboriginal Life in Australia*, London 1884, and the infamous *Dark Deeds in a Sunny Land*, Perth 1886. Ernest Gribble published three books: *Forty Years with the Aborigines*, Angus & Robertson, Sydney 1930; *The Problem of the Australian Aboriginal*, Angus & Robertson, Sydney 1932; *A Despised Race: The Vanishing Aboriginal of Australia*, ABM, Sydney 1933.

Private papers of John and Ernest Gribble can be consulted in the ABM Archives held in the Mitchell Library, in the National Library in Canberra and in duplicated form in the library of AIATSIS also in Canberra. Ernest Gribble is the subject of an excellent thesis by Christine Halse, The Rev. Ernest Gribble and Race Relations in North Australia, Ph.D., University of Queensland 1992. J. B. Gribble was the subject of a Bachelor of Letters thesis at the ANU in 1989. Gribble's battle with the Perth establishment was discussed by S. J. Hunt in a BA Hons. Thesis at Murdoch

University in 1978. Mary Bennett published a biography of her father, Christisson of Lamermoor, Alston Rivers, London 1927. In 1930 she published her powerful study *The Australian Aboriginal as a Human Being*, Alston Rivers, London.

There are a number of important manuscript collections with direct relevance to the humanitarian story. The papers of Constance Cooke are in the South Australian Archives; those of Bessie Rischbieth are in the Australian National Library. The papers of the Association for the Protection of Native Races are held in the Sydney University Archives. But by far the most important collection are the papers of the Aboriginal Protection Society and the Anti-Slavery Society which are both held at Rhodes House in Oxford. The 19th century papers have been microfilmed as part of the Australian Joint Copying Project and are available in the Mitchell and National Libraries.

The Joint Copying Project has also microfilmed the papers of the major British mission organisations to the extent that they relate to Australia and the Pacific. See for instance the Church Mission Society, the Methodist Missionary Society, the London Missionary Society. They are particularly important for such early 19th century missionaries as James Gunther, John Handt, William Porter, William Watson, W. Shelley, R. Hassall and L. Threlkeld. Much early missionary material will be found in the Bonwick Transcripts, Boxes 49–53 in the Mitchell Library. The Mitchell also holds the personal papers of G. A. Robinson, James Backhouse, Richard Windeyer and other missionaries and protectors including Joseph Orton, William Thomas and Richard Sadlier. The journals of Frances Tuckfield and James Dredge are held in Melbourne's La Trobe Library. For an excellent summary of missionary endeavour see J. Harris, *One Blood*, Albatross, Sydney 1990.

There are a number of books which are directly relevant to the present study. See G. S. Lang *The Aborigines of Australia*, Melbourne 1865; G. W. Rusden, *History of Australia*, 3 vols, London, 1883; R. Milliss, *Waterloo Creek: The Australia Day Massacre of 1838, George Gipps and the British Conquest of New South Wales*, McPhee-Gribble, Sydney 1992; T. Cribbin, *The Killing Times*, Fontana, Sydney, 1984; N. Green, *The Forrest River Massacres*, Fremantle Arts Press, Fremantle, 1995; and T. Egan, *Justice All Their Own*, Melbourne University Press, 1996.

INDEX

Index by Geraldine Suter